ASIAN ECONOMIC DEVELOPMENT

ASIAN ECONOMIC DEVELOPMENT

—

Edited by
Cranley Onslow

Foreword by Sir Sydney Caine

FREDERICK A. PRAEGER, *Publishers*

NEW YORK · WASHINGTON

BOOKS THAT MATTER

Published in the United States of America in 1965
by Frederick A. Praeger, Inc., Publishers
111 Fourth Avenue, New York, N.Y. 10003

Second printing, 1967

Library of Congress Catalog Card Number: 65–18459
Printed in Great Britain

CONTENTS

FOREWORD

BY SIR SYDNEY CAINE

In the last generation and especially since the end of World War II there has been a very great increase in conscious and theoretical discussion of the process of economic development. This is not because nobody was interested in the subject earlier or that nobody took any steps to encourage economic development; the whole history of modern times and particularly in the last century or so is evidence against that. What is new is the much more careful examination of what can be done by political authorities to bring about development, especially in what are generally called the under-developed countries, i.e. those in which the pace of development has in recent times been less rapid than in, say, Europe and North America. The attitude has been that it is no longer something which can be left to happen, with such occasional pushes and prods as governments may feel disposed to give, but must be a major preoccupation of governments. Equally, of course, it is expected that the governments of the more developed countries should accept a major preoccupation with the stimulation of 'growth', which is of course basically the same process.

Granted that this is a major task of governments, there has been a good deal of discussion as to how best to do it, whether on the basis of carefully worked out plans enforced by a central authority through suitable controls or largely by a private initiative operating within a favourable 'climate' established by suitable government policies. Different writers on the subject have taken different theoretical standpoints and the governments of different countries have adopted different policies. In the considerable volume of writing on the subject there has been a very strong tendency for those who lean towards the planning solution to discuss in terms of plans rather than achievements, i.e. showing how the plans *ought* to work, and equally for those who lean to the free enterprise or *laissez-faire* solution to explain equally theoretically how the beneficent hidden hand of classical economics *ought* to work.

What is comparatively lacking has been the really close study of what has happened in practice in different countries with different policies. The great merit of the studies which Mr Onslow has collected together in this volume and commented upon is that they try to look at the actual facts of achievement and not at what theory, whether of planning or free enterprise, would lead one to expect. The studies are concerned with a number of countries in southern and south-east Asia, which although very far from uniform in social or political structure do have substantial common features, each of them written from the point of view of a national of the country itself with a genuine sympathy with the aspirations of his country, but with a reasonable degree of objectivity and critical approach. They do give, therefore, some basis on which it is possible to begin to form a judgment about the relative success of different techniques aimed at the encouragement of economic development. Mr Onslow in Part II of the book has suggested the conclusions which seem to him to emerge. Whether or not one agrees with all of Mr Onslow's conclusions there can be no doubt that this kind of comparison of real facts rather than of theoretical possibilities is a most desirable development and one which I hope will be widely followed.

Clearly any conclusions emerging from this particular set of studies must be tentative. The processes which are being described are still in full play. Their long-term results can as yet be only dimly discerned and later experience may either confirm, disprove or qualify conclusions which appear to emerge at this still early stage. It is to be hoped that much fuller comparative reviews will follow. In the meantime anybody seriously interested in the actual processes which do go on rather than in the theoretical processes which might go on in a model world will find a great deal of interest in these studies.

EDITOR'S INTRODUCTION

FOR some years past there has been a growing dissatisfaction with the rate of economic progress in many parts of the less developed world.[1] Concurrently, there has been a growing feeling that part of the blame for the failure of economic performance to match political promises must be attributed to the official policies of the leading Western nations. This dissatisfaction and this feeling have now become widespread. But it has been very difficult to judge whether or not they are justified, if only because of the absence of a sufficient amount of impartial evidence.

This book is an attempt to remedy that deficiency. It consists, in the first place, of a series of individual studies of the economic progress, since 1945, of six Asian countries – Burma, Ceylon, India, Malaya, Pakistan and Thailand. These countries have been chosen primarily because they form a contiguous group, accounting altogether for some three quarters of the population of Asia outside Communist control. Each of the studies has been contributed by a leading economist who is a national of the country concerned. All the contributors were asked to express their personal opinions as freely and as vigorously as they wished, and I am most grateful to them for responding so liberally to the challenge.

These studies, which were completed at various times between January 1963 and February 1964, are arranged in alphabetical order in Part I of the book. Part II consists of a comparative analysis of the evidence thus presented. The aim of this analysis has been to examine critically the objectives and the

---

[1] I have generally used this phrase, and its antithesis, 'more developed', throughout, in preference to more conventional terms such as 'backward', 'underdeveloped' or 'developing'. All economies are to some extent developed, and developing: the differences are only differences of degree.

experience of the six countries as a group: for though there are clearly wide differences in individual circumstances within the group, there also appear to be many economic problems which are common to all.

On the basis of this examination, it has been possible to draw a number of conclusions which may be of value, not only to those directly concerned with the economic future of this part of Asia, but also for more general purposes. In the long run, the future peace and prosperity of Asia is certainly of greater international importance than that of any other part of the less developed world, because of the total population involved. But in the short term, other areas, and Africa in particular, are now entering much the same stages of economic development and facing problems similar to those which have been experienced in South and South-East Asia during the past two decades.

It must, however, be stressed at once that the conclusions I have drawn are not necessarily ones with which all the individual contributors would agree. In some cases, indeed, my own conclusions conflict directly with those contained in the original studies, just as some conclusions in one study conflict with those in another. In so far as this involves any criticism of the views of individual contributors, no discourtesy is intended: where I have felt it necessary to draw attention to apparently fallacious arguments, the reader remains free to judge the validity of these criticisms.

The limits of this necessarily brief analysis have also made it impossible to deal with every aspect of the whole subject of economic development. For obvious reasons, the treatment is highly selective. Some of the argument is closely compressed, and I have tried to avoid complex technicalities. Nevertheless, the conclusions set out in Part II are advanced in the belief that they are valid, and that they are supported both by the evidence of the studies as a whole and by general economic reasoning.

The major concern of the book as a whole is with the factors underlying economic development, and with the economic and social effects of actual policies. The reader may therefore like to keep these two subjects chiefly in mind when reading the studies in Part I. Even if he then disagrees with some or all of the conclusions drawn in Part II, I believe he will still find this a valuable exercise. I hope he will also agree that the problems of economic development and the policies pursued in this important region present formidable difficulties and dilemmas of major relevance to the contemporary scene.

PART I

Six National Studies

U TUN WAI *was born in 1922, and educated at Rangoon University, Bombay University (B.A.), Yale University (M.A., Ph.D.) and the London School of Economics.*

He was Lecturer in Economics, Rangoon University, from 1947 to 1949, when he joined the Staff of E.C.A.F.E. In 1955, he joined the International Monetary Fund, and served as Assistant Chief of the Finance Division and Chief of the Statistics Division before becoming Chief of the North West Africa Division in 1962.

He has published two books and a number of articles on economic affairs.

BURMA

BURMA emerged from World War II in a very bad condition after being fought over twice; once at the beginning of the war when the Japanese conquered the country and again at the end when the allies liberated it. The scorched earth policy and the fighting damaged or destroyed not only residential buildings but much of Burma's productive capacity. It is estimated that of the national capital (excluding land) amounting to Kyats[1] 3,500 million at prewar prices approximately half was lost by 1946.[2]

As a result of the war, the real gross domestic product in 1946–47 was only 61 per cent of the prewar level (*see* Table 1). Agricultural output was 59 per cent of 1938–39 and the production of minerals was negligible. Real income *per capita* had, of course, fallen by a larger amount because of the increase in population. Besides direct physical damage, wartime economic factors were also responsible for the extremely low output immediately after the war. For example, in agriculture the Japanese occupation had cut off Burma from her traditional export markets which had provided an outlet for about half the annual rice crop before the war. Therefore, there was no incentive to produce rice for export and by 1945–46 the acreage under rice (paddy) had declined to half that of 1938–39 and production had become geared to national subsistence only.

After the war, the authorities, therefore, faced the tremendous task of rehabilitating the economy to its prewar level and in later years of promoting economic development. To achieve this, all the postwar governments have relied on planning of one kind or another. In fact, efforts at economic planning began even before Burma obtained its independence when

---

[1] One kyat = 1s. 6d. sterling = $0·21 U.S.

[2] *Economic Survey of Burma*, 1951, p. 1, presented in Parliament by the Honourable Minister of Finance and Revenue, August 30, 1951.

Bogyoke Aung San convened the Sorrento Villa Conference in June 1947 to discuss problems of rehabilitation. Since then there have been four plans (including the current second Four-Year Plan) which have been implemented with varying degrees of success.

TABLE I COMPOSITION OF GROSS DOMESTIC PRODUCT[1]
(In millions of kyats at 1947–48 prices)

Industrial origin	1938–39	1946–47	1951–52	1956–57	1961–62[2]
1 Agriculture and Fisheries	1,907	1,147	1,440	1,753	1,813
2 Forestry	360	298	266	344	379
3 Mining and Quarrying	273	12	34	84	117
4 Rice Processing	182	90	119	144	147
5 State Marketing	633[3]	227	248	493	490
6 State Transport	117	47	48	76	89
7 State Banking	—	—	1	12	21
8 Other Public Utilities	31	8	10	31	68
9 General Government	153	216	314	487	626
10 Rental Value of Housing	165	149	162	203	230
11 Other Industries and Services	1,124	828	994	1,307	1,499
a Total in millions kyats	4,945	3,022	3,636	4,934	5,479
b Index 1938–39 =100	100	61	74	100	111

Source: Ministry of National Planning, *Economic Survey of Burma* (annual).

Despite the planning and even sixteen years after the end of World War II, the real gross domestic product of Burma is now only 11 per cent above that of 1938–39. The rate of recovery from the ravages of war has been rather slow and often quite erratic; it was only in 1956–57, ten years after obtaining independence, that the prewar level of production was reached (*see* Table 2). The average rate of recovery between 1946–47 and 1956–57 of 5·4 per cent per annum cannot but be considered slow because problems of recovery with idle agricultural

[1] Year beginning 1 October except for 1938–39 which is year beginning 1 April.
[2] Estimates.
[3] Refers to private marketing which has been replaced by State Marketing.

land, though difficult in the Burmese context, are usually minor in comparison with problems of genuine growth. It is, therefore, not surprising that in the subsequent period 1957–58 to 1961–62 the average rate of growth of 2·2 per cent per year was much smaller than the rate in the earlier postwar years.

TABLE 2 GROSS DOMESTIC PRODUCT AT CONSTANT PRICES

Year[1]	In millions of Kyats at 1947–48 prices	Index 1938–39 = 100	Percentage change over previous year
1938–39	4,945	100	—
1946–47	3,022	61	—
1947–48	3,557	72	18·1
1948–49	3,200	65	–9·7
1949–50	3,038	61	–6·2
1950–51	3,431	69	13·1
1951–52	3,636	74	7·3
1952–53	3,899	79	6·8
1953–54	4,046	82	3·8
1954–55	4,294	87	6·1
1955–56	4,456	90	3·4
1956–57	4,934	100	11·2
1957–58	4,770	96	–4·0
1958–59	5,106	103	7·3
1959–60	5,513	111	7·8
1960–61	5,408	109	–1·8
1961–62	5,479	111	1·8

Source: Ministry of National Planning, *Economic Survey of Burma* (annual).

Admittedly, political difficulties and lack of law and order caused by the insurgency beginning in 1948–49, were partly responsible for the slow rate of growth in Burma in the post-war period as a whole, but economic factors played a major role. It is the purpose of this essay to study the role of planning, the range of economic problems which confronted the country, and the policies adopted; all of these have influenced the postwar

[1] Year beginning October 1 except for 1938–39 which is year beginning April 1.

5

rate of growth. Some conclusions are also given so that they may serve as a guide to future economic policy.

PLANNING AND PERFORMANCE

The Two-Year Plan and the Insurgency

The Two-Year Plan of Economic Development, announced in April 1948, was the country's first attempt at planning. However, it was not a full-fledged plan but merely a list of physical targets considered achievable within the next two years. It did not have any financial framework and no attempt was made to relate the Plan to the government budget. It envisaged that by 1951–52 the level of agricultural output would reach the pre-war level. For industry, it enumerated a number of desirable projects but they were not supported by any technical studies for feasibility or cost-benefit calculations.

The Plan was never implemented in a formal sense because the insurrections broke out in the second half of the year and the attention of the government was diverted to restoring law and order in the country. However, there were a number of policy statements in the plan which guided the AFPFL governments in the course of their ten year rule. For example, the desire to promote economic growth through socialistic principles was followed. The Plan's objective of redistributing land and securing a fair share of the output led to the Land Nationalization Act which was passed in 1948, even though it was only in later years that it was gradually enforced; the proposal to set up a State Agricultural Bank was implemented in 1953. Furthermore, 11 out of the 12 industrial projects recommended in the Two-Year Plan were incorporated in later plans and have been implemented in course of time.

The insurgency and lack of law and order affected the country for more than a decade but were most serious for about three years. During 1948–49 and 1949–50 the lines of communication and transport facilities were so poor because of destruction by the insurgents that the volume of exports was limited as much by this factor as by the low level of agricultural output. The government had to deploy part of its armed forces to provide escorts for trains and boats in order to ensure that the agricultural products were exported.

6

The economy became more disorganized during the peak of the insurgency when even the villager was reluctant to cultivate in fields further away from the village or travel widely for trade. The real gross domestic product fell in both 1948–49 and 1949–50 to 61 per cent of the prewar level (*see* Table 2), and the earlier efforts at reconstruction were vitiated. The effect of the insurgency was seen not only in the foregone opportunity to produce goods and services, but more importantly in the large scale destruction of capital equipment which reduced the ability of the economy to grow rapidly. Trains, steamers, and bridges were blown up by the insurgents and it is estimated that from the outbreak of the insurgency until August 1950 about Kyats 426 million of government property was destroyed or looted.[1]

The Eight-Year Plan and the Korean War Boom

By 1951, the government was no longer fully occupied with the problem of law and order, and it began to devote its attention to economic planning and development. A group of American engineers and economists, financed initially by the US ECA programme, began preparing an Economic and Engineering Survey of Burma; their Preliminary Report was submitted in January 1952 and the Comprehensive Report in August 1953.

This Eight-Year Plan, also known as the KTA Plan and the Pyidawtha Plan, had the object of roughly doubling the gross domestic product in real terms between 1950–51 and 1959–60; the gross domestic product by the latter date would have increased by 31 per cent above the prewar level but *per capita* production by only 4 per cent above prewar because of the increase in population. The planners envisaged that it would be necessary to invest a total of K7,500 million over the planned period of which K4,020 million would be in the public sector and approximately K3,470 million in the private sector. Investment expenditures were roughly divided between rehabilitation projects with a capital–output ratio of 2:1 and new development projects with a capital–output ratio of of about 2·5:1.[2]

[1] See Honourable Finance Minister, *Budget Speech* 1950–51.
[2] No further statistical details are available, but practically all rehabilitation projects were in the government sector.

The average rate of investment planned for the period was 21·2 per cent of gross domestic product which was rather ambitious.

The Plan's objective of doubling output between 1950–51 and 1959–60 did not appear ambitious because there was unused agricultural land and the over-all level of production was still much below prewar. But, the assumption of the plan that it was necessary to have a very large investment programme in overhead social capital (infrastructure) and that these expenditures could be financed by the maintenance of the high level of rice prices prevailing during the Korean war boom was most unrealistic.

The desire to restore some of the infrastructure capital destroyed by the war and the insurgents is understandable. However, it should have been evident that if the objective was merely the restoration of prewar output with more or less the same composition of goods and services, then a capital investment of K7,500 million was not necessary because only half the prewar capital of K3,500 million was destroyed, and even after making allowance for a doubling of price of capital imports from abroad, the figure needed was less than K7,500 million.

The planners were most optimistic in the trend of agricultural prices especially for rice. The Korean war had caused prices of raw materials to rise rapidly in 1950–51 and rice prices also rose and continued to rise even when some raw material prices had fallen sharply in the spring of 1952. This undoubtedly led the planners to project a secular rice shortage and to predict that even in 1958–59 when production would have increased the price of rice would be only 14 per cent less than the peak price, that total export receipts would double, and that there would be balance of payments surpluses throughout the period of the Plan.

Although the planners did not realize that rice prices would break in course of time following the collapse of the boom, I pointed out in the summer of 1953 (at the time the KTA group published their Comprehensive Report) that by 1959–60 rice prices would be about 60 per cent of the level in 1950–51 and that the total value of export would be only about 10 per cent larger because despite the quantum increases in exports there would be this large decline in prices. Based on this and my

8

estimates for import demand, I concluded, unlike the planners who had projected surpluses in Burma's balance of payments that there would be deficits beginning with 1954.[1] All of these forecasts have been proved correct in subsequent years.

The capital investment programme of the Eight-Year Plan never reached the levels projected. In the beginning it was because of the physical bottlenecks in implementation such as decisions for ordering the right equipment and constructing the factories. Later, when the export boom collapsed it was due to the financial limitations of foreign exchange shortages. Foreign exchange reserves fell continuously from K1,269 million at the end of June 1953 to K628 million at the end of February 1955.

At this stage it became obvious to the government that the Eight-Year Plan was unrealistic and it therefore took drastic measures to stop the drain on foreign exchange. Cuts were made in the budget allotments for both current and capital expenditure for the remaining half of the fiscal year 1955–56. Many projects were abandoned or postponed and some orders for equipment were even cancelled. Only those projects on which work had started or on which unavoidable commitments had been made were allowed to be continued. For the private sector, the value of all import licences issued but not yet used was reduced by half and the system of Open General Licences was temporarily suspended. These measures put an end to the ambitious Eight-Year Plan.

The performance of the Eight-Year Plan fell short of its targets. As compared with an original investment programme of K7,500 million over eight years from 1952–53 to 1959–60, actual investment was only K5,174 million, a short-fall of 30 per cent. If the changes in prices of capital imports are taken into account (increases between 1952 and 1958 of 13 per cent for capital goods from the UK and of 26 per cent for capital goods from Japan) then the real performance was even more unfavourable.

In Table 3, the comparisons have been confined to the three operating years of 1953–54 to 1955–56 before the Plan was abandoned because the first year of the Plan, 1952–53, was

[1] See U Tun Wai, 'Outlook for Burma's Balance of Payments'. A paper read to the Burma Research Society on August 12 1953 and published subsequently in *Journal of the Burma Research Society*, December 1954, pp. 35–40.

practically over when the Comprehensive Report was published. It will be noted that actual investment in these three
years was about 25 per cent below the planned level and that in
relation to the smaller gross domestic product it constituted only
18·5 per cent as compared with the planned rate of 21·1 per
cent. Furthermore, the actual capital–output ratio was about
2·6:1 as compared with a planned rate of less than 2·5:1.

TABLE 3 PERFORMANCES OF THE FIRST EIGHT-YEAR AND
THE FIRST FOUR-YEAR PLANS

(In millions of Kyats)

	Eight-Year Plan Three operative years from 1953–54 to 1955–56		The First Four-Year Plan 1956–57 – 1959–60	
	Plan Average (Per Year)	Performance Average (Per Year)	Plan Average (Per Year)	Performance Average (Per Year)
Gross Fixed Capital Formation				
Government	668	505	507	484
Private	512	392	—	549
Total	1,180	897	—	1,033
As per cent of GDP	21·1	18·5	—	18·4
Net Fixed Capital Formation				
Total	812	617	—	709
As per cent of GDP	14·5	12·7	—	12·8

Source: Ministry of National Planning, *Second Four-Year Plan,* 1961–62 to 1964–65,
and *Economic Survey of Burma* 1962. (No further details on the private element of
gross fixed capital formation are available.)

Partly because of the lower level of actual investment and
partly because some of the investment was misdirected, the real
output grew at a much slower rate than planned; instead of
doubling between 1950–51 and 1959–60, domestic output in the

latter year was only 60 per cent larger than in the former (*see* Table 2).

The First Four-Year Plan

When the Eight-Year Development Plan was abandoned in 1955, the government revised downwards a number of its targets and these revisions for the last four years of the Eight-Year Plan came to be referred to as the First Four-Year Plan. This more modest plan was formulated in 1956 and covered only the public sector. For this reason no targets for the private sector are included in Table 3.

Apart from a lower level of planned investment the first Four-Year Plan was more realistic in the distribution of public investment between Agriculture and Irrigation (which now obtained a larger share) and Social Services, whose share was reduced (*see* Table 4). Industry retained its share of total investment, being largely a continuation of committed projects but there was some increase in expenditure for Power and for Transport and Communications despite attempts to scale down such expenditures.

The actual performance of the First Four-Year Plan in the government sector was very close to the programme and the annual rate of total net fixed capital formation was larger than in the three operating years of the Eight-Year Plan (*see* Table 3).

Second Four-Year Plan

The Second Four-Year Plan for 1961–62 to 1964–65 was adopted by the government of U Nu in August 1961. The objective was to achieve an annual rate of growth of 5·9 per cent per annum, and to lay the foundations for three additional Four-Year Plans which with increasing rates of growth would double real *per capita* income at the end of the sixteen-year period in 1977.

For the second Four-Year Plan 1961–62 to 1964–65, a capital–output ratio of 2·5:1 was assumed and net investment envisaged totalled K4,400–4,525 million.[1] Half of the total was for public investment and the other half was expected to be carried out by the private sector. There was greater emphasis in the allocation

[1] The lower figure was derived by adding up the cost of individual projects i.e. using the sectoral approach, while the higher figure was obtained by projecting national income and using assumed capital-output ratios.

TABLE 4 ALLOCATION OF INVESTMENT IN THE PUBLIC SECTOR

(In millions of Kyats)

	Eight-Year Plan 1952–53 – 1955–56	First Four-Year Plan 1956–56 – 1959–60	Second Four-Year Plan 1961–62 – 1964–65
Agriculture and Irrigation	154·6 (7·7%)	211·8 (10·9%)	316·7 (12·0%)
Forestry	30·6 (1·5%)	24·7 (1·3%)	67·8 (2·6%)
Mining	15·7 (0·8%)	8·6 (0·4%)	38·7 (1·5%)
Industry	186·6 (9·3%)	187·9 (9·7%)	279·8 (10·6%)
Power	202·6 (10·1%)	303·1 (15·6%)	203·8 (7·8%)
Transport and Communications	414·8 (20·6%)	496·5 (25·7%)	772·4 (29·4%)
Social Services (including construction)	438·9 (21·8%)	195·6 (10·1%)	497·2 (18·9%)
Law and order	370·1 (18·3%)	387·5 (20·0%)	303·0 (11·5%)
Others	199·2 (9·9%)	122·6 (6·3%)	149·6 (5·7%)
Total	2,013·1 (100%)	1,938·3 (100%)	2,629·0 (100%)

Source: Ministry of National Planning, *Second Four-Year Plan*, 1961–62 to 1964–65.

of investment in the public sector for agriculture and irrigation (12 per cent) at the expense of power (7·8 per cent). But transport and communications were given a larger share, amounting to 29·4 per cent (*see* Table 4).

The total actual net investment in the first year of the Plan, 1961–62 was only about к600 million as compared with a planned figure of к1,005 million. Part of the short-fall was due to the fact that U Nu's government did not implement all the projects included in the 1961–62 budget. But the main reason is that the military government under Bogyoke Ne Win postponed many projects and it was not quite ready to implement new ones when it came into power in the spring of 1962. Consequently, the real gross domestic product increased by less than 2 per cent as compared with the hoped for rate of 5·9 per cent in the Plan.

The present government has not published or announced any new plan, but neither has it rejected the second Four-Year Plan outright. It is continuing to implement a large number of existing projects but it has changed considerably the allocation of public capital expenditure in the Budget estimates for 1962–63 as compared with previous years. For example, the share allocated to agriculture and irrigation has increased from 11·2 per cent in 1961–62 and 12·0 per cent planned in the Second Four-Year Plan to 17·1 per cent in the budget estimates for 1962–63; the share for industry has increased from 4·9 per cent and 10·6 per cent respectively to 20·0 per cent for 1962–63. Cuts have been made in investment for administrative purposes and social services.[1]

As regards the total capital expenditure in the public sector,[2] the present government intends to raise this from к428 million in 1961–62 to к736 million in 1962–63 so that it can make up for the lost ground. This level of capital expenditure, if implemented, would compare very favourably with the annual rate of about к660 million planned in both the Second Four-Year Plan as a whole and in the budget of 1961–62, the first year of the Plan.

[1] See Ministry of National Planning, *Economic Survey of Burma*, 1962, pp. 132–3.
[2] This is a slightly broader concept than net fixed investment.

FACTORS INFLUENCING POSTWAR ECONOMIC GROWTH

It was noted earlier that the rate of economic growth in Burma has been rather uneven. Sometimes it has been very satisfactory: at other times the year to year changes in real gross domestic product have been negative. Over the postwar period as a whole (1947–48 to 1961–62) the rate of growth has been 4·3 per cent per annum but in recent years (1957–58 to 1961–62) it has slowed down to only 2·2 per cent per annum. The faster rate of growth in earlier years was due to the availability of idle resources which had not been used during World War II. Obviously no single factor has influenced either the uneven rate of growth or the time it took Burma to reach even prewar levels of output (reached only in 1956–57) but the major factors outside the formal development plan and their relative importance are considered in this part of the study.

Political and Social

With the attainment of independence in 1948 everybody expected that the country would recover quickly from the effects of the war and that under national leadership it would develop quickly without the restrictions of a 'colonial regime'. But the hard facts of economic life are the same for colonies and independent nations. This is not to deny that nationalism and the desire for a better way of life cannot be used as a force for development. In fact, the AFPFL government of U Nu used the method of Pyidawtha Discretionary Grants beginning in 1952–53 to get greater public participation in the development effort. Under this system, the government set up a Pyidawtha Discretionary Fund for constructing and rehabilitating communal facilities (wells, schools, roads, bridges, etc.) on the basis of κ50,000 per township on condition that public contributions of money, labour and materials were made available for these community projects.[1]

Another method used to channel national energies for development was public speeches, encouraging the people to

[1] In the first three years the total cost of the projects was about κ15 million per year and public contributions averaged 45 per cent. In later years there was less enthusiasm and partly because of government shortage of funds the total cost of the projects declined to κ2·5 million in 1957–58.

work harder and save more, coupled with promises of future riches.[1] This may have had some effect for a while, but after many years when there was hardly any difference in standards of living the people undoubtedly became discouraged and slackened their efforts. Furthermore, without adequate incentives the will to work harder could not be sustained, a point which is taken up below on economic policy.

The political wranglings that culminated in armed insurrections were an important factor in slowing down the development effort. Not only was there large scale destruction of equipment, but existing capital could not be utilized fully. Although this factor has sometimes been given undue importance to the exclusion of other factors, one cannot deny that without the insurrections, the country would have recovered much more rapidly.

Economic Policy and Planning

The various plans reviewed above indicate that there was a strong socialistic bias, determined by political theory, in the investment programme whereby the government was not only to provide the overhead capital in fields such as power and transportation, but also to own and operate breweries, cement factories, textile mills, oil refineries, etc. While there is no official economic rationalization for this approach one can perhaps understand it better from the line of reasoning given below.

Before the war, the country had relied on private enterprise, especially foreign owned, to ensure economic growth. While the rate of growth might have been satisfactory it was commonly felt that agriculture rather than industry was being developed, and that the Burmans were not permitted to play a sufficiently active role. After independence, the government wished to Burmanize the economy by cutting down the activities of foreigners. Since the Burmans had neither the finance nor the business experience, it was obvious that the government should follow a socialistic policy.

The above reasoning had one false assumption namely that the Burman's lack of experience in commerce and industry could be replaced and/or supplemented by experience in governing the country. It was of course quite disastrous to apply

[1] U Nu used to promise that there would be, figuratively speaking, 'rainfall of gold and silver'.

governmental methods to the Boards and Corporations which were created. Specific examples of the resulting bad management can be found in the cotton spinning and weaving factories and the cement works. It is only recently that a few of these nationalized concerns have been decentralized and run on commercial principles, for example BEDC (Burma Economic Development Corporation).

All postwar governments have followed an improper wage policy for their skilled personnel (technical and administrative) which has been detrimental to the socialistic policy. The relative remunerations in government service and enterprises *vis-à-vis* private pursuits such as law, medicine and petty business have been most unfavourable in postwar years whereas prewar it was just the opposite. Thus the best brains of the country have not been attracted to government service and instead have entered other professions. It was this new wage policy which caused the early retirement of experienced Burman officers soon after the country obtained its independence.

In addition Burma has faced a shortage of technicians to run all the industries and activities nationalized by the government, since the foreign technicians associated with previous foreign investment were no longer available to the country. Part of this deficiency has been met by the use of technical assistance experts from the United Nations and its specialized agencies, from the Colombo plan, and by bilateral arrangements with such countries as the USA, the Soviet Union, Israel and China. The value of technical assistance experts from the United Nations in 1953–56 averaged K3·1 million per year, while during 1961 and 1962 the average had increased to K7·6 million per year.

Another aspect of planning in Burma was that projects were at times included either for political considerations such as obtaining votes in an election or because of the personal preferences of one or more ministers. The methods used to implement the plans have also been inconsistent. The planning and executing machinery underwent many changes. First there was a National Planning Board in 1946, then the Economic Planning Board in 1947, then an Economic Council in 1949–50, then an Economic and Social Board around 1951–52 and so on. During this period the functions of the Ministry of National Planning and its relationship with other ministries were not always clear. Furthermore, the direct assumption by the Prime Minister of responsibility for the ministry or planning machinery may have centralized authority, but occasionally it caused planning to slow down as he was occupied with more urgent matters. At times, the composition of the Boards were so large that they became rather unwieldy.[1]

The planning bodies and successive governments were full of good intentions and ideas but sufficient time was not allowed to test or permit any method to succeed. For example, in the attempt to Burmanise the foreign trade and domestic industry, the planners became enamoured of co-operative societies (around 1948–49) and felt that this was the magic formula. But after two or three years it was abandoned in favour of the corporate form of enterprise. Then again a few years later the joint ventures with foreign private enterprises came in vogue e.g., the joint ventures with the Burma Corporation in 1951 and the one with the Burma Oil Company in 1954. Then, a few years later the joint ventures were made with domestic business firms, for example, JVC 1, JVC 2, etc.[2]

In the pure governmental sector also, many changing forms have been used. First there was the form of the Marketing Boards, e.g. State Agricultural Marketing Board, then the Development corporations, e.g. the Industrial Development Corporation and the Mineral Resources Development Corporations, and more recently the decentralized organization run along commercial lines, e.g. Burma Economic Development Corporation, which is basically a holding company with many subsidiaries. These changes, at times, led to improvements but the previous methods were not given a chance to yield results.

In the field of economic policy, one factor inhibiting private initiative and enterprise was that the boundary between industries reserved for the government and those intended for the private sector was never clear cut. Successive governments after declaring that light consumer goods industries would be left to private enterprise would then act in contradiction of their

[1] For details on changes in planning machinery see U Thet Tun 'Burma's Experience in Economic Planning', in *Open Mind*, Vol. I, No. 12, October 1960.

[2] In 1956–57 the government formed seven joint venture corporations (numbered JVC 1 to 7) with private Burmese businesses to handle the import and internal distribution of various commodities with a view to bringing down prices.

declared policy, as, for example, in the case of the nationalization of the Dyer Meakin brewery in 1954. From time to time the government would try to encourage the establishment of small industries by giving them partial exemptions from customs duties for imports of capital goods and preferential treatment on imports of raw materials. But frequently the newly established industries would then experience difficulties in obtaining certain raw materials because of changes in import policy or find themselves facing tough competition from finished goods when import controls were relaxed.

But the most debatable economic policy has been that of maintaining the internal price of rice unchanged since 1948 at K300 per 100 baskets of paddy (unhusked rice) for a representative quality (ngasein).[1] This represented a threefold increase over the prewar level (K100 per 100 baskets) but the price of goods (e.g. textiles, fish products and cooking oil) purchased by the farmer had increased much more. Therefore, rice farming has become much less profitable than before the war. The government's view in this regard has been that various other factors, such as controlled rents, low interest rates on government loans, cheap seeds and fertilizers distributed by the government, and the community development projects on roads, wells, etc, have tended to reduce the costs of production. While this argument may have been valid in 1948, it is hardly tenable in 1962. It is no accident that the acreage under rice in 1961–62 was still 84 per cent of prewar and production only 88 per cent whereas the 1961–62 production of groundnut and sessamum, which were not subject to price controls, were 199 per cent and 171 per cent of prewar level. Therefore, one method of raising rice production would be to provide incentives to the farmer through higher prices for rice.

Bottlenecks in Transportation and in Other Fields

Besides the political, sociological and psychological factors there are the purely economic factors, such as the sufficiency of savings to finance investment, the right allocation of resources between different fields, etc. In the context of planning

[1] This has been achieved by the government's monopoly in rice exports through the State Agriculture Marketing Board and by this organization buying rice at fixed prices for export.

in postwar Burma and the problems of reconstruction, there were also bottlenecks in some fields of production which at one time or another held back production in other fields.

One of the bottlenecks was transportation. Immediately after the war, agricultural stocks of wartime production and mineral stocks of prewar production could not be exported easily because of the shortage of railroad equipment, the lack of inland water boats and trucks, and the damage in the Port of Rangoon. From Table 1, it will be seen that recovery in transportation has lagged behind the rest of the economy: by 1956–57 it was still only 65 per cent of the prewar level whereas real gross domestic product had by then reached prewar level. During 1937–41 the Burma Railways handled about 3 million tons of freight and carried a total of 579 million ton-miles of freight traffic while in 1947–48 only 1·3 million tons were handled and 239 million ton-miles of freight were carried. By 1961–62, the total had risen to 2·5 million tons of freight handled and 405 million ton-miles of freight carried, but it was still below the prewar level.

The transportation bottleneck was most serious in the early postwar years but more recently (since about 1960) it is probably the lack of demand rather than any physical limitation of supply which has prevented freight transportation from expanding as rapidly as the rest of the economy. Indirect evidence supports this conclusion, in that since 1954–55 railway passenger traffic (measured both in numbers of passengers and in passenger-miles) has exceeded the prewar level and by 1959–60 it was even double the prewar figure.

Another example of a bottleneck in production is the immediate postwar shortage of plough cattle. In 1938–39 there were 3·6 million plough cattle in Burma, comprising 2·8 million oxen and 0·8 million buffaloes. Owing to war-time destruction there were only 2·6 million plough cattle in 1946 or 74 per cent of the prewar figure. As the area under cultivation expanded to 80 per cent of prewar level in 1947–48, there was a shortage of plough cattle. This shortage was partly relieved by the natural increase in cattle population and partly by U Nu's prohibition of cattle slaughter for meat consumption soon after the war. By about 1953–54 the ratio of plough cattle to land under cultivation exceeded that of prewar and there was no longer any shortage. In March 1962 the number of plough cattle was 13 per cent higher than prewar whereas the area under cultivation in 1961–62 was only 93 per cent of the prewar level.

Occasionally, the bottlenecks were the result of bad planning. A number of factories established by the government were not operated at full capacity. For example, the government spinning and weaving factory was unable to operate solely with home grown cotton and special strains of cotton had to be imported. As a result, the cotton yarn production of 1·8 million pounds in 1951–52 was only about 30 per cent of capacity, but it climbed to a peak of 70 per cent utilization in 1953–54 with production at 4 million lbs when better quality cotton was imported. Thereafter production declined to 3·1 million pounds in 1955–56 because of attempts to re-use inferior quality raw cotton and to substitute shorter staple local cotton.[1]

External Factors

These factors have been very important in determining the postwar rate of economic growth. Before the war, the economy relied heavily on foreign investment, mainly British, for its momentum. In postwar years, foreign investments have been very small and hence domestically financed investment, especially by the government, has had to replace foreign investment (*see* Table 5). While this has created a greater strain on domestic savings it has also meant that a smaller proportion of the gross domestic product is needed for paying interest and dividends to foreigners abroad. In 1938–39, out of a gross domestic product of K1,458 million about K85 million, or 6 per cent represented net income remittances overseas while in postwar years such payments have been less than one-half of one per cent of gross domestic product. (Over the postwar period as a whole these remittances, though subject to exchange control, have been allowed as long as income tax and/or company taxes have been paid.)

In the early years, the government took very little foreign aid, loans or grants from abroad. But in the mid-fifties, with declining rice prices, it had to seek large amounts of badly needed external finance in the form of Japanese reparations,[2]

---

[1] See *Economic Survey of Burma*, 1954, p.25, and *Economic Survey of Burma*, 1956, p.23.

[2] The first Japanese reparations agreement gave Burma a certain amount subject to further negotiation after reparations with other countries, such as Indonesia and the Philippines, had been settled. The additional reparations payments were finally agreed upon early in 1963.

BURMA

TABLE 3 DOMESTIC INVESTMENT AND EXTERNAL FINANCE

(In millions of Kyats)

	Gross Domestic Capital Formation[1]				External Finance[2]			
	Government	Private	Total	Per cent of Gross Domestic Product	Official Donations[3]	Official loans[4]	Private Capital	Total
1938–39	25	153	178	12·2	—	—	—	—
1950–51	177	299	476	12·9	22	—	6	28
1951–52	298	445	743	18·2	35	—	10	45
1952–53	482	394	876	19·0	21	—	8	29
1953–54	607	404	1,011	22·0	8	-136	-5	-133
1954–55	599	410	1,009	21·0	—	-75	21	-54
1955–56	501	429	930	18·1	32	71	9	112
1956–57	511	574	1,085	19·9	135	112	2	249
1957–58	552	631	1,183	22·0	159	82	10	251
1958–59	503	586	1,089	19·5	106	35	23	164
1959–60	432	687	1,119	18·7	104	79	2	185
1960–61	393	608	1,001	16·1	82	26	-12	96
1961–62	433	521	954	15·0	98[5]	55[5]	10[5]	163[5]

Sources: Ministry of National Planning, *Economic Survey of Burma* (Annual), and Union Bank of Burma, *Annual Reports*, 1952–57.

[1] Including changes in stocks.

[2] 1951 calendar data for 1950–51, and 1952 data for 1951–52 and so on until 1955–56 when 1956 annual data used.

[3] Including Japanese reparations and Russian gifts.

[4] Net long term loans from India, USA and IBRD.

[5] Estimates.

21

3

Russian gifts,[1] PL 480 from US and long-term loans from India, US and the IBRD. In two peak years 1956–57 and 1957–58 external finance contributed almost a quarter of the total resources for financing gross domestic investment. Although Table 5 indicates that the importance of external finance fell in 1960–61 it rose again in 1961–62. Furthermore, the second Four-Year Plan (1961–62 to 1964–65) envisaged that K809 million of foreign resources would be available for financing investment in the public sector.[2]

According to the 1962–63 budget estimates, the government expects a total of K278 million in 1962–63 consisting of K110 million of Japanese Reparations, K80 million loan from the Chinese, a credit of K24 million from USSR and Czechoslovakia, an AID loan of K35 million from the US, and a K29 million loan from IBRD.

It should also be noted that private foreign investment has played a negligible role. Successive governments have stressed the desirability of attracting private foreign capital and in 1959 the Burma Investment Act was passed. For duly approved projects, the Act offered (1) allocation of foreign exchange for importing necessary raw materials and equipment to be exempted from customs duty for three years, (2) income tax exemption for three years, (3) right to accelerated depreciation on original investment, subject to negotiation, (4) guarantee against nationalization for 10 years, (5) compensation in the event of ultimate nationalization and right to remit capital abroad, (6) dividends and profits after taxation may be remitted at the official rate of exchange.

In September 1961, the Investment Act was amended to permit guarantees against nationalization for any period the government fixes (in most cases 20 years or more). However, the Investment Act has not stimulated a large inflow of private foreign capital. Part of the reason is that other underdeveloped countries probably offer better investment climate and opportunities. According to the report of the US Trade Mission which visited Burma in early 1962, 'On a comparative basis, the

---

[1] The Russian gifts consisted of a technological institute, a hotel and a hospital. These were completed in 1960–61.

[2] Consisting of K380 million through reparations, K187 million from the US, K176 million from China, and K66 million from the IBRD.

Investment Act does not offer as liberal an incentive as may be available to American investors in other countries.'[1] The prospect of future foreign private participation no longer exists since the government's nationalization of all commercial banks in February 1963, and the announcement that all export and import trade and domestic industries would be taken over by the government in the near future.

The terms of trade (the relationship between export prices and import prices) are an important factor in determining the real income of an economy, its ability to save, and the level of investment. When export prices rise more rapidly (or fall less slowly) than import prices, the real income of an economy increases because more goods can be imported from abroad with the same quantity of exports. Reliable statistics are not available for Burma's import prices, and therefore in Table 6 the export prices of Burmese goods have been compared with export prices of British and Japanese goods as an indication of the price of imports into Burma. In determining terms of trade, the choice of an appropriate base year is crucial. But the data in Table 6 suggest that for the postwar period as a whole Burma's terms of trade have been rather favourable when compared to prewar. During the Korean war boom, Burma's export prices rose very sharply (*see* data with 1958 = 100) while the prices of manufactured goods from the United Kingdom did not rise. In recent years, if 1958 is taken as a base, it would appear that the terms of trade have become unfavourable for Burma, but they are still favourable when compared to prewar.

The reasonable level of Burmese export prices during the postwar period as a whole has not slowed down economic development. In fact the high rate of investment in relation to gross domestic product is explainable not only by governmental efforts but also by this factor. On the other hand, their fluctuations have had some adverse effects. As noted above in the section on 'The Eight-Year Plan and the Korean War Boom', the high prices for rice exports during the boom misled the planners and there was wastage of resources when some projects had to be abandoned or postponed.

[1] See US Department of Commerce, *Foreign Commerce Weekly*, April 9 1962, p. 587.

TABLE 6 EXPORT PRICES OF BURMA, UNITED KINGDOM, AND JAPAN

1953 = 100

	Export prices of the UK	Export prices of Burma
1937	31	10
1948	78	58
1952	104	89
1956	105	62
1960	110	56
1962	113	57

1958 = 100

	Export prices of the UK	Export prices of Japan	Export prices of Burma
1951	91	145	119
1953	92	113	162
1956	96	114	101
1959	99	104	92
1960	100	106	91
1961	102	105	96[1]
1962	103[1]	103[1]	92[2]

Source: International Monetary Fund, *International Financial Statistics* and its *Supplement to 1962–63 Issues.*

Other Economic Factors

The main factors have been outlined above, but there have been other minor factors such as an outmoded tax system which does not give sufficient incentives to private individuals to save and to invest, and where taxes on corporations are very much higher than on private business thus discouraging the formation of companies and corporations needed to pool savings.[3]

It was noted above that the level of government investment has been about half the total investment in Burma. These

[1] Based on data for nine months.

[2] Based on six months' data for export prices of rice.

[3] For a general review see U Tun Wai, 'Taxation Problems and Policies of Underdeveloped Countries' in *Staff Papers*, November 1962, pp. 428–48.

investments have been financed mainly by the profits of the State Agricultural Marketing Board on rice. Ever since 1948 the internal price of rice has been kept unchanged at a level much below the international price. As the SAMB has the monopoly of rice exports, it is able to make huge profits by buying rice domestically at a low price, and selling it abroad at a higher price. Profits from this source have ranged from 25 per cent to 40 per cent of total government revenue.

Monetary policy has been neither positive nor negative in promoting economic development. There was a large degree of monetary instability during 1952–56, but over the postwar period as a whole there was financial stability and stable exchange rates. However, there is still no stock exchange in Burma even though one existed in Rangoon before the war. The government probably could have encouraged the creation of development oriented financial institutions such as Development Banks and also done more to encourage savings and mobilize domestic capital besides selling post office savings certificates.[1]

In the field of commercial policy also, more might have been done to promote exports of minor commodities. There are still no commercial attachés abroad except at one or two embassies (for example, none exists at Washington, D.C.). The negotiation of trade agreements is influenced more by political than by genuine commercial considerations. While the diversification of the direction of Burmese exports and sources of Burmese imports should be welcomed, care should be taken that Burma sells in the highest market and buys from the cheapest supplier. As is well known, this has not always been the case and many of the trade agreements concluded with Soviet bloc countries have been very unfavourable to Burma. (One example is the case of cement delivered by the Soviet Union which was not only very highly priced but also of inferior quality.)

CONCLUSIONS

Economic development is a difficult process and in postwar

---

[1] For a monetary analysis and the measures which have been taken to develop money and capital market in Burma, see U Tun Wai, *Burma's Currency and Credit* (revised edition, 1962), pp. 209–31.

Burma, although gross domestic product grew at an average rate of 4·3 per cent per annum, the fact that real gross domestic product in 1961–62 was only 11 per cent above that of 1938–39 and that it was no different from the level in 1959–60 suggests that future prospects of growth are none too bright.

After a decade and a half of planning in Burma, successive governments have learned from the mistakes of their predecessors. The present government is also doing its best to produce quick results by giving priority to agriculture, which is commendable. But economic development is not only concerned with the economics of the government sector: it covers the private sector as well. Therefore, unless the efforts of all the people can be directed at achieving economic development the rate of growth must be unsatisfactory.

In the analysis of the factors affecting postwar economic growth both the positive and negative factors have been listed. It would seem that some lessons can be learned from the experience of 1946–62 and new policies should be evolved. Some of these new elements are increasing the price of rice as part of providing more incentives to work and save, adopting realistic commercial policies and better allocation of the savings for productive investments. While the present government seems to be avoiding the mistakes of its predecessors one cannot be certain that new mistakes are not being made; for example, the increasing share allocated for defence, while necessary for political reasons, may be reviewed from the point of view of economic development.

The large allocations on investment in overhead social capital and in industries for a decade and a half lead one to expect some basic changes in the structure of the economy. But unfortunately there has been little or no change. In 1946–47, 27 per cent of the gross domestic product originated from industries and services but by 1961–62 this percentage was still unchanged (*see* Table 1). The occupational distribution of working population in 1931 had 10·7 per cent employed in industry while in 1953–54, 9·3 per cent were employed in this sector.[1]

This is not to deny that new factories and industries have been established. In fact, a significant amount of industrial capacity

[1] See Ministry of National Planning, *Second Four-Year Plan*, 1961–62 to 1964–65, p. 19.

26

has been built up in Burma in such industries as cigarettes, canning and processing of foodstuffs, textiles, umbrellas, aluminium holloware, etc. Installed capacity of electric power in 1959–60 was 200,000 kW or over $5\frac{1}{2}$ times the prewar capacity of 34,000 kW. But there is always the question of allocating investment between consumer goods industries and in industries creating overhead social capital.

The commonly accepted view is that overhead capital is first needed while Messrs C. N. Vakil and P. R. Brahmanand have argued that wage goods (consumer goods) industries should be given preference.[1] The approach used by planners in postwar Burma has generally been first to rebuild transportation and organize power supply at the expense, at times, of agriculture. This approach may have unduly influenced the allocation of investment expenditures in favour of infrastructure in the past, but on the other hand the emphasis on agriculture in the 1962–63 budget of the present government should not be continued indefinitely. The proper balance between investment in consumer goods industries and that in capital goods industries depends on the actual situation at the beginning of each plan period. If the economy does not have excess transportation facilities or adequate fuel supplies, then it is not possible for the consumer goods industries to expand. On the other hand, there is not much point in creating basic overhead facilities if the consumer goods industries are not going to materialize. Therefore, allocation of investment between the two sectors must change from one plan period to another.

---

[1] For a review of their book *Planning for an Expanding Economy – Accumulation, Employment and Technical Progress in Underdeveloped Countries* see U Tun Wai, 'Planning for an Expanding Economy' in *Malayan Economic Review*, April 1958, pp. 42–51.

DR GAMANI COREA *was born in 1925, and educated at Royal College, Colombo, Cambridge University (M.A.) and Oxford University (D.Phil.).*

He joined the Central Bank of Ceylon in 1950, and was loaned to the Government of Ceylon as Economic Adviser, Planning Secretariat, in 1953. In 1957, he was appointed Director of the Planning Secretariat and Secretary of the National Planning Council. He was appointed Director of Economic Research, Central Bank of Ceylon, in 1960, and also became, in 1963, Assistant to the Governor of the Central Bank.

He has represented the Ceylon Government at a number of international conferences, and has also served with the United Nations, as leader of the UN Economic Planning Mission to British Honduras in 1963, and as consultant to the Secretary General, UN Conference on Trade and Development, 1963–64.

2

CEYLON

THE OVERALL GROWTH OF THE CEYLON ECONOMY

An obvious starting point in an appraisal of Ceylon's economic performance since Independence is a comparison of the growth rate of the economy as a whole with the growth rate of total population. In Ceylon, as in many other developing countries, the national accounts data needed for this purpose are by no means complete or wholly reliable. But at the same time there is no reason to believe that the broad picture conveyed by them is misleading. Between 1948, the year of Independence, and 1962 Ceylon's population increased rapidly – from 7·2 million persons to 10·4 million persons. The average annual growth rate of population was approximately 2·6 per cent – a rate significantly in excess of the rates experienced by many other developing countries. Over the same period, Ceylon's gross domestic product is estimated to have increased in real terms, (at 1948 prices) from about RS4,000 million[1] to RS6,000 million, representing an average annual rate of increase of about 3·0 per cent.[2] Real *per capita* product increased by approximately 0·7 per cent per year on average.

The broad picture conveyed by these data is that the Ceylon economy has succeeded, despite an exceptionally rapid rate of expansion in total population, in registering a moderate improvement in real product *per capita*. It would not, of course, be wholly valid to equate this improvement in *per capita* product with an improvement in the average 'standard of living'. But in the case of Ceylon there are at least three factors which suggest

---

[1] One rupee = 1s. 6d. sterling = $0·21 U.S.
[2] *Central Bank of Ceylon Annual Report for 1960*, p. 5. There were, of course, considerable annual fluctuations in the rate of change of gross domestic product over the period – corresponding in the main to fluctuations in export prices.

a rough correspondence between the improvement in *per capita* product and the improvement in living standards.

First, the available data point to a parallel expansion in *per capita* consumption. Real consumption per person is estimated to have increased, between 1948 and 1962, at an average annual rate of 1·4 per cent. Second, the process of rapid population increase was accompanied, as would be expected, by a shift in the age composition of the population in favour of the lower age groups. In other words, the rate of growth of the adult population tended to be lower than the rate of growth of total population and for this reason the increase in real product per adult, or even per family, was perhaps greater than the increase in real product per person of the population as a whole. Third, and no less significant, is the likelihood that income distribution in Ceylon might have changed in favour of the lower income groups. There are no precise statistics to provide an accurate picture of income distribution or its change in Ceylon. But the changing pattern of Government finance, with the growing emphasis on welfare outlays and transfer expenditure of one kind or another coupled with steep increases in taxation whose incidence on the upper income groups was particularly marked, does suggest that changes in income distribution are likely in Ceylon, more perhaps than in other developing countries, to have favoured the lower income groups. All this points to the possibility that the average standard of living or at least the standard of living of the mass of the population, may well have increased at a somewhat faster rate, though not at a markedly faster rate, than the average annual increment of 0·7 per cent in real *per capita* product.

How should this performance be appraised? The data cited above are of an overall or aggregative kind. It needs to be recognized at the outset that Ceylon, like many other developing countries, can point to a variety of individual projects that have been successfully completed, to the establishment of new facilities in different fields, and to several accomplishments and improvements of one kind or other. Over the years since Independence impressive advances have been made in such spheres as land development and colonization, health and education, transport and communications, power development and, more recently, manufacturing industry. Considerable tracts of new land have been brought under cultivation by means of extensive irrigation and colonization schemes. In consequence of this, and the raising of yields on lands already cultivated – which was itself the result of price incentives, extension programmes and tenurial reforms – Ceylon's rice production has increased and rice imports have been prevented from rising despite the large increase in population. The advances that have been made in the field of health and education are particularly notable and there is little doubt that few developing countries, if any, have paralleled Ceylon's achievements in this field. Rapid advances have also been made in social and labour legislation and trade union organization. All these and other gains are not recounted in the present paper. Yet it is necessary that they be acknowledged. The discussion that follows is essentially devoted to an appraisal of Ceylon's progress in terms of the aggregative indices of overall growth. It is based on the premise that Ceylon needs a higher rate of development than it has experienced in the past if it is to bring about a progressive transformation in living standards. It is when measured by the yardstick of overall progress that Ceylon's economic growth since Independence appears to have been inadequate and it is in this sense that Ceylon's performance is appraised in the pages to follow.

Ceylon's performance in overall terms appears inadequate on at least three main counts. The first concerns the very objective of economic development. Ceylon has succeeded over the last fifteen years in 'holding its head above water' in the face of exceptionally rapid population growth. But such an achievement, though not inconsiderable, can scarcely embody the goal of economic policy. In Ceylon, perhaps more than in many developing countries, the processes of universal franchise, which have been in operation since 1931, and the spread of education have resulted in a heightening of aspirations associated with the 'revolution of rising expectations'. The goal of economic policy in this context cannot be the mere preservation of existing living standards in the face of rapid population growth or the bringing about of only modest and marginal improvements in these standards. A rate of improvement in *per capita* product of 0·7 per cent per year, if projected over the future, would imply that it would take several generations before Ceylon could even hope to approach the living standards now prevailing in the more developed countries. In the meantime, economic growth in the developed countries would have proceeded apace and the so-called gap between Ceylon and these countries would have widened.

The growth rate displayed by the Ceylon economy has, moreover, been inadequate from the point of view of the basis it has provided for accelerated growth in the future. In the context of low levels of income, the scope for augmenting the resources-base for investment depends mainly on the channelling into investment of a significant proportion of the increment to income generated by the process of growth, rather than on the curtailment of existing levels of consumption. Clearly this process is frustrated where the increment to *per capita* income is only of a marginal character. On this score too it cannot be concluded that Ceylon has, over the years since Independence, succeeded in bringing about a substantial strengthening of the basis for future development.

The second count in terms of which Ceylon's performance may be judged to have been inadequate is of some interest. This relates to a comparison of growth rates in Ceylon with those of other developing countries in the Asian region. There are, of course, several limitations in the way of international comparisons of national income data. But if these are set aside some interesting evidence does emerge. A comparison of relative growth rates was recently made by the Economic Commission for Asia and the Far East.[1] Its conclusions afford little comfort for Ceylon. Out of 11 countries whose growth rates during the decade 1950–59 were examined Ceylon ranked 8th in terms of the increase of *per capita* real product. Although Ceylon's rate of population increase was higher than that of some of the other countries covered by the Survey, Ceylon's relative position was unchanged even where the comparison related to the growth rate of total national product itself.

It is true that these data should be viewed with some caution. Apart from limitations relating to the comparability of national

[1] *Economic Survey of Asia and the Far East*, 1961, United Nations, p. 11. According to the Survey, both *per capita* and total real product increased faster than in Ceylon in the following countries: Japan, Taiwan, Burma, Philippines, South Korea, Thailand, Indonesia. Countries showing slower growth rates than Ceylon were Cambodia, India and Pakistan.

accounts, there is the possibility that the relatively higher growth rates of some of the Asian countries were a reflection of the progress of reconstruction following the ravages of war. Exceptionally large inflows of foreign aid linked up with political and military considerations might also have been a factor. Nevertheless the fact remains, and this is borne out by other data as well, that Ceylon was amongst those developing countries which showed relatively low rates of *per capita* and overall growth during the postwar period. This result is disappointing in the light of several considerations.

Whilst it may well be the case that other countries were possessed of opportunities not available to Ceylon, it is also true that at the time of Independence Ceylon was favoured with many advantages which were not shared by all these countries. For instance, Ceylon started off with – and still enjoys – a level of *per capita* income or product higher than many other Asian countries. She has a substantial export sector producing tea, rubber and coconuts which accounts for about 30 per cent of national product and which is, in large part, efficient and organized on commercial lines. Moreover, Ceylon is also possessed of a relatively well developed framework of overheads both economic and social. In terms not only of transport and communication facilities but also of levels of education and literacy and of health services, Ceylon enjoys a position of relative advantage. Above all, Ceylon is favoured with a comparatively well developed administrative apparatus and with a large number of trained personnel. All these advantages might have led to the expectation that Ceylon was relatively well prepared to embark along the path of rapid economic growth, and the fact that despite these advantages Ceylon was not in the forefront of progress does give cause for concern.

The third count is perhaps the most important of all. This relates to the country's performance in terms of employment. Although, as mentioned, national product has kept up with and even slightly outpaced population there is little to suggest that the growth of employment opportunities has paralleled the increase in the workforce. It is not possible to provide a complete statistical picture of the course of total employment in Ceylon. But such partial data as exist do point strongly to the conclusion that the growth of employment opportunities has fallen markedly short of the increase in the workforce. The rate of growth in the size of Ceylon's workforce during the decade and a half since Independence was, of course, of a lower order than the rate of growth of population as a whole. The full impact on the size of the workforce of the increase in population during this period is still to come. Yet, according to available estimates Ceylon's workforce increased by some 1·3 million persons – from 2·7 million to 4·0 million between 1948 and 1962. This represents an average annual rate of growth of 2·9 per cent. Although, as indicated, there are no complete data, it is most likely that employment opportunities, both wage and non-wage, fell short of these magnitudes. A survey conducted by the ILO indicated that in 1959 some 375,000 persons were totally unemployed, representing about 11·0 per cent of the workforce. In addition the same survey estimated that 20 per cent of the workforce in the urban areas and 35 per cent of the workforce in the rural areas was underemployed.[1] Although no comparable data exist for the earlier period, these figures are hardly consistent with what could be expected had the employment situation been an improving one.

Evidence that the unemployment problem has been aggravated is also provided by statistics of registrants at the employment exchanges. These exchanges are located in the urban areas and the registrants are not necessarily confined to the unemployed alone. Nevertheless the trend is significant. At the end of 1948 the total number of registrants was 66,656 persons. At the end of 1962 this figure had risen to 152,209 persons. Equally, if not more significant is the falling ratio of placements by the Exchanges to the total number of registrants. Whilst placements amounted to 15·5 per cent of total registrants in 1948, by 1962 this ratio had fallen to 3·2 per cent. Other partial data confirm the picture. There has been evidence of growing unemployment amongst the resident population on the plantations and, above all, there has been an ever increasing pressure of population on land in the non-plantation rural areas.

In the light of this evidence there can be little doubt that even though Ceylon's performance has been adequate to enable *per capita* incomes to be improved upon in the face

[1] Quoted in *Central Bank of Ceylon Annual Report for 1962*, p. 64.

of rapid population growth, this performance has been inadequate on the employment front. This, possibly, is the least satisfactory aspect of the country's economic record since Independence.

Ceylon's experience on the employment front corresponds to that of many other developing countries and points to a conclusion of relevance to the concept of a minimum acceptable rate of growth for such countries. The General Assembly of the United Nations has specified a rate of growth of 5 per cent per annum as a minimum target to be reached by developing countries by 1970, the end of the 'Development Decade'. The adequacy of such a target, however, is clearly open to question. A growth rate of this magnitude would not only fall short of what is required to bring about a significant improvement in living standards and to set in motion a process of accelerated growth. It is also likely to prove inadequate for the realization of employment objectives in the context of rapid population growth. In most, if not all, developing countries there remains considerable scope for improvements in the productivity of labour, particularly in the field of agriculture. In such circumstances, an overall growth rate of only 5 per cent may well be compatible with a deteriorating employment situation.

Ceylon's experience illustrates this very conclusion. Much of the gain in national product in Ceylon has been associated with improvements in yields per acre in the plantation sector, particularly in tea production, and in the domestic agricultural sector, particularly in rice. These improvements have not been associated with substantial increases in total employment. In terms of increasing employment and in terms of bringing about a significant improvement in living standards it would appear, therefore, that targets for developing countries would need to be higher than hitherto assumed – possibly in the neighbourhood, by way of rough illustration, of 6 to 7 per cent per annum.[1] Only growth rates of this magnitude would appear sufficient in the light of rapid population growth and the aspirations of developing countries for appreciably higher standards of living.

---

[1] Ceylon's Ten-Year Plan which aimed at virtually the full absorption of the workforce by 1968 provided for an annual average growth rate of 6·3 per cent.

THE BACKGROUND TO CEYLON'S PERFORMANCE

External factors

The preceding section has set out the main aggregates which provide a measure of Ceylon's overall economic growth. The rest of the discussion is devoted to a broad analysis of the several factors which, in one way or another, influenced or determined the pace of growth. Naturally both external and internal factors were of significance in this connection. Many of them, particularly the external factors and even some internal ones, were outside Ceylon's control during the period under review. Others may be regarded as falling within the purview of official policy. It would hardly be possible, of course, to assess the precise part which each of these factors played in determining Ceylon's progress. But an identification of them would be of some assistance in understanding Ceylon's experience and in illustrating their role as a determinant of growth in a developing country.

The present section is confined to a discussion of external factors. The crucial role played by the external trade sector in the economic growth of developing countries has been highlighted in many recent studies. This stems from the central importance of imports in the development process. Economic growth is closely dependent on the availability of machinery and equipment, raw materials, and even consumer goods of different kinds. Not even the largest of the developing countries are able to provide their entire requirements of these items from within their own boundaries. The smaller countries with scarce raw materials and limited internal markets are particularly dependent on imports from abroad for meeting their needs. In this situation the ability to import – as determined by the course of external receipts – becomes an important determinant of the pace of economic growth.[1]

For Ceylon the role of the external trade sector is particularly important. Two of Ceylon's major products, tea and

[1] Studies by the United Nations Secretariat suggest that for the developing countries as a whole, import requirements tend to increase at a somewhat faster rate than national income. For example, the attainment of a 5 per cent target rate of overall annual growth would require a rate of growth of imports of about 6 per cent annually.

rubber, are produced almost wholly for export whilst about a half of Ceylon's other important product, coconuts, is also exported. Although the share of exports in Ceylon's domestic product amounts to between 30 and 35 per cent, the role of these commodities in the economy as a whole is even greater than is suggested by these figures alone. Exports, for instance, represent a greater proportion of the monetised sector of the economy. Moreover, a host of ancillary activities embracing commerce and distribution, transport and finance, not to mention Government activities themselves, is intimately bound up with the tempo of activity relating to the major exports.

A corollary to the dependence on exports is the particularly severe dependence on imports. In the absence of a sizeable industrial sector Ceylon has to look to external supplies for virtually the whole complex of her requirements of manufactured consumer and capital goods. But this is not all. Ceylon's dependence on imports extends also to primary products, including nearly half her requirements of rice as well as substantial proportions of her requirements of fish, milk and meat products, and even fruits and vegetables.

In this situation the crucial importance of the prices fetched by Ceylon's exports and of the prices Ceylon has to pay for imports – the terms of trade – becomes readily apparent. In Ceylon, as in other 'export-import' economies, there is a dichotomy between real domestic product and real domestic income. There is a sizeable 'import constituent' to real income in Ceylon and the latter is dependent, therefore, not only on the course of real domestic product but on the terms on which Ceylon's exports could be exchanged for imports. The prices fetched by Ceylon's exports are of significance, therefore, not only from the point of view of their relevance to the course of export production. They are also, in combination with the prices of imports, of significance from the point of view of the availability of resources in Ceylon for consumption and investment.

Now it is a fact that in the years since 1948, with the exception of two brief intervals, the price trend of Ceylon's exports has been generally downwards. The exceptions relate to the years 1950 and 1951, the period of the Korean War, when export prices, particularly the price of rubber, shot upwards and the

37

years 1954 and 1955 when there was a sharp increase in the price of tea. For the rest of the period Ceylon's export prices were singularly lacking in buoyancy. In this respect Ceylon shared the experience of other primary producers who had to face the repercussions and consequences of the relatively low income elasticity of demand for their products on the part of the advanced countries. In addition, the years since Independence have witnessed the growth of several new forces which, far from strengthening the market position of these primary products, have served on the contrary to undermine it and to render it even less stable than in the previous period.

There were several such disequilibrating forces of consequence for Ceylon's exports. In the case of rubber there has been the advance of synthetic production in the major consuming centres, particularly the United States. Until recent times it was believed that although synthetic rubber had quality advantages over the natural product or was competitive with it over a wide range of uses, there still remained about a third of the consumption field where the natural product enjoyed distinct quality advantages. In the more recent period, however, with the evolution of 'natural synthetic' rubber even this protection appears to be in the process of being removed. The existence of strategic stockpiles in the consuming centres is a further source of potential pressure on natural rubber prices. Although such stockpiles have served as an instrument of stabilization of natural rubber prices their very existence in the hands of a major consumer cannot naturally constitute a source of assurance for producers of natural rubber. The concern of producers on this score is enhanced by the prospect of the size of the stockpile being reduced through sales in the light of modern strategic requirements. This last consideration is of relevance from yet another point of view. The price of rubber appears to be less responsive than before to international political tensions.

The problem of world markets was also a cause of concern in the case of tea and coconut products. With tea, apart from the slow growth in demand, there has been the emergence of new sources of supply in East Africa and other parts of the world. The quantities involved have hitherto been of a relatively small order but are likely to expand as new areas come into production. There has been an additional factor as well. Whilst Ceylon's high grown teas enjoy a quality preference in the UK market, Ceylon's low and mid grown teas depend largely on the markets of the Middle East countries. The balance of payments and foreign exchange problems of the Middle East countries, however, have resulted in the intensification of restrictions on Ceylon teas and the consequent prospect of the curtailment of consumption. These developments have imparted a new element of uncertainty and instability to Ceylon's tea industry, particularly the section producing mid and low grown teas in which the ownership of plantations by nationals predominates. Although Ceylon has endeavoured to meet these difficulties through the instrument of bilateral trade and payments agreements, the scope for such expedients is limited in view of Ceylon's limited needs for the products of the Middle East countries and her weak bargaining position on this score. In the case of coconuts too, there have been similar problems. The world market for coconut products has been threatened not only by the rapid development of synthetic detergents and other products but also by the expanded production of other natural substitutes particularly soya oil and fish oil.

The background to Ceylon's export trade during the period since Independence has thus been one of uncertainty and anxiety. The major sectors of activity in the Ceylon economy have subsisted under the shadow of depressed prices. This situation, moreover, has coincided with far reaching technical developments on the side of production. Technical research and experimentation have resulted in the evolution of new high yielding strains of planting material in the case of both rubber and tea which hold promise of more than a doubling of the average yields per acre on lands now under cultivation. There has been no comparable technical 'revolution' with coconuts, but even here a significant increase in output is possible by means of the increased application of fertilizers and other measures of rehabilitation. These developments have posed a particularly difficult problem for Ceylon. On the one hand, the very fact of depressed and deteriorating external prices reinforces the urgency of reducing production costs through the raising of yields and of productivity. On the other hand, and this is particularly true of tea where Ceylon is a substantial supplier of the world market, the increase in output would add to world supplies and thereby aggravate the market position. A solution on the lines of a raising of yields on the basis of a restricted total acreage is rendered difficult by the absence of suitable and remunerative alternate crops.[1]

As already indicated, the output of Ceylon's export crops, particularly tea, expanded significantly during the period since Independence. Tea exports alone increased by 54·0 per cent from 296·0 million pounds to 455·9 million pounds between 1948 and 1963. This increase, however, was not due to replanting with high yielding varieties – a development of comparatively recent origin – but to such factors as the increased application of fertilizers. There was also an increase in the exports of coconut products, though of a more moderate order. Here the increase in total output was partly absorbed by the increase in domestic consumption consequent upon population growth. Rubber output, on the other hand, did not increase substantially. This was largely the result of the increase in yields in areas under production being almost wholly offset by the losses in output brought about by the uprooting of old trees for replanting under a Government subsidized scheme. Overall, the index of export volume increased by 40·7 per cent between 1948 and 1962. The course of the terms of trade is, of course, also dependent on the course of import prices. Ceylon's import price index has taken an upward course between 1948 and 1962. In particular, the price of rice, one of Ceylon's major imports, has shown an upward trend over the period. This was of particular significance to Government finance in view of the distribution of rice by Government to consumers at subsidized prices. A sharp rise in the price of rice was one of the major causes behind the acute financial difficulties of Ceylon in the immediate aftermath of the Korean War.

There can be little doubt that had Ceylon faced a stronger and more favourable terms of trade situation her economic performance since Independence would have been considerably

---

[1] The problem of competition from synthetics is one of growing concern to primary producers the world over. It is probably the case that a scheme of compensatory financing in respect of declines in prices or the terms of trade of developing countries offers the most practicable solution to the problem – a solution which would enable developing countries to bring about the structural adjustments made necessary by the emergence of synthetics.

better.[1] An improvement in the terms of trade would have resulted not only in a higher rate of growth of imports and of national income but it would also have strengthened the resources-base for capital formation. In the impact on savings and Government revenue in Ceylon, there is a difference between a rise in incomes in the export sector and a corresponding rise in incomes in the domestic sector. An increase in incomes in the export sector through, for instance, a rise in prices is concentrated, particularly in the case of tea, amongst a relatively few producers, both companies and individuals. This makes possible not only a corresponding increase in savings, but also a channelling away to Government revenue of a substantial part of the increment to incomes, through the medium of the export duty and the income tax. An increase in incomes in the domestic sector brought about by general economic development, on the other hand, tends to be more diffused. It accrues to a larger number of persons many of whom fall outside the network of direct taxation. Nothing could have been more conducive to a stepping up of the rate of investment in Ceylon, and hence the rate of growth of the economy as a whole, over the decade and a half since Independence, than a background of rising export prices and of improving terms of trade. The absence of such a background must, therefore, clearly be counted as one of the important factors responsible for the relatively retarded pace of growth of the Ceylon economy.

Population growth

There is another factor which, though not of an external kind, was nevertheless beyond Ceylon's control in the short-run and which serves to explain the relatively retarded pace of improvement in *per capita* income in Ceylon over the period under review. This is the factor of rapid population growth. Ceylon's rate of population growth averaging 2·6 per cent per annum over the period 1948 to 1962 was more rapid than the rates experienced by most developing countries over the same period.

---

[1] The extent to which the deterioration in the terms of trade negatived Ceylon's efforts at increasing export production is illustrated by the fact that whilst between 1948 and 1963 Ceylon's export volumes increased at an annual average rate of 2·1 per cent, the purchasing power of her exports increased at an average rate of only 0·9 per cent per annum. Cf. *Central Bank of Ceylon, Annual Report for 1963,* Part I.

The cause of the rapid increase was not a rise in the birth rate – Ceylon's birth rate has remained at a level of around 36 births per 1,000 for nearly fifty years – but rather a sharp and spectacular decline in the death rate. Ceylon's death rate fell from 21·0 per thousand in 1939 to 13·2 per thousand in 1948 and 8·0 per thousand in 1961. The fall in the death rate was associated with improvements in health and nutritional standards, leading in particular to a reduction in infant and maternal mortality, and credit is commonly given to the role played by DDT in the elimination of malaria which was endemic over large parts of the country. In many senses Ceylon was a pioneer amongst the developing countries in the process of reducing death rates. For this reason the process of rapid population growth set in somewhat earlier in Ceylon than in other developing countries, and Ceylon had to cope with the problems posed by rapid population growth to a greater extent than these other countries.

The significance of rapid population growth to Ceylon's economic performance is not limited to the simple arithmetic of the relationship between overall growth rates of national product and *per capita* growth rates, although this is in itself of some relevance. Had Ceylon's population increased by say 1·5 per cent or 2 per cent, an overall growth rate of gross national product of 3·5 per cent would have resulted in a *per capita* growth rate of 2 per cent or 1·5 per cent. This would have had obvious implications for the course of living standards, not to speak of unemployment levels. But even more important is the significance of high rates of population growth to levels of capital formation.

A progressive increase in the amount of capital per head of population or per head of the workforce is of the essence of economic development. Yet a rapid rate of population growth renders this process a difficult one in at least two ways. In the first place it requires the diversion of a larger part of the increment to income that arises through economic growth to consumption rather than to investment. Second, and no less significant, it results in the imposition of strong pressures for diverting such resources as are available for total investment into investments in the field of social capital, including health, education and housing. This last point is of some importance.

Countries with rapidly growing populations are obliged to devote increasing amounts of resources to the field of social capital, not for bringing about actual improvements in existing *per capita* standards, but merely for the purpose of sustaining existing standards and of preventing a further deterioration. The importance of pressures of this kind in determining the pattern of resource-allocation is amply illustrated by Ceylon's experience and played no small part, as will be shown later, in preventing a more purposeful allocation of resources for rapid growth.

During the period under review Ceylon did not, as already mentioned, have to face the full impact of population growth on the size of its workforce. The main impact of population growth found reflection in the growing size of the school-going population. The consequences of population growth on the employment situation will be felt more fully over the years ahead. But, as indicated above, population growth was not without relevance to Ceylon's economic performance during the period since Independence. The factor of population growth was, of course, beyond Ceylon's control in the short run. A slowing down in the rate of growth of population can occur through a reduction in the birth rate, but spectacular results on this score could hardly be achieved over the short period. Yet it is of some interest to note that, unlike certain other countries, Ceylon has yet to formulate and implement an official policy relating to the population problem. The 'Ten-Year Plan' of Economic Development published in 1959 drew pointed attention to the problem and stressed the need for the formulation of policy and for the appointment of a population commission. Yet no significant steps in this direction have yet been taken. An agreement was signed between the Ceylon Government and the Government of Sweden for studies in the field of family planning covering attitudes to birth control and so on. But apart from this, and the establishment of a voluntary non-official association, no concrete steps in the way of an extensive programme have yet been taken. In fact, it would be correct to assert that the official attitude to the population question has up to now been a hesitant one.

Yet the importance of the problem to Ceylon cannot be overstated. There can be little doubt that unless Ceylon's rate of population growth, now running at nearly 3 per cent per year, can be slowed down in the future, the problem of bringing about an effective improvement in *per capita* incomes and of laying a sound economic base for accelerated growth would be formidable indeed. There have, in recent years, been signs of a modest falling off in the birth rate, but it is doubtful whether such a process, if based exclusively on spontaneous forces, will be sufficiently rapid in its impact to afford effective relief to the development problem.

Social and political factors

The comparatively unfavourable external background and the rapid increase in population influenced the scale of total investment in the Ceylon economy and the manner in which it has been distributed over the several sections of the economy. The size and pattern of investment will be discussed in more detail in a later section. But it is of some importance in the context of Ceylon to understand some of the wider political and social factors which also influenced the size and pattern of investment and which, in one way or another, made it difficult for Ceylon to concentrate more heavily on development. Indeed Ceylon's experience of the relationship between economic development and social and political change may be of interest to other newly independent countries as well.

It is important to recognize that Ceylon's development effort since Independence had to be made against a background of not only a relatively unfavourable external situation but also of an enlivened internal democratic process. The nature of the external factors has already been outlined; but the difficulties they posed for development were particularly great when placed in the context of the political processes at work in Ceylon. It is to the credit of Ceylon that she has succeeded in maintaining a democratic political system throughout the period since Independence, a system which stood the test of a change of Government. Yet the compulsions of the democratic process had their own implications for development policy.

Universal adult suffrage was introduced into Ceylon as far back as 1931. During the three decades that have since elapsed there has been a marked increase in the political consciousness of the electorate. Whilst it might often be true that in the initial

44

phase following the introduction of universal franchise the mass of the voters tend to be relatively passive in the exercise of the franchise – often supporting the traditional leadership – this is no longer the case as their experience of the electoral process lengthens.[1] There can be little doubt that during the period since Independence Ceylon has witnessed the functioning of a lively and active system of parliamentary democracy.

The important ways in which the political and social processes at work in Ceylon influenced development policy are outlined in the remainder of this section. Generally speaking, it is true that a policy aimed at raising the rate of investment requires effective restraints on the growth of consumption. However, policies directed at restraining consumption and at deploying resources towards investment can not be carried out independently of political and social realities. They have to take account of the pressures emanating from the political process. Whilst the satisfaction of some of these pressures is itself dependent on a rapid pace of development, the process cannot be wholly postponed until such time.

In a general sense, one of the obvious manifestations of the democratic process has been the pressure to make amends for the past neglect of substantial sections of the population. Historically, the emergence of 'dualism' in the economy was accompanied by an emphasis in Government policy on the needs of the modern plantation and commercial sectors of the economy and a relative neglect of the traditional rural sector based on peasant farming. The traditional sector was peripheral to the economy as a whole and was not even the main provider of the country's supplies of food. As the result the traditional sector was sparsely provided with educational and health facilities, with transportation and communication systems, and so on. It was inevitable, therefore, that in the workings of the democratic process a new emphasis would be placed on remedying some of the shortcomings of the past.

In more specific terms, the changing political and social background may be viewed as exerting its influence on the

---

[1] It may be observed in passing that the initial phase of universal franchise and epresentative institutions appears to provide an opportunity for initiating a purposeful development policy. For Ceylon, however, this initial phase coincided with the Great Depression and the Second World War and preceded the era of conscious development planning and policy.

country's development effort in three important ways. First, there was the inevitable emphasis on social welfare in the programmes and policies of Government. Even before Independence the representative legislature established under the Donoughmore Constitution of 1931 placed particular emphasis on schemes for the provision of social amenities of one kind or another. But this emphasis gained in intensity in the postwar period. Following the report of a Commission on Education in 1945, Ceylon adopted a system of free and compulsory education 'from the Kindergarten to the University'. Similar facilities were sought to be provided in the field of health and sanitation services. The claims made by these services on the financial resources of the Government in the context of a rapidly growing population were not only large but subject to continuous increase.

Most significant of all were the subsidies on food. During the period of the Second World War the Government took over the import and distribution of rice and introduced a scheme of rationing to consumers. The role of Government as sole importer and distributor of rice has remained to this day. During the period of the Korean War it was decided to reduce the price of rice to the consumer as a means of relieving the cost of living. Such a step was, at the time, well within the financial capacities of the Government whose revenues were augmented by the boom in commodity prices. The aftermath of the Korean War, however, saw not only a decline in the prices of Ceylon's exports but also an acute world shortage of rice and a sharp increase in international rice prices. In those circumstances, the maintenance of the fixed price of rice to the consumer imposed the severest strains on the Government budget and resulted in the diversion of resources that might have been applied to investment and in the emergence of overall budget deficits which aggravated Ceylon's adverse external payments position and hastened the decline in external reserves. In 1953, in an attempt at corrective action, the Government increased the price of rice to levels equivalent to import costs, but the move resulted in political disturbances and was followed by the reconstitution of the Government itself.

The history of consumer rice prices since that time has been one of successive reductions leading to a progressive increase in the costs of the subsidy as a whole and of its share in the total of Government outlays. An attempt by Government in 1962 to reduce the burden of the subsidy encountered such strong resistance that it had, almost immediately, to be withdrawn. As mentioned, the burden of the food subsidy and other welfare expenditures have clearly implied the diversion of resources that would otherwise have been available for economic development. Ceylon, it is true, has been spared the need for devoting substantial outlays to defence. In this sense, Ceylon has been in a favoured position relative to many other developing countries. But this does not alter the fact that resources that would otherwise have been available for development were diverted to the social services and that political compulsions, at the present stage of the political process at any rate, stand in the way of an effective reversal of priorities and a significant reallocation of resources in favour of development.

The second way in which the processes of political and social change have affected economic development in Ceylon is more complex. The rapid growth of population coupled with the spread of education and the workings of the electoral system have proved to be powerful levers of social change in Ceylon. These forces have exerted far reaching effects on the leadership pattern, particularly in the rural areas, and have prompted the emergence of new élites and groups who have challenged and at times replaced the authority and influence of the traditional leadership. These changes have been accompanied by a new awakening on the part of broad sections of the people who had hitherto been outside the vortex of political power and influence in public life. This awakening has been accompanied by a reassertion of traditionalist sentiments and a resurgence of new nationalisms based on linguistic, religious and cultural values.

In a basic sense these changes are progressive in character in that they are a reflection of the emergence of a new dynamism in the country which could potentially be mobilized for purposes of economic and social change. The growth of a new rural élite, for example, whose position and influence is based on education rather than the ownership of property or family status, augurs well for the introduction and dissemination of modernized techniques and systems of organization. Nevertheless, in the circumstances of a plural society, these changes have

47

given rise to some acute problems which have tended to divert and distract the nation from the tasks of economic construction. In particular they have been associated with the generation of divisive conflicts and antagonisms between the different sections of the Ceylonese community. Several of such conflicts could easily be identified and have, in fact, appeared on the surface in varying degrees during the period under review.

In the first place, there has been the reaction against the Western or English educated élite. The educational system during the colonial period was designed primarily for the creation of an English educated class that could assist in the administrative and commercial life of the country. It was this class created, so to speak, in the image of the colonial power, that inherited the managerial and administrative authority of the British. Yet, by virtue of the very education it had received and the cultural patterns it had adopted, the Western educated found themselves alienated and cut adrift from the new groups and the new nationalisms that were arising throughout the country. A growing dichotomy began to emerge between the locus of political power and that of administrative, executive and managerial authority. This dichotomy tended to weaken the capacity of the Western educated to provide the leadership in the drive for economic development by reducing its authority and initiative. For a developing nation the dilemma was a real one indeed. On the one hand, it is the Western educated class which is possessed of the skills and aptitudes for promoting development and for bringing about the adoption of modern technologies and methods of organization. On the other hand, it is partly against this class and the privileged position it has enjoyed under the colonial era that the force of the new nationalism is directed. The path of escape may be through adaptation, adjustment and educational reform. But the reconciliation would largely have to be achieved by the new rather than by the older generation and in the meantime the goal of economic progress may well be hampered by the conflicts and antagonisms of the adjustment process.

One of the important manifestations of the conflict described above was the strong pressure for the replacement of English by 'Swabasha' or the national languages, as the official language of the country. But the movement to replace English soon took

the form of a conflict between Sinhala and Tamil which culminated in the adoption of 'Sinhala Only' as the official
language of the country – with provisions for the 'reasonable
use' of Tamil on a regional basis. These developments soon
resulted in protracted linguistic conflicts and controversies
between the majority Sinhalese community and the minority
Tamils. It resulted in communal and linguistic riots in 1958.
All these events naturally did not help to create a background
or an atmosphere in which the attention of the nation could be
focused on the tasks of economic development. There was yet
another conflict of a divisive character which resulted in similar
consequences. This was the religious conflict associated in part
at least with the resurgence of Buddhism and in part with
reforms in the educational system which have resulted in the
take-over by the State of private assisted schools, mostly
Catholic schools. Undertones of the conflict were, of course, to
be found outside the educational sphere extending, for example,
to pressures against the disproportionate number of Catholics
in the public service. Apart from preventing a concentration of
energies on development, these developing antagonisms could,
if they are not reconciled or contained within limits, result in
bringing about a sense of alienation or non-participation on the
part of important minorities which by virtue of education and
skills are well placed for playing an important part in the
development process.

It needs to be noted that in virtually all these cases the
antagonisms were directed against groups which, largely for
historical reasons, had hitherto enjoyed positions of privilege
in the community. During the period of British rule both the
Tamils and the Catholics, who are mostly low country Sinhalese, were in a favoured position in respect particularly of the
availability of educational facilities provided largely through
the efforts of private religious bodies. The Sinhalese Buddhists
in comparison were less well placed and began only relatively
recently to receive the benefits of a State organized educational
system. Together with the lead in education went positions of
advantage in commerce, the professions and public service. For
all these reasons it would perhaps be correct in large part to
view the conflicts and antagonisms of the period as a manifestation of an equalizing process through which the large

sections of the community, hitherto relatively under-privileged, are striving to obtain correction and redress.

It is because the privileged groups have happened largely to be linguistic or religious minorities that the conflicts have assumed a religious or linguistic character. The economic background to these conflicts was also sharpened by the relatively slow rate of growth of the economy, particularly the inadequate expansion of employment opportunities referred to earlier. This is yet another example of the innumerable 'vicious circles' that characterize the problems of the developing countries. The inadequacy of development generates conflicts and antagonisms that in turn make difficult the attainment of an adequate rate of development. Not all the problems requiring correction and redress are, of course, dependent for their solution on a high rate of development. Corrective measures of one kind or another could be introduced by legislation, for example by language laws, educational changes, etc. But the success which these steps would have in blunting the sharper edges of conflict would clearly be much enhanced if expanding opportunities for employment and rising standards of living are also made possible by economic growth.

There is still a third way in which the processes of political and social change have had their impact on Ceylon's economic development over the period since Independence. The heightened political consciousness of the voter has been accompanied by the growth of a greater egalitarian sentiment which has resulted in an undertone, at least, of hostility to private capital and enterprise and to the adoption of predominantly 'free enterprise' prescriptions for economic development. It is not without significance that all the major political parties in Ceylon, from left to right of centre, describe themselves as socialist. The policies of successive Governments since Independence have rested on the concept of a mixed economy in which positive roles have been enunciated for both the public and the private sectors. But the fact that the private entrepreneural class in Ceylon was limited in numbers and in affluence and tended to confine itself to the ownership of plantations and, to a lesser extent, to commercial activity, led to the gradual extension of the activities of the State in the economic sphere. The corollary to this was an ever increasing burden of taxation on private incomes, both corporate and individual, which greatly reduced the surpluses available for investment in the private sector, even taking into account the partial relief afforded through tax concessions of one kind or another. It is a fact that in the context of an electoral system based on universal franchise, the small size of the investing class implies the virtual non-representation of the direct tax payer in Parliament.

Another facet of the extension of State activity has been the reservation of specific fields of enterprise, the so-called basic industries, and the importation of essential foodstuffs, to the State, and also the emergence of measures of nationalization or public ownership in such fields as public passenger transport, port handling operations, life insurance business, and commercial banking. It is difficult to say what effect these measures exerted on the 'climate' for private capital. Although successive Governments have repeatedly announced their desire to attract foreign capital, the inflow of new capital was relatively sparse. Measures for the nationalization of foreign owned plantations, though included in the manifesto of the party that formed the Government since 1956, were never adopted. But at the same time it has to be recognized that Ceylon was not in a position to afford the kind of political environment and policy framework that would have been particularly attractive to the private foreign investor. The question of the type of policy framework that would have proved effective in securing private foreign capital is, of course, a difficult one. The fact that private foreign capital was not particularly responsive during the period prior to 1956 when Government policy was in many senses more favourable to it, did not pass unnoticed in Ceylon.

The extension of the role of the State in economic life, whether due to political or other influences, need not, *a priori*, have resulted in a retardation of the pace of economic growth. But it it is a necessary condition for the success of a mixed economy that both the public and the private sectors are possessed of the flexibility and dynamism needed for economic growth. One of the main requirements for a process of economic development in which a growing public sector plays an active part is that public sector enterprise should be capable of yielding surpluses for augmenting the investment base of the economy. This objective would clearly be jeopardized in conditions where the operation and policies of public sector enterprises are subjected to the welfare influences that contribute mainly towards a raising of consumption levels. If such enterprises are regarded primarily as instruments for lowering prices to consumers or for raising the wages of the workers engaged in them, the role they could play in the development process would necessarily be a restricted one. In this situation it is quite possible to envisage a developing country, pursuing the concept of a mixed economy, getting the worst of both worlds – where the private sector is itself restrained and inhibited and the public sector is in turn lacking in flexibility and dynamism.

In Ceylon, public sector enterprises have encountered the type of problem referred to here. Public resistance to price increases – as in the case of Ceylon Transport Board – and the pressure of wage demands from employees could prove to be amongst the factors that result in financial losses on the part of these enterprises. It needs, of course, to be recognized that with the rapid extension of State activity, public enterprise in Ceylon was faced with a host of other problems, particularly of an administrative and organizational nature. It is possible that with growing experience in the management of these enterprises and with the emergence of a trained cadre, their performance in the future will improve. But such success is nevertheless dependent on the transformation of public enterprises into active instruments of development rather than of welfare policies.

ECONOMIC GROWTH AND INVESTMENT PATTERNS

The preceding section has outlined some of the political and social factors that have been in operation in Ceylon as well as the manner in which they have influenced economic policy. However, as mentioned earlier, the relatively slow rate of increase in Ceylon's national income during the period under review can also be explained in terms of the composition and quantum of investment. Indeed, it is through their impact on investment that these political and social factors exerted their most direct effects on the pace of economic growth. A brief analysis of Ceylon's experience in the field of investment will, therefore, be of help in completing this appraisal of the country's economic performance since Independence.

It was indicated earlier that much of the increase in Ceylon's gross domestic product was due to improvements in yields per acre in both the plantation and the domestic agricultural sectors. Increases in service incomes were also an important contributory factor. Yet it is unlikely that these increases in output were the consequence of substantial investments in fixed capital. On the contrary, in cases like tea and rice production, the rise in output was largely the result of increased fertilizer application and of the adoption of improved cultivation techniques. There are no statistical data to show precisely the distribution of investment in fixed capital in Ceylon by sectors for the economy as a whole. But the evidence at hand does not suggest that there was a particularly close correspondence between the relative increase in income in the different sectors and the distribution of investment. This poses a question of some interest. Since the level of gross investment in Ceylon averaged around 12 per cent of gross domestic product over the period, it is relevant to ask why the process of investment did not make a more significant contribution towards raising total production and towards stepping up the overall rate of economic growth? What was the character of the investment that did take place and what appraisal could be made of its possible impact on the economy? It is to these questions that it is necessary now to turn.

The first point that needs to be noted in this connection is that there has been a shift in the pattern of investment in Ceylon towards a greater emphasis on the public sector. In 1948 private sector investment in Ceylon amounted to 55·6 per cent of the total of investment, and public sector investment to 44·4 per cent. By 1959 the rates were significantly reversed with the share of the public sector in total investment rising to 57·0 per cent and the share of private sector investment falling to 43·0 per cent. Not all the outlays classified as public sector investments represent asset formation within the public sector. Capital subsidies and other payments to the private sector are also included in the public sector total where they are channelled through Government. The trend, nevertheless, is unmistakable. As in most developing countries, the extension of Governmental functions in the field of economic activity has resulted in an increase in the relative importance of public sector investment.

In the light of this development, it is appropriate to ask

53

5

whether the shift towards public sector investment has affected the course of the national product in Ceylon. It is difficult, of course, to provide an answer that is absolutely conclusive. But at the same time there are considerations that stand out clearly. In the first place, the rise in public sector investment has been accompanied by an increase in taxation – although in the more recent periods Governmental borrowing has also increased substantially. Between 1948 and 1962 the volume of Government investment increased by Rs428·4 million whilst Government tax revenues increased by Rs837·7 million. It is difficult to say whether the transfer of resources from the private to the public sector has resulted in a corresponding reduction in private sector investment. The increase in taxation may have led in part at least to a curtailment of private consumption. Moreover, even when taxation impinges on private savings, it does not imply that it has been at the expense of productive private investment. Private investment in fields which expand the productive capacity of the economy depends on many factors besides the availability of financial resources. Nevertheless, it is also true that with the important exception of residential construction which normally takes up a fair proportion of private investment, such private investment as takes place is generally of the kind that leads to a direct increase in output. The profit motive itself results in compulsions of this kind. It follows from this that within a given total of investment a shift in relative shares against the private sector and in favour of the public sector could result in a reduced impact on total output unless the public sector investments were themselves of a directly productive kind.

In Ceylon there were at least two important factors which influenced the character of public sector investments and weakened the relationship, in the short run at any rate, between such investments and increases in total domestic output. The first of these factors was the heavy claim made by the social services sector on the investment resources of Government. Outlays on school buildings, hospitals, sanitation and water supply schemes and housing have taken up an appreciable proportion of the total public sector capital budget. Expenditures on education have been particularly heavy since, as already explained, educational expansion has loomed large in Government policy since the introduction of the scheme of free and compulsory education. It would, however, be misleading to depict the relative emphasis on the social services in terms of a policy preference for welfare as against production. The stress on the social services sector does admittedly reflect a response to pressures emanating from the political process. But it is also as much a consequence of rapid population increase. With a rapid rise in the school-going population more schools need to be built if existing standards of facilities per pupil are to be maintained. Similarly, more houses need to be constructed merely to prevent the housing situation from getting worse, and water supply schemes have to be extended to preserve urban standards in the face of a growing population. To curtail the capital programme in the social services sector is more often than not to permit a deterioration in existing standards and this is a decision which Governments could hardly be expected to take.

Whatever the reasons for the scale of investment in the social service sector, the resulting benefits in terms of raising total production have been limited at least over the period under review. In recent years much attention has been focused, in discussions of the problems of developing countries, on the importance of investment in human resources as a pre-condition for rapid economic growth. Ceylon provides an example of a country where such 'investment in men' has received considerable emphasis. It is evident, at the same time, as the Ceylon example well illustrates, that this approach will not always ensure an immediate and rapid acceleration in the pace of overall economic growth.

There are at least three factors which are of close significance to the relationship between economic growth and investment in human resources. First, an early manifestation of social policies, particularly in the field of health and nutrition, is a rapid reduction in the death rate and a consequent stepping-up of the rate of population increase. Second, the initial impact of population growth is a rapid rise in the population of school-going age and this results in a consequent need for devoting progressively larger resources to education if the objective of investing in human resources is to be satisfied. Nevertheless, though the spread of education can exert a far-reaching influence on the productivity of labour and on the capacity of a country to

55

bring about a technological transformation in its economy, the process involves a considerable time lag. This is a consideration of some importance in Ceylon's case. The long period of gestation which characterizes investments in education and in health may mean that Ceylon might reap substantial benefits from her efforts in these fields in the years to come. But, for the period under review, the large investments made by Ceylon in the social sector cannot be said to have contributed markedly towards a stepping up in the rate of overall growth.

The third factor is also of much importance. The impact of social investments on economic growth depends not only on the magnitude but also on the character of these investments. Outlays on education, for example, could have a greater or lesser impact on productivity according to whether the type of education imparted has a technical and scientific or literary bias. It has been one of the criticisms of the educational system in Ceylon in the past that it has not been adequately geared to the development needs of the country and that it has laid too much stress on turning out candidates suited to white collar and non-technical employments. There has been an increasing awareness of these shortcomings in the recent period. But there is still a great distance to be covered in bringing about a more complete integration between programmes in the social service sector and plans for general economic development.

The needs of the social services sector have been one factor influencing the relationship between investment in the public sector and general economic growth. The other factor has been the nature of public sector investments in the field of the economic services themselves. Apart from investments in state-owned industrial enterprises which have attained some importance in the more recent period, most public sector capital outlays in the economic field have been directed to infrastructure items embracing transport and communications, power supplies, irrigation and land development, and so on. Here again the investments are of a kind that have a relatively long gestation period and influence the course of production in more indirect ways. Although it is hardly possible to measure the extent to which investments in this field affected the pace of economic growth over the period under review, it is possible and likely that their immediate effects were limited.

Investments in land development and irrigation have occupied a prominent place in the development programmes of Government in the postwar period. These investments, by bringing new land under cultivation, could exert a more direct impact on production than some of the other investments in the economic field. But in addition to being of a relatively long-term character, most of the important projects in this category have hitherto succeeded in merely extending the area of relatively low productivity systems of peasant agriculture. The transformation of cultivation techniques leading to higher yields per acre has yet to take place – there are only signs that the process is beginning at present – whether in the older areas already under cultivation or the new areas brought into use by investment in the field of irrigation and agriculture. Mention must also be made in this connection of Governmental capital subsidies to private owners for the replanting of rubber and tea land with new high-yielding strains. This category of public sector investment outlays has assumed some importance – for rubber since 1953 and for tea since 1959 – but the impact on production has still been negligible as the replanted areas have yet to come into production. This is yet another example of a long gestation period serving to limit the relationship between investment and output during the period since Independence.

Whilst the composition of investment in Ceylon partly explains the limited impact which investment appears to have had on output during the period since Independence, it is possible, as discussed above, that its benefits might emerge with greater force in the period ahead. In a general sense this should be true of investments in health and education which improve the aptitudes of the future workforce and increase its receptivity to technological change. It is also true of the investments in the economic overheads which strengthen the infrastructure for future development. The potential benefits of investments in irrigation and land development may also be greater, not merely because of the long gestation period between the commencement and completion of construction activity, but also because of the large scope which exists for transforming production techniques. At current levels of productivity, capital–output ratios for irrigation and land development schemes in Ceylon are exceptionally high. But these ratios may change radically, even for schemes already undertaken, if productivity improves markedly with the modernization of agricultural techniques. All this is not to say, however, that the pattern of priorities governing public sector investment during the period under review was an appropriate one. Although the concept of more active state participation in the development process gained recognition in Ceylon during these years and came to be reflected in an expanding public sector programme, it cannot be claimed that this has extended to the adoption of a consistent framework of priorities in determining the composition of public sector investments. Although such a system was made articulate enough in successive planning documents, there has been but little acceptance in practice of the discipline which close adherence to a plan involves.

Ceylon's slow rate of economic growth was also the outcome, of course, of an inadequate quantum of investment. There is little doubt that had Ceylon succeeded in raising the ratio of investment to national income the pace of economic expansion might well have been faster. A relatively low ratio of investment is a common feature of most developing countries. But what is particularly interesting in Ceylon's case is that the investment ratio has remained low despite a relatively successful effort on the part of the Government at mobilizing financial resources, particularly through taxation. In Ceylon, Government revenues amounted to 26 per cent of national income, a proportion considerably higher than attained by most developing countries. Government borrowing from non-bank sources amounted to a further 3 per cent of national income. Despite this and despite substantial recourse to inflationary financing in recent years, total gross capital formation constituted 12 to 13 per cent of national income, and public sector gross capital formation to 7 per cent of national income. This large disparity in scale between the financial resources mobilized by Government and the resources devoted to investment is a manifestation of the severe pressures created by current expenditures on the total of resources available to Government. The nature of these pressures has been discussed in previous sections. Apart from large current outlays on health and education, food subsidies have accounted for nearly 11·2 per cent of the total expenditures of Government and for 15·7 per cent of total current expenditures. The political considerations which stand in the way of a reduction of these subsidies have already been referred to. What is of significance in the present context is the financial and monetary consequences of the Government's attempts to pursue simultaneously the dual objectives of accelerated welfare activities and more rapid economic development. In the more recent period in particular, these consequences have given rise to problems which have deeply affected the country's monetary situation.

In a sense, it is only partly true to describe capital and current expenditures as being competitive with one another. This would only be valid in the context of a given volume of financial resources. Where the claims of both current and capital expenditures are particularly pressing, however, there is also the tendency to expand the volume of financial resources through an expansion of the money supply.[1] Ceylon was unable to have recourse to devices of this kind in the period of the Currency Board system which prevailed up to 1950. But with the establishment of a Central Bank in that year, the country came to be possessed of a more flexible monetary system which made possible the financing of overall budget deficits through an expansion of the money supply. There were two phases of the period since Independence when Ceylon experienced substantial overall borrowings from the banking system. The first phase followed the aftermath of the Korean boom, when Government revenues were adversely affected by the fall in export prices and when the steep rise in the world price of rice swelled the Government's outlays on food subsidies. The second phase, which still continues, commenced towards the end of the nineteen fifties when the subsidy bill which had previously been reduced by unpopular action was enlarged once more through a lowering of consumer rice prices. Each of these phases is rich in illustrations of the limitations which confront a country like Ceylon in attempts to sustain or enlarge the volume of Government expenditures through resort to excessive deficit financing.

Ceylon obtains a substantial part of her requirements of

[1] Foreign aid could, of course, also constitute a supplementary source of resources. Ceylon has been the beneficiary of both multilateral and bilateral aid. However, only a relatively small percentage of total investment was financed through aid, although the proportion has recently tended to increase. US aid to Ceylon has ceased since 1962 because of the question of the amount of compensation payable to the nationalized petrol distributing companies.

consumer goods through imports. This applies, not merely to manufactured goods, but to primary products as well. In consequence, a general increase in money incomes through expansionist budget deficits is rapidly translated into an increased demand for imports which could well exceed the level of Ceylon's external receipts. As long as the country is in possession of adequate external reserves, the increased demand for imports could be met by increased supplies that are financed through a drawing down of those reserves. In this situation the resort to excessive expansionist financing does not tend to have a significant impact on domestic price levels. It results rather in a deficit in the balance of payments on current account. Once the country's external reserves have been substantially used up, however, the situation changes drastically. If the monetary expansion is continued after this point there is no alternative but to resort to direct restrictions on imports in order to preserve a minimum level of external reserves and to safeguard the external value of the currency. However, the reduction in the supply of imports, in the face of a continuance of monetary demand would tend naturally to impart an upward pressure to price levels. If these pressures are sustained the rise in price could be cumulative and be fed by successive increases in wages and costs. The external prices of exports could not, however, be raised in response to an increase in domestic costs. The continuance of a domestic inflation could, therefore, affect export production as the margin of profits in the export sector declines. This would further aggravate the country's balance of payments position and necessitate a further restriction on imports, thereby aggravating the inflationary process still further.

The first phase of substantial deficit financing in Ceylon after the Korean War did not proceed beyond the point of a running down of external reserves. In 1953 the budgetary deficit was virtually eliminated by the removal of the rice subsidy before stringent restrictions on imports became necessary. The phase did not involve, therefore, a significant increase in the domestic price level. The corrective action of the time was further aided by a fall in world rice prices and a boom in the price of tea. By 1955 Ceylon's budget was in overall surplus and Ceylon's external reserves started to rise once more. The second phase which commenced in the late nineteen fifties, on the other hand, was not followed by policy measures of a similar kind. Since 1961 when external reserves had fallen to a low level – a decline that was further aggravated by a reduction in export prices and, in 1963, by a rise in import prices – Ceylon has imposed increasingly heavy restrictions on imports. The reduction in the supply of imports, however, was not matched by a contraction in the size of the budgetary deficits and hence by a reduction in monetary demand. The result has been the emergence of pressures on the domestic price level. The process, however, is still at an initial stage and price increases have up to now been of a moderate order. Prices have been restrained by such factors as the availability of stocks previously imported, the rise in the domestic production and the liberal licensing of essential imports. But in the absence of measures to curtail the monetary expansion or of a favourable turn in the terms of trade, there is a possibility that the process will continue and that Ceylon will face increasing difficulties in the years ahead.

It needs to be recognized, of course, that a process of development in countries hitherto dependent on exports of primary products could generate inherent tendencies of an inflationary kind. Development involves an increasing demand for imports of capital goods, raw materials and even consumer goods. If external receipts do not increase in the same proportion, due for instance to inadequate external demand, balance of payments problems are bound to arise necessitating restrictions on imports and shortages of various kinds. A distinction needs to be made nevertheless between balance of payments problems and inflationary tendencies generated by attempts at bringing about structural changes in the economy through accelerated development, and difficulties caused by attempts to sustain welfare programmes through resort to expansionist finance. Ceylon's difficulties in recent years were as much the result of attempting to sustain consumer subsidies and other transfer outlays as of striving to accelerate the pace of development. There can be little doubt that had the same magnitudes of deficit financing actually experienced by Ceylon been accompanied by larger investment outlays the prospects for economic growth would have been notably better.

There is, however, a development of the last year or two that needs to be noted. Under the stimulus of import controls a number of industrial ventures have begun to emerge, producing substitutes for imports. This has been the first manifestation of significant structural changes in the economy. The total output of manufactured goods has of course been too small to exert a marked impact on the course of national income. But it is a fact that the creation of an assured market for domestic ventures through restrictions on imports has proved to be a more powerful stimulant than incentive legislation or the creation of a favourable 'political climate' for business expansion. A protected market for domestic industry could, of course, have been provided in other ways. Ceylon never had an effective policy of tariff protection for domestic industry, and import restrictions introduced for balance of payments purposes are not the most rational means of providing such protection. Items subject to import control – mostly luxuries and inessentials – are not necessarily the items most suited to domestic production. But the fact that a beginning has been made in the field of industry is notable and, given a rational policy in the future, these beginnings could form the basis for the establishment of a viable industrial structure in Ceylon.

CONCLUSION

The discussion in the foregoing pages has outlined the salient features of Ceylon's experience in the field of development. Since 1948, the year of Independence, Ceylon has had four general elections, and in 1956 the Government of the ruling United National Party gave way to a Government constituted by the Sri Lanka Freedom Party. However, though the changes in administration were accompanied by some changes in policy and emphasis, these were not such as to bring about major differences in the approach to problems of development. Both administrations strove to maintain and expand the social programmes in the fields of health, education and housing, and both were subjected to the pressures of population growth and social changes in the context of democratic institutions. Similarly, both administrations were instrumental in extending the role of the public sector, although there was some acceleration in the process after 1956 with the nationalization of certain activities and the establishment of several new public corporations in industrial and other fields. For a general analysis of growth problems, therefore, a division of the period since Independence in terms of the successive administrations would be of limited significance.

As shown above, the economic growth of Ceylon over the last decade and a half was affected by a host of factors both internal and external, and political and social as well as economic. Nevertheless one of the striking features of the Ceylon scene over these years has been the absence of a systematic 'drive for development'. The expansion of state initiative and intervention in several fields was not matched by a corresponding approach towards a serious effort at planned development. The public sector activities, though increasing in scale, were often the result of *ad hoc* improvisation or endeavours at 'partial' planning. Ceylon did not suffer from an inadequacy of development plans during this period. On the contrary, successive planning documents, including a report of a World Bank Mission, two six-year plans, a ten-year plan, and a three-year Implementation Programme, analysed and laid bare with varying degrees of elaboration and articulation the logical course for action and policy. Yet for the most part these plans, though acknowledged by Governments and even implemented in parts, have largely remained inoperative as effective focal points for action. The political will to implement them has been lacking. Some of the reasons which handicapped the pursuit of a vigorous policy for development have already been outlined. But it is evident that in the absence of a strong resolution to pursue the goal of development the rewards that could be expected would remain limited.

Ceylon's performance in the field of development cannot, of course, be entirely attributed to internal problems and policies. As shown earlier, the absence of a favourable external situation also played a large part in retarding the pace of growth. It need hardly be emphasized that if the prospects for Ceylon's external trade continue to deteriorate in the future, even the greatest discipline and resolve in respect of internal policy would yield but limited results. But given a favourable external context and a disciplined and coherent internal policy the potential for future development is substantial.

Ceylon's Ten-Year Plan spelt out a strategy of development

REVENUE, EXPENDITURE, OVERALL SURPLUS OR DEFICIT AND FINANCING

(Rupees Million)

	Revenue	Current Expenditure	Current Account Surplus	Capital Expenditure	Overall Surplus (+) or Deficit (−)[1]	Expansionary Finance
1947–48	540·6	433·3	107·3	157·4	− 52·3	n.a.
1948–49	576·0	451·2	124·8	218·2	− 115·1	n.a.
1949–50	623·3	461·1	162·2	258·5	− 172·4	n.a.
1950–51[2]	910·2	690·8	219·4	259·3	− 58·5	− 71·1
1951–52	954·0	866·0	88·0	379·9	− 287·7	242·1
1952–53	952·5	788·2	164·3	358·3	− 247·0	149·9
1953–54	1,026·2	673·2	353·2	293·0	+ 5·0	− 89·7
1954–55	1,158·6	762·3	396·3	357·3	+ 90·5	− 171·3
1955–56	1,257·2	862·8	394·4	430·9	− 65·5	6·1
1956–57	1,260·5	976·7	283·8	395·9	− 245·5	147·9
1957–58	1,280·0	1,118·2	161·8	498·6	− 273·3	107·8
1958–59	1,330·4	1,274·4	56·0	493·0	− 442·8	241·0
1959–60	1,403·8	1,365·4	38·4	495·7	− 458·6	247·1
1960–61	1,513·9	1,471·3	42·6	519·1	− 490·8	241·4
1961–62	1,621·4	1,498·1	123·3	585·6	− 476·9	186·4
1962–63	1,593·4	1,524·9[3]	68·5	498·3	− 396·3	178·5

Source: Central Bank of Ceylon.

1 The overall deficit is the difference between revenue and total payments including extra-budgetary capital expenditures as distinguished from the net cash operating deficit which is the difference between revenue and budgetary payments.

2 The gross receipts and payments of the Railway and Electrical Departments have been included in the general budget only from 1950–51.

3 Provisional figure

appropriate for the country. It depicted the scope for expansion that still exists within the agricultural sector of the economy. The agricultural export sector producing tea, rubber and coconuts is capable of more than doubling its present output through replanting with new varieties and through other measures of rehabilitation. The domestic agricultural sector is capable of a substantial increase in output through the raising of productivity on existing land and the development of new land in the 'dry zone' by means of irrigation. However, as shown in the Ten-Year Plan, agriculture alone cannot constitute an indefinite source of expansion or of labour absorption. Given the physical and technical limits to the potential in this field, it is apparent that Ceylon has necessarily to turn to industrialization as well. It is essentially through the creation of an industrial sector that Ceylon can envisage a process of cumulative expansion that will suffice to provide continuing avenues of new employment for her growing workforce.

There are several manufacturing activities that could be established on the basis of Ceylon's domestic market alone and the latter is certain to increase progressively in the course of overall economic growth. Nevertheless, it is also very evident that in the long run large-scale industrialization for Ceylon will involve extensive production for export markets as well, particularly within the Asian region. It is only in this way that industry in Ceylon could make the fullest use of the economies of scale. Today, industrialization for export is hampered by, amongst other factors, the restrictive policies of industrialization pursued by developing countries that are obliged to follow the path of self contained or autarchic development. These policies could only be replaced by arrangements for regional economic cooperation. Ceylon, like many of her neighbours, has much to gain by the move towards economic integration and cooperation in the Asian region. Indeed, such a move may well provide the key to the future development not only of Ceylon, but of the entire South-East Asian region as well.

PROFESSOR V. K. R. V. RAO *was born in 1908, and educated at Bombay University (M.A.) and Cambridge University (B.A., Ph.D.). In 1948, he was awarded the degree of B.Litt. by Delhi University in recognition of his work as Chairman of the United Nations Sub-Commission on Economic Development.*

Professor Rao was Principal and Professor of Economics at the S.L.D. Arts College at Ahmedabad before joining the University of Delhi as Professor and Head of the Department of Economics in 1942. He was the founder and first Director of the Delhi School of Economics, and for three years was Vice-Chancellor of Delhi University. He then served as Director of the Institute of Economic Growth, Delhi, and in 1963 was appointed a member of the Indian Government's Planning Commission.

Professor Rao is the author of a number of books on economic subjects, and has served on numerous Indian Government Committees and Commissions.

3

INDIA

INDIA's economic position on the eve of independence was not such as to cause optimism. Our career as an independent nation began with the unhappy heritage of a war-economy financed largely by inflation and unaccompanied by any significant increase in national production. The problems created by this heritage certainly did not gain in ease of solution by the events that came in the wake of independence, such as the influx of refugees and the military developments consequent on the Kashmir dispute. The country was also faced by a serious food shortage which had to be met by rising imports and controlled distribution and procurement of domestic output. There was also the problem of the large number of semi-autonomous princely states which had to be integrated with independent India by peaceful and persuasive means. The country had to frame its constitution – a time-consuming process – while, alongside, the Government was faced with the rising and possibly somewhat extravagant expectations which the people now entertained of an immediate improvement in their economic condition and which they expected their new popular Government to fulfil.

High prices, shortages, controls, transport difficulties, transition from a war-time to a peace-time economy, refugees, princely states, the Kashmir fighting, labour unrest, and extravagant expectations of economic improvement consequent on independence – all these made for a sombre beginning. The one favourable factor, however, was the people's confidence in their leaders who now constituted the government and, in turn, the leaders' dedication to the country and confidence in their power to do good to their people. Also on the positive side were to be counted the preliminary work which had already been put in on programmes and projects of postwar reconstruction during the closing years of the war, and the sterling balances which had been accumulated by the sale of Indian goods and services to the allies in their campaigns in the Middle East, the Near East and the Far East theatres of war.

The first three years after independence were mainly occupied with the politics of integration and constitution making, the politico-economics of transition to a peace economy, and refugee relief and resettlement. With the liquidation of princely authority, the enactment of India's republican constitution, the freezing of the Kashmir problem, and the satisfying of the people's immediate felt needs following the termination of war, the Indian Government could turn their attention to the country's basic economic problem. This was the problem of poverty and economic stagnation. Agriculture was the principal economic activity; and the *per capita* income it gave was low not only because of under-investment, traditional techniques, and low productivity, but also because the holdings were small and the pressure of population on land higher than in most other parts of the world. Modern industry accounted for but a small part of the national economy and it consisted mostly of consumer goods with hardly any significant element of basic or capital goods industries. Literacy was conspicuously low, even primary education was not available to a large majority of children of school-going age, scientific and technical education was woefully inadequate, and there was hardly any provision for organized scientific research within the country. The output of basic minerals like coal and iron ore was low even in absolute figures and much more so in *per capita* terms. The position was similar with regard to electric power, while oil hardly figured in domestic output. Domestic savings and investment were estimated at about 5 per cent which, on a capital–output ratio of 3:1 and the current rate of population growth, barely prevented the *per capita* national income from falling, while there was but little significant injection of foreign capital to lift up the level of economic growth. A low basic level of economic activity, a high rate of population growth, a pre-industrial structure, a low rate of savings and investment, and a snail's pace of economic growth – these were the salient features of the Indian economy, the overall picture being represented by a *per capita* national income of RS266·5 or £10 for the year

68

1950–51, which placed India almost at the bottom of a list of the then independent countries arranged in order of the size of their *per capita* annual income.

There could be no doubt that India's problem No. 1 was the conquest of mass poverty. This could not be done by a process of redistribution, the basic need being one of expansion of production. What the country required was economic development. The official view of the development problem was quite clear. Domestic savings were low; foreign loans or grants or investments were negligible; investment was therefore low; and without investment, equipment was low and with it both productivity and production. The other important stimulant of economic development, namely, use of modern methods of production and application of science and technology to economic activity was also of a significantly low order of magnitude. The number of engineering colleges, polytechnics, research laboratories, and other professional institutions relevant for the efficient utilization of resources was also most inadequate for making any significant impact on the Indian economy. It is true that the country had ample resources, both natural and human, but if these were to be geared to economic growth, and the economic potential converted into actual increase in output, it was necessary that there should be a significant increase in investment and in the application of science and technology to economic activity. To bring about a release in productive energies and secure an all round increase in the tempo of economic activity presupposes an adequate build-up of social and economic overheads in the economy, and there was no guarantee that this would take place even if there was an increase in investment. Economic analysis showed that the necessary stimulus to economic development was not likely in the absence of deliberate measures, and that this required not only a much bigger economic role for Government and the public sector generally, but also a considerable measure of co-ordination, anticipation, regulation and programme – in other words, economic planning. Moreover, the constitution adopted by the Constituent Assembly contained directive principles of state policy on economic and social matters, the implementation of which could not be effected in the absence of economic planning. Finally, even before the transfer of power from Britain to

6

India, the then Government had taken some steps for postwar economic reconstruction and development on a planned basis to be brought into force on the conclusion of peace, and a special department for the purpose had been set up. Leading industrialists had also issued a joint memorandum, popularly known as 'The Bombay Plan' which set out an ambitious programme for the planned economic development of India. Moreover, the party which constituted the Government after independence, namely the Congress Party, had accepted the necessity for economic planning long before it came into power; Prime Minister Nehru himself having functioned as Chairman of a National Planning Committee which the party had set up in 1938. Under the circumstances, it was clear that there was no alternative to planning as the methodology for economic development; and it was not surprising therefore that this became the official policy of the Government of India in March 1950, when they turned their attention seriously to the solution of the country's long-term economic problem.

India's first Planning Commission was set up by Government Resolution in April, 1950.

The First Five-Year Plan was produced in draft form in July 1951 and, after public discussion and debate, in its final version in December 1952. The Plan covered the five year period from April 1951 to March 1956. Its analogy with the Soviet First Five-Year Plan, however, was more in name than in content or ideology. There was neither a revolutionary background nor a totalitarian regime behind the Indian Plan. Nor did it visualize the application of planning to the production, distribution or exchange of the entire economic output of the country. It was concerned more with effecting the postwar and post-partition readjustments required by the economy rather than dealing with the entirety of the country's long term economic problem. It was true that the Plan did contemplate a closer integration of the private sector with the public sector and the guidance of the former by the latter, but essentially it was concerned with rationalizing and increasing capital expenditure in the public sector, rather than with controlling and directing all private investment. Moreover the Commission had neither a blank nor a clean slate on which to write its Plan. Public expenditures on economic development, both capital and revenue, had been in progress during the postwar period on the part of both the central and the state governments, and had already involved large sums of money. It was obviously impossible to scrap these schemes and thus to waste the millions of rupees that had already been spent on them. Inevitably it followed that the Commission could not draw up a plan on an *a priori* basis of assessment of requirements on a national scale, but had to some extent to content itself with the task of coordinating and integrating the central and state programmes of expenditure already in operation, eliminating some and economizing on others. Its task thus became one of bringing order out of the chaos of existing public expenditure, rather than one of drawing up a plan *de novo* for the economic development of India. Moreover, war-time and postwar inflation, combined with the economic and political consequences of partition, needed attention before anything spectacular or significant could be attempted by way of economic development.

Political and administrative factors also limited the scope of the Commission's recommendations. The Congress Party was not then a socialist party. True, its leader, Mr Nehru, professed admiration for socialist ideas; but he was too good a democrat to subordinate his party to his own personal views, especially when he himself was not convinced of their immediate practicability. Moreover, the administrative personnel was already overstrained and could not stand the much greater stretching that would be involved in any large extension of public ownership and operation of economic activity. Nor could the country's public finance afford the expenditure which, consistent with the principle of compensation enshrined in the Constitution, such extension would necessitate. Then again the country was committed to the democratic process, and its government functioned on the basis of parliamentary responsibility. Planning had, therefore, to proceed without the ease of operation afforded by a totalitarian regime. At the same time, *laissez-faire* and free enterprise could not secure planned development, nor were they politically acceptable to the vast majority of the population. Under the circumstances, the rather anaemic compromise of a mixed economy naturally became the political background against which the Commission had to project its Plan for economic development. Thus it was inevitable that India's first

Five-Year Plan should be moderate and modest rather than grandiose or doctrinaire, and that it should take the form largely of rationalizing and increasing public expenditure on development rather than of calling for over-all ownership, operation or even control by the Government of the country's entire productive resources.

In its final version, the first Five-Year Plan did place before the country targets or expectations of its programme of long term economic development. Thus it contemplated a doubling of the *per capita* income by 1977, i.e. in about 27 years, provided certain assumptions were fulfilled regarding major parameters in the economy, the most important of which related to rise in the pre-plan rate of saving and investment of about 5 per cent to that of 20 per cent by 1968–69 and its continuance at that level thereafter. For the first five-year period, however, the increase in national income contemplated was only 10 to 11 per cent and of *per capita* income 5 to 5½ per cent with savings and investment rising to the modest figure of 6¼ per cent at the end of the period. The First Plan itself, however, was quite modest and visualized a total investment of RS35,200 millions or £2,640 million over the period 1951–56. Of this, about 51 per cent represented what the private sector was supposed to undertake and hardly figured as an integral part of planned development.

The real planning was in the public sector where an investment of £1,470 million over 5 years became the responsibility of Government. Agriculture, including community development and irrigation, claimed the lion's share, accounting for 31 per cent of the planned investment. Transport and communications accounted for 27 per cent, power for 13 per cent, social service for 23 per cent, and industry had to be content with an allocation of about 4 per cent of the total investment. The bulk of the finance needed was to be found from domestic resources and sterling balances, with foreign aid and deficit financing playing only marginal roles. Nature was also friendly and the first Plan period saw two favourable monsoons which led to bumper harvests in its concluding years. The Plan thus got over-fulfilled. National income rose by 17·5 per cent at the end of the Plan instead of the targeted figure of 11 per cent; and *per capita* income by 10·5 per cent instead of 5·5 per cent. Prices actually recorded a decline, sterling balances still remained a substantial nest-egg, deficit finance was significantly below what the planners had been prepared to acquiesce in, and there was no balance of payments problem. Truly, planning was not only successful but also appeared to be painless; and the country saw the close of the first Plan period with a great feeling of optimism and self-confidence. There were, of course, some blemishes in the picture. Even the modest industrial target was not achieved, land reforms got blocked up in legal tangles and unwillingness of the landed interests to give up their privileged positions, and the community development programme, while releasing a new wave of expectations in the rural areas, did not succeed in sufficiently canalizing it into positive channels of self-reliance and economic betterment. All the same, the total picture looked good and the country set out on its Second Five-Year Plan with a feeling of accomplishment and therefore preparedness to face up to something bigger and more difficult in its desire for economic development.

The Second Plan was formulated on a more ambitious scale; and it was more of a Plan in the orthodox sense of the word than the First Plan. Emphasis was now shifted to industry; and not just industry, but basic industry, steel, cement, coal, power and oil which provide the sinews of industrial development, and machine tools, machine building, heavy engineering and heavy chemicals which give the country its growth potential in the physical sense, and will set it on the road to self-sustaining and self-accelerating economic development. To get the economy to 'take-off' became the objective; and there was readiness to make more use of deficit financing as well as eagerness to make more use of foreign aid. The strategy of the Second Plan was to make investment not only more massive but also more growth-oriented and more based on foreign resources, and to leave consumer goods to small scale and cottage industries and less capital-intensive methods of production. The volume of investment contemplated, including what is called current outlay or current expenditure of a developmental character was RS77,000 millions or £5,775 millions of which £2,325 millions was expected to be in the private sector. Governmental investment was placed at £3,450 millions over the five-year period. This time, agriculture, including irrigation and power, accounted for only 30 per cent of the public outlay as against 44 per cent in the

First Plan. While transport and communications retained their First Plan proportion in the public outlay, social services recorded a decline from 23 per cent to 18 per cent.

The most significant change was in the investment on industry and minerals in the public outlay. This increased from 4 per cent to 20 per cent, and out of a total that was double that of the First Plan. There was also a big rise in the investment on industry in the private sector. Mainly because of this emphasis on industry, there was a big increase in foreign exchange requirements, the total deficit in the balance of payments being estimated at £825 million. After allowing for a withdrawal from our sterling balances to the tune of £150 millions, the Plan estimated the foreign aid required at £675 millions as against the foreign aid of £153 millions used for the First Plan. In absolute terms, foreign aid requirements were estimated at more than four times that actually used in the First Plan period. Domestic resources, in spite of a substantial increase in their absolute amount, also showed a larger gap, with the result that deficit financing was now placed at £900 millions, or more than three times the amount used for the First Plan. National income was expected to rise by 25 per cent as against the realised increase of 17·5 per cent during the First Plan period, thus showing the longer gestation period of the investment contemplated during the Second Plan and the consequent rise in the capital–output ratio. *Per capita* income was expected to increase by about 18 per cent as against 11 per cent achieved during the First Plan period. Domestic saving was expected to rise from 7 per cent to 9 per cent, investment increasing faster from 7·3 per cent to 10·7 per cent.

The Second Plan was thus not only bigger in both the effort required and the targets put forward, but also in its dependence on both deficit financing and foreign aid. The Plan also required a more careful and detailed measure of planning and programming, and in a field, namely, basic and heavy industries, in which the country did not have enough experience. The Second Plan quickly ran into difficulties. Laxity in the administration of licensing and import controls led to a much larger volume of private investment and private imports than the Plan contemplated. Import prices rose, partly on account of the Suez crisis and partly on account of growing full employment and inflationary conditions abroad, and swelled our foreign exchange requirements. Plan estimates of expenditure on investment turned out to be gross under-estimates in some major projects with the result that some of the investments contemplated had to be postponed, while others cost much more than had been anticipated. Agricultural production failed to increase, especially during the first three years of the Second Plan period; and domestic prices of both food grains and raw materials rose with inevitable repercussions on public expenditure, both developmental and non-developmental, and on exports. Deficit financing on the vast scale provided for in the Plan added to the difficulties of the situation more especially as output failed to rise to the anticipated extent. The country was faced with a balance of payments crisis almost from the first year of the Second Plan period, sterling balances were drawn upon well beyond the amount visualized in the Plan document making it necessary to lower the legal limit of India's statutory foreign exchange reserves, and foreign aid was asked for and resorted to on a much bigger scale than originally contemplated. Imports of foodgrain also had to be increased substantially under PL 480 agreement with the United States, in order to exercise a curb on rising domestic prices and augment the country's food supplies. Altogether, the Second Plan woke up the country to the real implications of planning for a rapid rate of economic growth and made the people realize that economic development was in some respects like war involving sweat and toil; if not also tears.

It must be added however that the Second Plan did not prove a failure, as had been anticipated by some gloomy prophets. While over-all achievement was less than targeted and while there were short-falls in output and postponements in investments, what was accomplished was nevertheless truly impressive. National income rose by 20 per cent and food production increased by 15 million tons in 5 years. The index of mineral production showed an increase of 42 per cent and that of organized industry 39 per cent. Some of the major basic and heavy industries increased their output in startling fashion, basic industrial chemicals by 143 per cent, fertilizers by 149 per cent, basic metals by 84 per cent, machinery by 170 per cent and petroleum products by 57 per cent. During the same period, imports of machinery of all kinds rose by nearly 40 per cent. The number of villages covered by community development and national extension services increased from 143,000 to 364,000; the number of pupils in primary schools from 23·9 million to 34·8 million, in high school from 8·5

TABLE I NET NATIONAL OUTPUT AT 1948–49 PRICES[1]

Sector	Value (in £ million)		Percentage distribution	
	1950–51	1960–61	1950–51	1960–61
Agriculture, animal husbandry and ancillary activities	3,255	4,433	49·0	46·4
Mining, manufacturing and small enterprises	1,110	1,582	16·6	16·5
Commerce, transport and communication	1,245	1,845	19·0	19·3
Other Services[2]	1,043	1,740	15·6	18·2
Net domestic output at factor cost	6,653	9,600	100·2	100·4
Net earned income from abroad	15	37	−0·2	−0·4
Net national output at factor cost = national income	6,638	9,563	100·0	100·0

million to 9·5 million and in universities from 574,000 to more than one million. Progress was particularly rapid in engineering and technology, the number of pupils in engineering colleges practically doubling itself during this period, with admission capacity reaching the figure of 13,860 for degree and 25,570 for diploma courses in engineering and technology. Viewing the progress of the economy objectively during the Second Plan period, there can be no doubt that it had become both advanced and diversified and added substantially to its growth capacity.

[1] Based on Tables 10 and 10.1, *Estimates of National Income, 1948–49 to 1961–62*, Government of India.
[2] Comprising professions and liberal arts, government service, domestic service and house property.

Before proceeding to a discussion of the Third Plan which is now half-way through its third year and has in the meanwhile got overlaid with the national emergency resulting from Chinese aggression, it may be useful to look at the results and lessons of the first ten years of planning. The over-all results of the first two Five-Year Plans are seen in Table 1 (opposite). This shows that national income rose by about two-fifths during the first ten years of planning. During the same period, population rose by 21·4 per cent. *Per capita* income therefore increased from £18·6 in 1950–51 to £22·3 in 1960–61 or by about one-fifth. There could be no doubt that the Indian economy had broken away from the path of stagnation thanks to planning, though the progress achieved was not satisfactory from the point of view of Indian requirements.

These figures do not, however, reveal the salient features of India's economic growth during this period. The table shows practically no structural change in the economy except that the share of agriculture has recorded a small decline of 2·6 points in favour of the miscellaneous sector comprising all services. This is a misleading picture, as the income under services has not been deflated for the rise in prices during the period, while that has been done in the case of all the other sectoral incomes. Moreover, details of the meaningful sub-groups under each sector have not been worked out at constant prices, while they are available at current prices. To get at the dynamics of income growth during the period, therefore, it is better to use the national income data at current prices. Table 2 (pp. 78–9) gives details of national income by industrial origin at current prices for the pre-plan year 1950–51 and the final year of the Second Five-Year Plan 1960–61, together with the index of growth in each sector during the period as well as the difference this has made to its share in the net domestic product:

We may further classify the sectors by type of methodology of production, under three categories, namely, modern, traditional, and others. Table 3 (p. 80) gives details of the increase in the value of net domestic output, percentage increase over 1950–51, and change in the percentage share of the total.

It is seen that the modern sector increased its net output by RS1,630 millions or by 122 per cent, whereas the traditional sector increased its net output by RS26,400 millions or by only

TABLE 2 NATIONAL INCOME BY INDUSTRIAL ORIGIN[1]

Category	1950–51 (millions Rs)	1960–61 (millions Rs)	Increase in 1960–61 over 1950–51 (millions Rs)	Percentage increase 1950–51	Change in % share of total
(1)	(2)	(3)	(4)	(5)	(6)
Agriculture					
Agriculture, animal husbandry, etc.	4,780	6,690	1,910	40	−3·0
Forestry	70	110	40	57	+0·1
Fishery	40	100	60	150	+0·3
Total	4,890	6,900	2,010	41	−2·6
Mining, Manufacturing and Small enterprises :					
Mining	70	160	90	129	+0·5
Factory establishments	550	1,320	770	140	+3·5
Small enterprises	910	1,120	210	23	−1·7
Total	1,530	2,600	1,070	70	+2·3
Commerce, Transport Communications :					
Communications (Post, telegraph and phones)	40	60	20	50	nil
Railways	180	360	180	100	+0·7
Organized banking and insurance	70	160	90	129	+0·4
Other commerce and transport	1,400	1,760	360	26	−2·3
Total	1,690	2,340	650	38	−1·2
Other Services :					
Professions and liberal arts	470	740	270	57	+0·3
Govt (administration)	430	910	480	112	+1·9
Domestic service	130	190	60	46	−0·1
House property	410	530	120	29	−0·5
Total	1,440	2,370	930	65	−1·6

[1] Based on Table 3, *Estimates of National Income, 1948–49 to 1961–62*, Government of India.

TABLE 2 *continued*

Category	1950–51 (millions Rs)	1960–61 (millions Rs)	Increase in 1960–61 over 1950–51 (millions Rs)	Percentage increase 1950–51	Change in % share of total
(1)	(2)	(3)	(4)	(5)	(6)
Net domestic product at factor cost	9,550	14,210	4,660	49	
Net income from abroad	—20	—50	+30	150	
Net national output at factor cost = national income	9,530	14,160	4,630	49	

36 per cent. But because of the much greater weight that the traditional sector has in the Indian economy, the domestic output at factor cost increased by only 48·8 per cent. The modern sector, in spite of a rate of growth that was *nearly three times* that of the rest of the economy, could increase its share in the total by only *seven per cent*, reaching a figure of 20·9 per cent in 1960–61 as against 14 per cent in 1950–51. Herein lies one of the major reasons for the comparatively slow growth of the national income as also an indication of one of the major requirements for accelerating its rate of growth in the future. Obviously what is required is not only an increase in the size of the modern sector and in its efficiency, but also an increase in the efficiency of the traditional sector. In other words, without a substantial improvement in the productivity of agriculture and in that of small industry and small commerce, it will not be possible to bring about a substantial increase in domestic output within a short period. Hence the renewed emphasis on agriculture and small industries in the Third Plan pattern of investment and policy assistance.

The second feature we have to notice about the first ten years of planning is the extent to which the structure of the economy in terms of its growth potential has been emphasised in the

TABLE 3 NET DOMESTIC OUTPUT AT FACTOR COST[1]

Category	Increase in 1960–61 over 1950–51 (million Rs)	Percentage increase in 1960–61 over 1950–51	Change in percentage share of total
(1)	(2)	(3)	(4)
I. *Modern Sector:*			
1. Mining	90	129	+0·5
2. Factory establishments	770	140	+3·5
3. Communications (Posts, telegraph and telephones)	20	50	nil
4. Railways	180	100	+0·7
5. Organized banking and insurance	90	129	+0·4
6. Govt (administration)	480	112	+1·9
7. Total	1,630	122	+7·0
II. *Traditional Sector:*			
1. Agriculture and allied activities	2,010	41	−2·6
2. Small enterprises	210	23	−1·7
3. Other commerce and transport	360	26	−2·3
4. Domestic services	60	46	−0·1
5. Total	2,640	36	−4·1
III. *Others:*			
1. Professions and liberal arts	270	57	+0·3
2. House property	120	29	−0·5
IV. *Grand Total*	4,660	49	

[1] Based on 'India's Industrial Revolution in Progress', Walchand Memorial Lecture, 1961, by Professor V. K. R. V. Rao.

pattern of investment. The bulk of public investment has been devoted to the creation of economic and social overheads, including not only transport, power and irrigation, but also minerals, steel, basic industries, and scientific and technical education. Even in the private sector, the emphasis has been on basic industries like heavy chemicals, machine building, electrical equipment and light engineering, while in agriculture special attention has been paid to industrial raw materials like jute, cotton and oil seeds. There is no doubt that this emphasis on structural change, with its inevitable lengthening of the period between investment and output, has had an adverse effect on the growth of the national income in the short term, but this is an inevitable accompaniment of any type of planned development that aims at the long term growth of the economy. Viewed analytically, it is the same thing as stepping up the rate of domestic saving beyond what it is likely to reach in the absence of economic planning; and it constitutes an essential part of the strategy of economic development. This of course involves a heavy price in the case of a country like India with its low basic levels of current output, but there is no getting away from the fact that any attempt at accelerating economic development is bound to mean some sacrificing of the present in the interests of the future. But as the investments complete their gestation periods and begin to fructify, and as the response of private enterprise to the stimulus of investment opportunities created by the building up of economic and social overheads and the physical means of capital formation begins to emerge and expand, the effect will be felt in a stepping up of the increase in national income.

This brings me to the role of the private sector in India's planned development and the interminable controversy of the public *versus* the private sector. Taking the investment in the public sector, it will be seen that the bulk of the outlay is not only of a non-competitive character with the private sector but is actually aimed at providing investment opportunities for the private sector and facilitating a larger return for private enterprise than it would otherwise have made. Thus the investment outlay on agriculture, national extension and community development, and irrigation and flood control are all intended to raise productivity in agriculture and not to bring agriculture under public ownership. At the same time they constitute items of investment that no individual or combination of individuals in the agricultural field would either be able or willing to undertake. Similarly the investment outlay in the field of social services is intended to raise the productive capacity of labour, including the large number of self-employed persons or small entrepreneurs, by improving their health and imparting them skills or, at any rate, the possibilities of acquiring skills; and it is obviously expenditure that private individuals would neither be able nor willing to undertake. The power that is going to be produced in the public sector is largely intended to service the private sector; in fact, it will not only serve existing units of private enterprise but also service their expansion and facilitate the emergence of additional units of private enterprise.

The biggest item of investment outlay in the public sector is on the consolidated item of transport and communication. The bulk of the items falling under this head are all items that are beyond the capacity of the private sector to undertake and have, in addition, been traditionally within the public sector in India long before India got its own independent Government. In fact, they constitute the essential economic overheads without which it is impossible for private enterprise even to function, let alone expand. It needs no elaborate arguing to show that unless there is expansion of India's capacity in transport, harbour and communication facilities, there can be no expansion of opportunities for private enterprise either in industry or in agriculture or in commerce. Here again, expenditure in the public sector is not only non-competitive with the private sector but is, in fact, an essential preliminary for the expansion of the latter. Even in regard to public investment in industry proper, it is almost exclusively concerned with minerals and basic industries requiring investment on a scale that is beyond the reach of the private sector in India. The three steel plants that have figured in the Second Plan would quite certainly not have come into existence if they had been left to private enterprise; and the same is true of the significant expansion that is now taking place in India's output of crude oil.

In view of the considerations stated above, I suggest that too much has been read into the figures of investment outlay in the public sector by the accredited champions of private enterprise.

In fact, it is this heavy investment in economic and social over-heads that has created the necessary background for the stimulation of industrial production in the private sector. The private sector has also been stimulated by the closed economy that has accompanied planning, with its severe restrictions on imports of consumer goods and the greater availability of foreign exchange for capital goods and maintenance imports. The more or less guaranteed domestic market that this has created has acted as a tonic to private industry and led to its growth and expansion on a larger scale and in a more diversified manner than was actually contemplated in the Plan targets. The private sector has also been assisted in securing foreign exchange for its capital requirements by government sponsorship before foreign financial organizations like the International Bank, the International Finance Corporation, the Export-Import Bank and some other banking institutions. Direct government help to the private industrial sector in securing domestic finance has also been considerable through different financial institutions like the Industrial Finance Corporation, the Industrial Credit and Investment Corporation, the National Industrial Development Corporation and the Refinance Corporation of India. According to Shri K. P. Mathrani of the Industrial Finance Corporation, such direct financial assistance by way of loans and credits given to the private sector in industry has totalled RS2,240 millions during this period or about 24 per cent of the total estimated investment of RS9,450 millions made in the organized industries in the private sector during the two Plan periods. In addition, the International Finance Corporation and certain other institutions have been given guarantees for deferred payments and under-written capital issues, aggregating to RS400 millions during this period. If this amount is added to the assistance given to the private sector in organized industry in actual cash, the contribution of the State to private industrial finance during the period comes to nearly 28 per cent of the total investment. The government has also given substantial indirect financial assistance to private industry by way of tax concessions aimed at promoting investment, such as double depreciation allowances, development rebates, and tax holidays. While it is not possible to give a quantitative estimate of this assistance, there can be no doubt about its substantial character as is seen by the comparatively small increase in tax contribution out of the gross profits earned in the private industrial sector during the last ten years. It is surprising therefore to hear from time to time a suggestion that the public sector has been developing at the expense of the private sector. On the contrary, the bulk of the investment and current outlay incurred by Government during this period has been for the purpose of facilitating development in the private sector; and that this policy has also succeeded is amply borne out by the phenomenal increases in output and diversification that have taken place in the private sector in organized industry during this period. By way of illustration, I may point out that during the nine years ending with 1959–60, there were many private sector industries that increased their output by amounts varying from 350 per cent to more than 1,000 per cent. These include bicycles, sewing machines, razor blades, winding wires and screws, domestic refrigerators, caustic soda, chlorine liquid, sheet glass, rayon-viscose yarn, diesel engines, electric motors, staple fibre and rubber cables. It must also be pointed out that, contrary to the impression found in some circles, development of industry in the private sector has not only been in the field of consumer goods, but also extends both to intermediate goods and capital goods. Thus, steel has an important place in the private sector and so have coal, petroleum products, and fertilizers. The private sector is dominant in cement, chemicals, some types of prime movers and electrical equipment, aluminium, road vehicles, rubber goods, textile machinery, sugar machinery and cement machinery.

I have dealt at some length with this topic mainly because I want to dispel the illusion that somehow the public sector has been grabbing the whole field of intermediate and capital goods, and the even stranger illusion that public policy has aimed at crippling the growth of the private sector rather than, as has been actually the case, promoting its expansion. I must hasten to add that development in the private sector in organized industry also owes a lot to the energy and ability of the entrepreneural classes in the country. There can be no doubt that the last ten years have seen a significant advance in the quality and equipment of private enterprise, and this has had a very important effect on the development of industry and contributed to the country's industrial revolution. The public sector has created opportunities for the private sector; and the latter has shown itself ready to take advantage of these opportunities and go ahead with the expansion and diversification of industry.

Another important feature of Indian economic planning has been the massive extent to which foreign exchange resources have been used for development, whether by way of pre-plan savings or foreign loans and grants. The country started the First Five-Year Plan with a sterling balance equalling RS9,114 millions. By the time the first two Five-Year Plan periods were

TABLE 4 UTILIZATION OF AID UP TO 31 MARCH 1961[1]

	Aid authorized (Rs million)	Aid utilized (Rs million)
USA[2]	17,910·5	9,774·5
USSR	3,849·3	761·7
United Kingdom	1,234·7	1,223·0
Canada	1,063·6	957·1
Australia	132·8	126·4
New Zealand	34·3	32·3
West Germany	1,421·5	1,275·4
Japan	276·2	160·1
Czechoslovakia	231·0	
Switzerland	109·0	
Yugoslavia	190·5	
Norway	25·3	25·3
Poland	143·0	
IBRD	3,230·0	2,566·1
UN Special Fund	41·5	
UN Expanded Technical Assistance Programme	16·6	16·6
Ford Foundation[3]	192·0	116·8
Total	30,101·8	17,035·3

[1] See 'Foreign Aid and India's Economic Development' by V. K. R. V. Rao and Dharm Narain, p. 4.

[2] Includes P.L. 480 Titles II and III, gross value of Imports under P.L. 665 and P.L. 480 Title I, and Third Country Currency Assistance.

[3] Excludes utilization of Ford Foundation grants to the private sector, for which information is not available.

7

over, this had been reduced to RS1,358 millions. During the same period, foreign loans and grants, including PL 480 funds, had been utilized to the tune of RS17,035 millions. Table 4 (p. 85) gives figures of aid authorized and utilized up to 31st March 1961.

The bulk of the aid came from government sources, nearly 84 per cent being of a bilateral character. About 75 per cent of the aid was tied to purchases within the donor countries, which not only restricted freedom of choice in the purchase of imported goods but also resulted in India's generally having to pay higher prices for what she purchased. Loans accounted for 75 per cent of the foreign aid utilized during the period. Nearly one-third of the aid came from PL 480 loans used mainly for the purchase of foodgrain, while 18 per cent was used for industry, 12 per cent for railways and 4 per cent for power. Details are given in Table 5 (p. 87).

As regards the effect of foreign aid, broadly speaking it has tended to strengthen the public sector and increase the governmental share of the country's productive capacity. This has been so not only in respect of the infrastructure but also in respect of the producer goods industries. To this extent, we may say that foreign aid has facilitated the implementing by India of her declared social ideology. On the other hand, the emphasis placed on private enterprise by the World Bank, the Cooley clause in the administration of PL 480 funds, and part of the aid received from western countries have all led to the strengthening of the private sector in Indian industry. Along with this, there has also taken place a strengthening of what may be called modern capitalist ideology. The incentives which have been strengthened are mainly monetary reward and economic betterment of the individual entrepreneur, rather than the kind of social and community-centred motivation that goes with a socialist pattern of society. Social systems and social attitudes have been getting more and more similar to those prevalent in western capitalist countries and there has been little change of the nature of a social revolution. The status quo is changing, with traditional values and institutions in retreat, but the change is more in the direction of the liberal and capitalist ideology of the west than in that of the totalitarian and socialist ideology of the east. How far this is the result of the impact of

TABLE 5 SECTOR/PURPOSE-WISE CLASSIFICATION OF AID UTILIZED[1]

Sector/Purpose	Aid[2] (Rs millions)	Percentage of total aid utilized
A. *Agriculture, Community Development and Irrigation*		
(i) Agricultural production	147·4	0·9
(ii) Community Development	64·4	0·4
(iii) Animal Husbandry and Dairy Development	27·2	0·2
(iv) Fisheries	22·2	0·1
(v) Forest and Soil Conservation	1·7	
(vi) Irrigation	150·1	0·9
(vii) Others	47·1	0·3
B. *Industry and Power*		
(i) Manufacturing	3,081·3	18·0
(ii) Minerals and Oil	185·4	1·1
(iii) Power	679·9	4·0
(iv) Others	99·3	0·6
(v) Uncommitted	1,305·0	7·7
C. *Services*		
(i) Transport		
(a) Railways	2,082·8	12·2
(b) Road	43·1	0·3
(c) Civil Aviation	95·3	0·6
(d) Shipping	106·4	0·6
(ii) Other services	1,024·1	6·0
D. *Community Aid*		
(i) Consumer Goods	7,149·1	41·9
(ii) Industrial Raw Materials		
(a) Steel	398·5	2·3
(b) Fertilizer	222·8	1·3
(c) Cement	29·7	0·2
(d) Cotton and others	75·1	0·4
Total	17,037·9	

[1] This table is not exhaustive but covers the bulk of the aid utilized up to approximately the end of the Second Plan period.
[2] See 'Foreign Aid and India's Economic Development', p. 42.

foreign aid and how far of indigenous political and socio-economic forces is a question to which it is not possible to give an answer. All that we can say is that foreign aid has helped to modernise Indian society to some extent and simultaneously strengthened both the public and the private sectors in the Indian economy. As for the proclaimed socialist ideology of the Indian Government, foreign aid, on the whole, has not been of much help; if at all its impact has been in the opposite direction.

Foreign aid has also given rise to many problems, the most important of which relate to repayment. On April 1 1961 – i.e. after 10 years of planning – repayment obligations of net liabilities in foreign currency, due during the Third Plan period alone, totalled RS5,043 millions. The magnitude of this figure can be appreciated when it is realized that it works out at 60 per cent of the targeted increase in exports in the Third Plan period over exports actually achieved during the Second Plan period. The annual level of exports during the Fourth Plan period has to be double that during the Second Plan period if India's foreign exchange requirements on account of repayment obligations and of maintenance and developmental imports are to be met. Doubling the annual volume of export within ten years is not going to prove easy, especially when such a large proportion of our exports is of traditional goods that are facing increasingly effective competition in foreign markets. All the same, the effort has to be made if Indian planning is to succeed in giving the country a self-reliant economy. 'Export or perish' is becoming an even more vital slogan for India than it was for Great Britain during the early years of the postwar period.

Apart from the problem of balance of payments and the related question of foreign aid, our first ten years of planning have also revealed the existence of a number of other problems to which we have not yet found satisfactory answers. The most important of these is that of agricultural production, especially of foodgrains. The country requires a substantial increase in its output of food grains not only for raising the present low levels of food consumption, but also to meet the food requirements of the increasing population. It also requires a substantial increase in the output of raw materials to meet the increased requirements of its industrial development and also its export needs.

Increase in agricultural production therefore constitutes the key factor in India's plans for economic development. In both the First and Second Plans, emphasis was placed not only on irrigation, flood control and soil conservation, but also on increased catering for agricultural imports like fertilizers, agricultural implements, pesticides, etc – in short, better farming. Credit facilities for agriculture were enlarged and co-operative organizations encouraged. Land reforms were introduced with a view to increasing the security of tenure for the actual cultivator, as well as facilitating the acquisition of the land he farms. A nation-wide programme of community development was organized with the primary object of carrying an agricultural extension service to India's 550,000 individual villages. Maximum food prices were also guaranteed for certain food crops.

With all this effort, however, agricultural production has not increased to the extent required. No doubt the increase which has taken place, namely 36·4 per cent in ten years, is substantial, but requirements still exceed domestic supplies. The country has been importing about 4 million tons of foodgrains every year, and but for the availability of PL 480 facilities this would have proved an intolerable burden on the country's limited foreign exchange resources. An annual increase of 5 per cent in agricultural production is what the country requires for the next few years; and this is no easy task, when the number of cultivator households is 60 millions, the average holdings are less than 5 acres with many million holdings of below 2 and 3 acres, and more than half the cultivated acreage is dependent on the vagaries of the monsoon. Then there is the problem of population. India's population is currently increasing at a rate of more than 2·2 per cent a year, which means an addition of between 9 and 10 million persons a year; and this acts as a heavy drag on the growth of the *per capita* income, besides giving rise to an increasing scale of secular unemployment. There is also the problem of administrative failings and deficiencies inevitable in planning the economic development of such a vast country as India. Domestic effort and foreign aid have both shown a significant increase during the first ten years of economic planning; but both are inadequate when viewed in the context of the requirements for making a massive impact on the economy.

The Third Five-Year Plan was formulated against this background of achievement in terms of the country's historical record in the pre-plan period and of inadequacy in terms of her current and future requirements. While larger than the Second Five-Year Plan, the Third Plan contemplated a more moderate rate of increase over the previous Plan as compared to that of the Second Plan over the First Plan. The total investment it envisaged was RS104,000 millions, of which the public sector accounted for RS63,000 millions. Agriculture, power and irrigation now accounted for 30 per cent of the investment outlay as compared with 25 per cent in the Second Plan. Organized industry and minerals claimed 25 per cent as against 23 per cent in the Second Plan, while transport and communications were given a smaller share at 17 per cent as against 21 per cent in the previous Plan. Social services were also lower at 16 per cent as against 19 per cent in the previous Plan. Except for the increased emphasis on agriculture and power indicated by the rise of 5 per cent, the accent still remained on industry, and heavy industry at that, except that minerals, particularly iron ore and petroleum, were now given greater importance. There was a larger degree of dependence on foreign aid, the amount of aid visualized, including PL 480 funds, being RS32,000 millions as compared with RS14,060 millions in the Second Plan. In contrast, there was a drastic reduction in the volume of deficit financing provided for in the Third Plan, the figure being RS5,500 millions as against RS12,000 millions in the Second Plan. The Third Plan also required a great deal of project preparation and programming because of its emphasis on minerals and industry. National income was expected to rise by 30 per cent as against the realized increase of 20 per cent in the Second Plan period, and domestic savings were expected to reach about 11·5 per cent of the national income as against 8·5 per cent at the end of the Second Plan period, with net investment reaching 14·5 per cent from the 11 per cent reached at the end of the Second Plan period. The Third Plan has also started facing difficulties from the outset; and investments and achievements so far have not been up to targets, notably in agriculture and some of the heavy engineering and heavy chemical industries. But the Third Plan has only completed two years so far and there are still three years to go. It is too early therefore to say with confidence what the achievements will be at the end of the Third Plan period. What is clear, however, is that the stresses and strains experienced during the Second Plan period will continue into the Third Plan period as well.

On the top of all this, we now have the emergency caused by the Chinese invasion and the continuing military threat arising from their occupation of some Indian territory in the north and their massive military build-up in Tibet. India has had to go in for an unprecedented increase in her defence expenditure and a certain measure of reorientation in the priorities and direction of her development programme. But she has risen nobly to the challenge; and the country is making a heroic effort to meet the twin needs of both defence and development. The future is certainly grim in terms of the strain this is imposing and will increasingly impose on the people and on the possibilities of significant increase in their current level of living despite the massive investment effort they are making. The one happy feature in the situation, however, is the fact that modern defence and economic development are complementary rather than competitive in terms of industrialization, agricultural production, and scientific and technical education. Defence can therefore grow side by side with development; only a part of the current fruits of development will get frittered away in meeting unproductive defence needs with the result that the people will have to wait a little longer for the promised doubling of their current levels of consumption.

All in all, there is no need to be pessimistic about the future of the Indian economy. On the contrary, the achievements so far are truly massive against the background of the economic stagnation that preceded the introduction of planned development in the Indian economy. What experience shows, however, is the difficulty of forcing the pace and the enormity of the social and economic discipline that is entailed on the part of both the classes and the masses in the country. In one sense, we in India have added to our economic burden by sticking to national independence, democracy, and a free society. But the cost is worth incurring when the stakes are high. With luck, a more massive domestic effort on our part, and a more understanding and more generous policy of aid by our foreign friends, the Indian economy will not only help to preserve our independence but is also sure to reach the take-off stage by the end of the current decade, though it will still continue to be faced by balance of payments problems. It should not however take more than five or at most ten years from then to give the country a tolerable minimum standard of living and set it securely on the road of self-sustaining and self-accelerating growth, which indeed is the goal of all planned economic development.

SHORT BIBLIOGRAPHY ON INDIAN PLANNING

BALOGH, T. *Some aspects of economic growth of under-developed areas :* three lectures. New Delhi, National Council of Applied Economic Research, 1961.

BAUER, P. T. *Indian economic policy and development.* London, Allen and Unwin, 1961.

BETTELHEIM, C. *Some basic planning problems.* Indian Statistical Institute, Indian Statistical Series, No. 12. Bombay, Asia Publishing House, 1961.

DATTA, Bhabatosh. *Essays in plan economics : a commentary on Indian planning experience.* Calcutta, The World Press, 1963.

Datta, Bhabatosh *et al. Economic development and exports : a study of the impact of Indian economic development on exports.* Calcutta, 1962.

DESHMUKH, C. D. *Economic developments in India, 1946–65 :* a *personal retrospect.* Dadabhai Naoroji Memorial Prize Fund Lectures. Bombay, Asia Publishing House, 1957.

GADGIL, Dr. R. *Planning and economic Policy in India, 1961.*

INDIA, Planning Commission. *Papers relating to the formulation of the Second Five Year Plan,* New Delhi, 1955.
    First Five Year Plan.
    Second Five Year Plan.
    Third Five Year Plan.

LEWIS, John P. *Quiet crisis in India : economic development and American policy.* Wisconsin, 1962.

MAHALANOBIS, P. C. *Talks on planning.* Indian Statistical Institute, Indian Statistical Series, No. 14. Bombay, Asia Publishing House, 1961.

MALENBAUM, Wilfred. *Prospects for Indian development.* London, 1962.

RAO, V. K. R. V. and DHARM NARAIN: *Foreign aid and India's economic development.* Delhi, Institute of Economic Growth, Studies in Economic Growth, No. 4. Bombay, Asia Publishing House, 1963.

REDDAWAY, W. B. *The development of the Indian economy,* London, 1962.

SINHA, M. R. (ed.). *Decade of economic development in India.* Bombay, 1962.

VAKIL, C. N. and BRAHMANAND, P. R. *Planning for an expanding economy : accumulation, employment and technical progress in under-developed countries.* Bombay, 1956.

WARD, Barbara. *India and the West.* London, Hamish Hamilton, 1961.

MR LIM CHONG YAH *was born in Malaya in 1932, and educated at the University of Malaya (M.A.).*

After serving in the Singapore Administrative Service from 1955 to 1959, he returned to the University of Malaya as a Lecturer in Economics. He has written a number of articles on economic affairs.

4

MALAYA

INTRODUCTION

In the past, the term 'Malaya' was generally applied to the whole area comprising both the Federation of Malaya and also the territory of Singapore. But since the Federation of Malaya achieved Independence, on August 31, 1957, 'Malaya' has been increasingly used to mean the Federation only; and it is used in that sense in this study.

Malaya, then, comprises an area of approximately 51,000 square miles, nearly four-fifths of which is covered by dense jungle, and one-quarter of which lies more than 1,000 feet above sea level. It has a population of slightly more than 7,000,000 of whom about 50 per cent are, by ethnic origin, Malaysians, 37 per cent Chinese, and the great majority of the remainder Indians and Pakistanis. All those who regard Malaya as their home and country call themselves Malayans whatever their ethnic extraction.

The population of the country is concentrated largely in the coastal regions on the western side of the Malayan Peninsula. There is a fairly well-developed system of roads, railways, ports, posts, telecommunications, electricity supply and other basic facilities. The two most important primary industries are the production of natural rubber, and tin, where, in both cases, and for many years, Malaya has been the world's largest producer.

On December 8, 1941, the Japanese bombed Pearl Harbour. Next day, Japanese troops began their invasion of Malaya. In less than two and a half months, to the shock of the entire Malayan population, and in spite of the resistance of the British, Australian and Malayan defending forces, the whole Peninsula, including Singapore, was overrun by the enemy.

With the Japanese occupation, Malaya entered a period of

95

economic ruin. This was not so much the result of the actual fighting, although the scorched earth policy of the retreating Allied forces, the damage done by the advancing Japanese, and general looting all contributed to the country's rapid impoverishment. The root cause was the fact that occupied Malaya was cut off from the outside world, an isolation later made complete by the Allied sea blockade.

In prewar days, Malaya produced mainly rubber and tin, almost all of which was exported to industrial countries, in particular to Great Britain and the United States. With the proceeds of these exports, Malaya bought rice from neighbouring countries like Thailand and Burma, and industrial goods and machinery from the industrialized countries of the West and Japan. The figures of Malaya's *per capita* income and consumption, though low by Western standards, were amongst the highest in Asia.

The isolation of Malaya under the Japanese occupation inevitably resulted in the closing down of all export industries, with a consequent catastrophic decline in income and employment. In the absence of any significant imports, the domestic prices of all goods rose persistently, and inflation was aggravated by the occupation government's reckless printing of currency to finance local military expenditure. Hundreds of Malayans could be seen literally starved to death in the major towns; the plight of the unemployed rubber estate workers was particularly severe.[1]

After the Japanese surrender, British troops returned to Malaya at the end of 1945, and the postwar administration immediately began to tackle the problem of putting the country back on its feet. This was certainly no easy task. Law and order had to be restored. Corruption, despotism, profiteering, food shortages, black markets, destitution, malnutrition and high

[1] To show how productivity was affected by the occupation, it is only necessary to take the example of the rice industry. Paddy growing was, and still is, a domestic industry, consisting of thousands of smallholders producing primarily for their own requirements, and thus ought not, on the face of it, to have suffered as the export industries. Indeed, since the occupation caused a food famine in Malaya, the Japanese administration went all out to encourage food production. But in spite of this, rice production declined from 338,000 tons in 1939 to 225,000 tons in 1946, although the amount of land under paddy increased by 63,000 acres in the same period. This large drop in terms of yield per acre was due almost entirely to the effects of the occupation.

mortality rates – all associated with, and direct products of the occupation years – had to be eradicated. Rubber holdings, tin mines, oil-palm estates, drainage and irrigation installations, education and health services, and the rest of the social and economic infrastructure of the country, all neglected and run down during the occupation, had to be rehabilitated and re-established. The pent-up demand for goods and services, denied to the population during the war years, had to be met.

But, for all the difficulties, postwar recovery and progress was rapid. By 1947, the Malayan economy had, by and large, shaken off the effects of the war. In that year, the production of rubber, the country's largest industry, was already greater than in any prewar year, and the stage was now set for further growth.

Malayan Growth Statistics

Before one can go on to examine the pattern and causes of this growth, however, it is necessary to state that Malayan national income data, in any form, are only available for the period 1955–60. But earlier aggregate Pan-Malayan national income estimates – covering both the Federation of Malaya and Singapore together – are available from three different sources, published and unpublished. These three sources are F. C. Benham's *The National Income of Malaya, 1947–1949* (Singapore: Government Printer, 1951), the report of the World Bank Mission which visited Malaya in 1954, published under the title *The Economic Development of Malaya* (Baltimore: Johns Hopkins, 1955), and the unpublished estimates of P. A. Wilson, a member of the Economic Advisory Unit of Singapore.

In this study, statistics from these three sources have been put together to form a series of roughly comparable aggregate national income figures for the years 1947–54. But it has first been necessary to split up these figures to obtain their Malayan and Singapore components. This has been done on the basis of relative population and total foreign trade changes in the two territories. (It is hoped that a note on the details of this 'split operation' will be published elsewhere.)

All the Gross Domestic Product (GDP) data thus obtained are expressed in terms of current market prices. However, there were important changes in general price levels during the period

1947–60; the GDP figures have therefore been adjusted in order to obtain the figures of Real Gross Domestic Product (RGDP). Because of the paucity of statistical data, this adjustment has to be made on the basis of official retail price indices only. The use of the term 'Real' is not intended to imply that all the inherent and other shortcomings in these data, for comparative purposes, have been overcome: the data are intended to be indicative of broad changes only.

Most of the other statistical data quoted in this study are either taken directly or derived from official figures published by various Malayan Government Departments, the Statistics Department in particular.

NATURE AND CAUSES OF GROWTH

During the years 1947–60, the Malayan economy experienced three major forward movements, each of which put the country on a higher level of economic development. The first big jump took place during 1950 and 1951, the second during 1955–56, and the third in 1959–60. The fact that each of these major forward movements lasted for approximately two years is perhaps coincidental.

It could be said that, in the years 1947 to 1949, the growth of the economy was scarcely discernible. In 1947, the RGDP was $2,982 million.[1] In 1949, it was $3,027 millions, an increase of only 1·5 per cent over the two-year period.[2] At the same time, it must not be forgotten that 1948 saw the outbreak of the emergency.

But in mid-1950, with the outbreak of hostilities in Korea, Malayan economy 'took off' to a much higher level of development. Between 1949 and 1950, the RGDP increased by 61 per cent. The economy continued to expand in 1951, though with a slower momentum: the increase, compared with 1950, was 3 per cent.

[1] All money values quoted in this study are in Malayan dollars. The exchange rate is Malayan $1 — 2s 4d sterling — $0·33 US.

[2] F. C. Benham, in his book *The National Income of Malaya, 1947–1949*, in fact found that the GDPs, in terms of current prices, actually declined each year, from $2,654 million in 1947 to $2,494 million in 1948, and $2,391 million in 1949. Benham's original figures, which were Pan-Malayan, have been split up to arrive at the Federation estimates.

The upswing of 1950–51 was followed by a big downswing, which started in 1952, and the position deteriorated further in 1953. RGDP fell from $5,000 million in 1951 to $4,153 million in 1952, and still further, to $3,883 million, in 1953. The period 1950–54, which covers the two years of upswing and the three years of downswing may be described as the first postwar Malayan 'cycle'.[1]

The second major forward movement began in 1955, and lasted till 1956, after which another period of decline set in, which lasted for the years 1957–58. The growth rate in 1955 was 27 per cent. In 1956, the growth momentum slowed down to 0·3 per cent. In 1957 RGDP decreased by 4 per cent and in 1958 there was a further fall of 3 per cent. This period, 1955–58 can be described as the second postwar Malayan cycle.

The third major forward movement started in 1959: and once again, the big momentum lasted for one year, and slowed down in the following year. RGDP increased by 15 per cent in 1959, but 1960's increase was only 9 per cent. There are unfortunately no GDP data for 1961, and it is therefore not possible to examine the economy in GDP terms. But there are indications that the 1959–60 upswing may have to be described in future years as the upswing phase of the third postwar Malayan cycle.

What were the main causes of these three major forward movements? The first of them, it will be remembered, coincided with the outbreak of the Korean War, which produced a sudden increase in stockpile demand for strategic raw materials such as rubber and tin. As a result, prices of such primary products skyrocketed. The average rubber price in Singapore increased from 38 cents per pound in 1949 to 108 cents per pound in 1950 and 170 cents per pound in 1951. The average tin price increased from £606 per ton in 1949 to £745 per ton in 1950 and £1,077 per ton in 1951.

In 1951 rubber and tin accounted for approximately 86 per cent of the Malayan Gross Export Proceeds (GEP). And these sudden and spectacular rises in export prices inevitably put the

---

[1] 1954 RGDP was actually slightly higher than that of 1953: but 1954 has been included in the first cycle because the increase was only very slight, and also because of the low level of RGDP. 1954 was much closer to 1953 than to 1955.

Malayan economy on a much higher plane, in terms of GEP, and therefore also of GDP: for although import prices also rose, the rise was much smaller. It is true that other raw material producing countries also benefited from the Korean War boom: but the United Nations 'World Economic Report' for 1950–51 shows that producers of rubber, tin and wool benefited most, as the prices of these three commodities – two of which were Malaya's principal exports – rose much more than those of other raw materials and foodstuffs. Rubber and tin were also the principal exports of countries like Indonesia, but the Indonesian economy was much larger than that of Malaya in terms of GDP. A change of this sort must therefore have greater repercussions on the Malayan than on the Indonesian economy, for the Indonesian export sector constituted only about 11 per cent of Indonesia's GDP, whereas it accounted for about 48 per cent of the GDP of Malaya.

It is clear, therefore, that the big forward movement of 1950–51 was export induced, and the same is true of the upswing of 1955–56. These years (1955–56) were years of prosperity in Western Europe and North America. And the impact of this prosperity was an important rise in the prices of rubber, petroleum and metals. The United Nations 'World Economic Survey, 1955' shows that the terms of trade moved in such a way that only those low-income countries which produced large quantities of rubber, petroleum and metals benefited from the 1955 boom. Again, Malaya was favourably placed: while the terms of trade and balance of payments position of many low income countries deteriorated, those of Malaya improved considerably.[1]

The average rubber price in 1954 was 67 cents. In 1955, it rose to 114 cents; and in 1956 it was 97 cents, still 44 per cent higher than the 1954 price level. The price of tin increased from an average of £719 per ton in 1954 to £740 per ton in 1955, and £788 per ton in 1956, an increase of 3 per cent and 10 per cent over the 1954 price level respectively.

The third major forward movement had its roots in the same cause. During this period the average annual GDP of Malaya

[1] In 1955 Malaya exported about 23 per cent of her rubber to the US dollar account countries, 29 per cent to OEEC countries and 24 per cent to the United Kingdom. Source: Federation of Malaya *Rubber Statistics Handbook 1961*, pp. 38–9.

increased by 15 per cent compared with 1957–58, and GEP increased by an average of 33 per cent, repeating the old story of greater fluctuations in the export sector, compared with the economy as a whole. Once again the main cause of the upswing in export proceeds is to be found in the rise of rubber and tin prices. The price of rubber increased from 80 cents in 1958 to 102 cents in 1957 and 108 cents in 1960, increases of 27 per cent and 35 per cent respectively over the 1958 level. Principally because of these increases, rubber export proceeds rose from $1,197 million in 1958 to $1,722 million in 1959 and $1,829 million in 1960. In 1958, the price of tin was £735 per ton: it went up to £785 per ton in 1959, and to £797 per ton in 1960.

These statistics are intended to show roughly how Malaya's natural income changed in the period 1947–60, and the main reasons for this fluctuating growth. Let us now turn to consider the part that Government played in this growth process.

GOVERNMENT AND GROWTH

The first point that must be stressed is that the main problem which faced the Government after the war, and once most of the work of post-occupation reorganization and reconstruction had been completed, was the Emergency caused by Communist insurrection. This officially broke out in 1948, and at once it became the Government's top priority to end the Emergency as soon as possible. The costs involved were very considerable; for example, at the height of the Emergency, in 1951 and 1952, some 40 per cent to 45 per cent of the Federal budget had to be set aside for expenditure on internal security. But by 1955, it was increasingly apparent that the situation was being brought under control, and in 1960 the Emergency was officially declared at an end.

Meanwhile, throughout the Emergency period, the Government's object was to contain the insurrection within as small an area of the country as possible. In this it was increasingly successful, and by and large, the main lines of economic activity suffered relatively little disturbance during the years 1948–60. Rubber production, tin production and the entrepot trade of Penang went on as usual. As exports flowed smoothly, more and more foreign exchange was earned. With more foreign earnings more imports became possible, and the standard of living rose considerably, with prosperity and depression largely determined by rubber and tin price levels.

Throughout this period free private enterprise has continued to dominate the economic scene, with all rubber estates, all tin mines, all rice fields, all oil palm estates and all the trading houses and firms owned and managed by private individuals or companies. This is not simply because of the Government's preoccupation with its fundamental role of restoring and maintaining law and order. Rather it is the result of the Government's deliberate and conscious policy that the economic sphere should be left to private enterprise, with the Government's role being generally confined to the protection of private industry, and to arbitration, where necessary, between private entrepreneurs, through the agency of the appropriate Government departments.

This does not mean that there has been no Government interference in the activities of free enterprise in postwar Malaya. But interference has been the exception rather than the rule, and when it has occurred, it has come as a conscious departure from the Government's basic free-enterprise philosophy.

What is probably the most important example of such Government intervention in an otherwise free economy can be found in the gigantic rubber replanting programme. At the end of the war, most of the rubber trees had passed tappable age: and because very little replanting had been carried out, the rubber industry was facing senility and decay, as well as the danger of growing competition from synthetic rubber. In this situation, the Government rightly stepped in. Taxes were imposed on rubber exports, and the proceeds channelled into funds specifically designed to subsidize replanting by means of substantial grants per acre replanted. This scheme, which was instituted in 1952, has achieved striking results in spite of some shortcomings. In 1947, replanting on rubber estates amounted to only about 25,000 acres, and, in the smallholding sector, the figure was as low as 2,000 acres. But in 1956, the replanting acreage on the rubber estates had risen to 70,000 acres; the same figure was reached in the smallholding sector in 1957. In

1960, in addition to the replanting of 70,000 acres in the small-holding sector, a further 25,000 acres were new-planted.[1]

Altogether, about 30 per cent of the total Malayan rubber acreage had been replanted by 1955, and this had risen to 46 per cent by 1960. Today, there is no doubt that Malaya has one of the most efficient and progressive rubber industries in the world, and it is not surprising that the drafters of the Second Five-Year Plan should have considered this rubber replanting programme as one of the outstanding achievements of post-war Malaya.[2] All in all, the rubber replanting programme has been a spectacular success. The replanted trees can yield three to four times as much as the plants they replace: and if the replanting trend continues, and there seems to be no good reason why it should not, Malayan rubber production should double its present level by 1975.

A second important sphere in which Government has departed from a pure *laissez-faire* philosophy must also be mentioned. Land alienation and development virtually came to a standstill for many years after the war, due mainly but not entirely to the Emergency conditions prevailing in the country. But by 1956, conditions had improved to the point where it became possible for the Government to launch a new land-development campaign. Thousands of acres of primary jungle were cleared and opened up for cultivation of crops, the main crops planted being rubber, fruit trees and rice.

By 1960, twenty-two land-development schemes covering about 30,000 acres, enough for 3,500 families, were already in existence. Under the current Second Five-Year Plan (1961–65), the aim is to open up another 250,000 acres of virgin jungle. Each year it is planned to carry out 12 land-development

[1] P. T. Bauer, in an article which first appeared in the *Political Science Quarterly* in 1957, and which was reprinted in T. H. Silcock's *Readings in Malayan Economics* (Singapore: Donald Moore, 1961) strongly advocated a policy of new-planting as against replanting. Probably, Bauer has under-stated the advantages of replanting in the circumstances that then faced the Malayan rubber industry, although he was correct in stressing the importance of alienating more land for cultivation; cf. p. 117.

[2] For more information on this subject, see *Report of the Mission of Enquiry into the Rubber Industry of Malaya*. Kuala Lumpur, Government Printer, 1954. Also Federation Government *White Paper on Taxation and Replanting in the Rubber Industry*, Kuala Lumpur, Government Printer, 1955: and Lim Chong Yah, 'Malayan Rubber Replanting Taxes'. *Malayan Economic Review*, Vol. VI, No. 2, Oct. 1961, pp. 43–52.

schemes, each of which will provide about 400 families with individual holdings of 7 acres of rubber or oil palm land, and 3 acres for paddy, vegetables, fruit and other crops. The fruits of this project, which is being carried out by the Federal Land Development Authority, will begin to be reaped when the rubber or palm-oil comes to the market; but meanwhile the land-development programme is providing and will continue to provide, directly and indirectly, useful employment for thousands of Malayan citizens. Indeed, if Malaya accelerates the present tempo of expansion in the oil palm sector, as no doubt should be the policy, it is very probable that she will emerge as the world's largest palm oil producer in the next decade.

Elsewhere, in the field of industrialization, the Government has played an important role in promoting growth, but not in participating in it. The two main fiscal measures designed to attract more foreign capital to Malaya, and to divert more local capital and enterprise to the manufacturing industries have been the granting of free tax holidays (i.e. freedom from Company Tax for specified periods) to pioneer industries, and, where necessary, the provision of tariff protection. Other measures include the establishment of industrial estates, and the setting up of the Malayan Industrial Development Finance Corporation. By 1960, more than 50 firms, manufacturing 238 products, and with a called-up capital of some $27 million, were awarded pioneer status. At the end of 1961, the number of pioneer companies reached 72.

There is one respect in which the Government does participate directly in the economy. This is in the vital field of basic services – the industrial, commercial and agricultural infrastructure of the country. The Malayan Government owns all the roads, ports, airports and railways in the country. It also owns all the water supply lines, and runs the greater part of the electricity services through the agency of statutory corporations like the Central Electricity Board. Irrigation works are also owned and maintained by the Government.[1]

[1] Under the First Five Year Plan, drainage and irrigation accounted for about $38 million out of a total of $228 million spent on public investment in the agricultural sector. Under the Second Five-Year Plan, expenditure under this heading is to be increased to $100 million.

But the main, and by far the most important, field of Government activity in the postwar period has been that of the social services: education, health, and welfare. In prewar Malaya, the official education services were limited to the provision of free primary education to Malays in Malay-medium schools, and the running of a number of English-medium primary and secondary schools in the large towns. The Chinese-medium stream was left to flow as it liked, supported almost entirely by private individuals. There was not a single university in Malaya, although there were two small colleges in Singapore: the handful of university graduates in Malaya had all been educated in Great Britain, mostly at their own expense.

After the war, however, there emerged in Malaya a great and increasing demand for education at all levels, and there has been a correspondingly great increase in Government expenditure on the financing of education. In 1947, there were only 468,000 school-going children in Malaya; in 1960, there were 1,272,000. In 1947, there were 3,673 schools; in 1960, 5,409. In 1947, there were 13,994 teachers; by 1960, the number of teachers of all grades had risen to 49,177. To provide the teachers needed, emergency teacher training schemes were mounted in a number of places in Malaya, and two special training centres were also organized in the United Kingdom, where hundreds of trainees were flown annually from Malaya for training. Whereas there was no University in Malaya before the war, there are now three in the Federation of Malaya and in Singapore, catering for some 8,000 students, most of whom are financed by Government scholarships or bursaries: and there are probably an equal number of Malayan students in places of higher education abroad.

The result is that education expenditure now constitutes the most important single item of expenditure in the Malayan Budget, having risen from a recurrent total of about $16 million in 1947 to a total of some $190 million in 1961. During the same period, there has been a similar, and only slightly less dramatic, increase in health expenditure, which has risen from a recurrent total of about $18 million in 1947 to a figure of $88 million in 1961.

In all this, it is possible to see the practical expression of the Malayan Government's basic belief in a free economy. By and large, the Government has been, and still is, content to leave the operation of the economy to free enterprise. Only where free enterprise cannot operate successfully does the Government step in to give a lead to the development process – as in the land development schemes, and in the field of industrialization. At the same time, the development of the economic and social infrastructure of the nation remains the proper responsibility of the Government, for clearly it cannot be left to private enterprise to develop such essential basic facilities as roads, railways, or irrigation works, any more than private enterprise could be expected to meet the vastly increased needs of the nation in the provision of the education and health services of modern Malaya.

Mention must also be made of another role of the Government – that of preserving the continued stability of the Malayan currency. Unlike many other countries, Malaya has never experienced any balance of payments difficulties. This is because of the nature of her currency system, which is fully backed by the UK pound sterling. The rate of exchange between Malaya and the United Kingdom has remained at 2s 4d to the $ since 1906. This stability of the Malayan currency has not only helped to retain in the country the foreign investment that existed before Independence, it has been a vital factor in making Malaya a safe, and therefore attractive, place for new foreign investment. In short, it has helped to promote trade and the flow of finance between Malaya and other countries.

But before one can pass judgment on Malaya's postwar progress, there are three important subjects that deserve to be considered. The first of these is the extent to which development has been consciously planned by the Government. The second is the Government's approach to the financing of public expenditure. And the third is the extent, if any, to which the Government has failed to meet the real needs of the national economy.

PLANNING ECONOMIC DEVELOPMENT

This is the age of planning. The decision in developing countries today is not 'to plan or not to plan', but rather 'how much to plan', and 'how to plan'. If a country like Malaya has no formal

Plan, that does not mean that planning does not exist, nor does it mean that Government does not interfere at all in the major facets of the economy. Similarly, even if there is a formal Plan, that does not necessarily mean that there is more planning, or that the Government has by implication taken over more and more economic functions.

The point is that, in Malaya as in most other countries, 'planning' has always existed, through individual departmental plans, and through the central control and co-ordination of governmental activities. In any well-organized society, departments have to face the Treasury each year, and it is through the machinery of the Treasury that a certain measure of co-ordination is effected, and priorities determined.

In fact, Malaya has had three formal Plans. The first of these was the Draft Development Plan, sometimes called the Yellow Book, which extended from 1950 to 1956, both years inclusive.[1] However, it must be said that this simply consisted of a catalogue of the development projects which each major Government department hoped to carry out over the Plan period. There was no co-ordination of projects, nor was there any co-ordination with the private sector. Indeed, even important statutory public corporations like the Central Electricity Board and the Malayan Railways were not included in the Plan. Malaya was still, at that time, a British colony, and the administration in Malaya wanted to put up proposals to the British Colonial Office as a basis for the assessment and allocation of grants under the Colonial Development and Welfare Act, by which a sum of £120 million was set aside by the UK Government for the development of British colonies and dependencies. Malaya was entitled to a share in this sum, and the Draft Development Plan was hastily put together to support the claim for assistance from the metropolitan country.

At the same time, there is an important lesson to be drawn from the fact that the Yellow Book was destined to be soon forgotten. (It was given only a passing mention in the comprehensive report of the World Bank Mission to Malaya in 1954.) In Malaya, as elsewhere, formal planning is meaningless unless the planners know, or succeed in estimating, what the main

[1] Federation of Malaya *Draft Development Plan.* Kuala Lumpur, Government Printer, 1950.

changes in the economy are going to be during the Plan period; and the longer the Plan period, the more difficult it is to form a correct estimate of such changes. In the case of Malaya, it is rubber and tin prices that are the determining factors. The levels of these prices govern national income, internal prices and consumption, the levels of imports and capital formation, the levels of wages, and last but not least the amount of revenue available to the Government. (During the Great Depression years of the early 1930's, one Commissioner of Police even claimed that he could forecast the country's crime figures simply by looking at rubber and tin prices, on the reasonable argument that, as these prices collapsed, so starvation, and so crime, would spread.)

The Yellow Book was drafted in 1949, before the first major forward movement, at a time when the Government was quite pessimistic about future prospects. It was based on a rubber price of 45 cents per pound. But the whole picture was fundamentally altered in 1950–51, when the first big jump occurred. As Malaya was at that time producing about 1,600 million lbs of rubber per year, an increase of only 10 cents per pound in the rubber price would have meant that the country would automatically be richer by $160 million. In fact, the price of rubber in 1951 rose to 169·55 cents per pound, and the gross rubber export proceeds increased from $990 million in 1949 to $2,445 million in 1951. In 1949, the Government had a Budget deficit; by 1951, there was a large surplus. Government reserves, which stood at $40 million at the end of 1949, totalled $415 million by the end of 1951.

The recommendations of the World Bank Mission were overtaken by events in much the same way. The Mission submitted to the Malayan Government a plan of action, involving only the public sector, extending from 1955 to 1959: this was based on a rubber price of 75 cents per pound in 1955, 'and of 65 cents in the following four years'.[1] But the price of rubber in 1955 rose to 114·16 cents per pound, and in all the other years of the period it exceeded 80 cents per pound. To show the effect of this, in 1955 gross rubber export proceeds exceeded the Mission's estimate by some $558 million, or nearly three-quarters of the total capital expenditure recommended by the Mission

[1] World Bank Mission Report, p. 141.

for the period 1955–59. To provide another illustration: the Mission estimated that the revenue from rubber export duties would bring in about $100 million in 1955, and $85 million each year thereafter. The actual duties collected were as follows: 1955, $335 million; 1956, $217 million; 1957, $181 million; 1958, $137 million; and 1959, $227 million – in every year except 1958, more than double the Mission's estimate.

Nevertheless, the World Bank Mission's recommendations proved useful when the Malayan Government came to prepare its position for the financial and economic discussion with the British Government that preceded final Independence. The Mission's estimates were recast, and formed the basis of the 'Report on Economic Planning in the Federation of Malaya', which five years later became known as the First Five-Year Plan.[1] This report, like the Yellow Book, was nothing but a synthesis of the various departmental projects for the years 1956–60. Little was subsequently heard of it until the publication of the Second Five-Year Plan (1961–65).[2]

What should be noted here is that the second big forward movement was still in progress in 1956, and that 1960 was the peak year of the third big jump. Thus, if a comparative assessment is made between 1956 and 1960, the result appears very satisfactory. But a comparison between 1956 and 1958 yields a much more gloomy picture, for in the latter year there was large-scale unemployment in the tin mines, and the Government had to face a large budget deficit. This illustrates the point that in an export-dominated, and more or less monocultural economy like Malaya's, the country's economic fortunes are very largely outside the control of the Government; and, so long as such an economic structure exists, it is quite as wrong to give the Government most of the credit for prosperity, as it is to give the Government most of the blame for depression. It makes little difference who is in power in Kuala Lumpur; if the USA sneezes, Malaya will still catch influenza.

With the passage of time, however, Government planners in Malaya have come to realize the overriding importance of

[1] *Report on Economic Planning in the Federation of Malaya*, Kuala Lumpur, Government Printer, 1957.
[2] *Second Five Year Plan*, Kuala Lumpur, Government Printer, 1961.

rubber prices as a factor in planning. And the Second Five-Year Plan does make clear the crucial part that the price of rubber will play in determining the degree of actual success or failure in the Plan. For it is the price of rubber that largely determines the extent of available resources, in both the public and the private sector, and therefore the amount of possible investment and consumption, as well as the degree of necessity for any foreign borrowing. But it is still questionable whether the full implications of this situation have been sufficiently appreciated by the planners. Under the Second Five-Year Plan, *per capita* income in Malaya is expected to rise very slightly if the price of rubber remains at the 1960 level throughout the period – that is, at 108 cents per pound; but it is most unlikely that the price will remain at this high level. Although the Plan also thinks in terms of the price falling to 80 cents per pound, there is no explicit recognition of the fact that this must inevitably entail a fall in *per capita* income. Nor does the Plan entertain the possibility of a fall to a still lower level, though this can by no means be ruled out.

FINANCING DEVELOPMENT EXPENDITURE

It is obvious that no Government can carry out its social and economic policies unless it has the financial resources. A Government cannot manufacture financial resources, nor can it exist endlessly on credit. Where, then, has the Malayan Government obtained the money that has enabled it to increase Government expenditure three-fold between 1949 and 1960? It has obtained it mainly from taxation.

Before the war, Malaya was a paradise for private enterprise. There was no company tax, and no personal income tax. Export taxes were rudimentary, and import taxes very low. A large part of the revenue of all the State Governments was in fact derived from the taxation of opium smokers and toddy drinkers.[1]

After the war, there were revolutionary changes in the tax system. Personal income and company taxes were introduced, export taxes were expanded, and import duties were extended

[1] For more information on this subject, see Li, Dan J., *British Malaya: An Economic Analysis*, New York, The American Press, chapter on public finance.

to cover virtually the whole range of imported goods, and the rates of all these taxes have from time to time been raised. If it had not been for this growth of the tax system, the public sector would in fact have derived much less benefit from Malaya's economic prosperity, and the Government would have been forced, by sheer lack of funds, to make far less contribution to economic and social development. Before the war, because of the absence of a well-developed tax system, the greatest part of the profits of every export-induced boom was allowed to flow abroad unhampered in the form of inflated company profits and family remittances.

Indeed, the Malayan economy could have reached a much higher level of development before the war, if only a well-developed tax system had been in existence then. There may be a danger of over-taxation today, but before the war, there was certainly serious under-taxation. The conditions were such that prewar Governments could have raised millions of dollars from taxation without hampering or discouraging the activities of private enterprise. Even today, with company profits tax standing at 40 per cent, a graduated personal income tax structure, and fairly high import taxes, it is still possible for some $250 million per annum to leave Malaya in the form of foreign company profits.[1]

To show the practical effects of the rapid postwar growth of the tax structure, coupled with the great increase in national income, upon Government finances, it is only necessary to quote a few statistics from the years of the first major forward movement. At the end of 1949, the Government had a Budget deficit of slightly over $2 million, and reserves of about $40 million. Because of the Emergency and other pressures, the Government was forced to increase its expenditure from some $360 million in 1949 to $563 million in 1951. If Government revenues had remained at the 1949 level, or even a little above it, there must have been a huge deficit in the 1951 Budget. In fact, and despite the terrific increase in Government expenditures,

---

[1] There is unfortunately little published literature on the growth of the tax system in Malaya. See, however, three articles by the writer on 'The Taxation Policy of the Federation Government', *Sunday Mail*, January 8, 15, and 21, 1961, and an article by the same writer, 'Export Taxes on Rubber in Malaya – a Survey of Post-War Development', *Malayan Economic Review*, Vol. V, No. 2, October 1960, pp. 46–58.

there was an unprecedented Budget surplus of $189 million in that year; the Government reserves rose from $144 million in 1950 to $415 million in 1951.

Another important feature in the field of public finance has been the Government's action in respect of forced savings. To provide old age security on a national basis, the Government has introduced a scheme whereby most employees in the country have to contribute a percentage of their monthly earnings to an Employees Provident Fund, a similar sum being contributed by the employers. The main purpose of the scheme is, of course, old age security, but meanwhile, as the Fund has begun to accumulate, it has become an important source of loan capital to the Government and the Statutory corporations. Under the First Five-Year Plan (1956-60), the Government was able to borrow a total of $394 million from the Fund out of a total Plan capital expenditure of $1,007 million. And, under the Second Five-Year Plan, it is intended to borrow a further $500 million from this source for a Plan public expenditure of $2,150 million.

The expansion of voluntary savings, through the Post Office Savings Banks, has also helped to tap private resources for public development purposes. In 1947, total POSB deposits in Malaya and Singapore amounted to $54 million: by 1960, these had risen to $200 million, an increase – even after allowing for changes in the purchasing power of money – of about 225 per cent.

THE RICE SECTOR

Thus far, it must be said, the picture of Malaya's postwar economic development has been a fairly bright one. In the years 1947-60, the country's population increased from 4,900,000 to 6,900,000,[1] at a compound rate of 2·7 per cent per annum: in the same period, the RGDP increased at the compound rate of 4·5 per cent, thus surpassing population growth by the useful margin of 1·8 per cent per annum – which is approximately the compound growth rate in *per capita* RGDP for 1947-60. But there is one very important sector of

[1] The main cause of this 'population explosion' was a fall of about one-half in the country's mortality rate, from 19·4 per 1,000 in 1947 to 9·5 per 1,000 in 1960.

the economy where the picture is by no means so bright. This is the rice sector.

The rice sector of the Malayan economy is, in terms of labour employment and land utilization, second only in importance to the rubber industry. Some 17 per cent of cultivated land is under rice or paddy, and about 19 per cent of the total economically active population is in this sector.

In terms of sheer physical productivity, over the period 1947–60, the rice industry has fared very well, and certainly much better than the rubber industry. Taking 1947 as the base year, the index of rice production in 1960 was 228, whilst that of rubber production was only 109. The compound rate of increase in rice production during this period was 3·3 per cent per annum, and that of rubber production only 0·2 per cent. In 1955, the Rice Production Committee rightly claimed, with the support of statistical data, that physical productivity per acre in the Malayan rice sector was one of the highest in South-East Asia, and this achievement is also stressed by the Government in its 1962 Annual Report.[1]

But let us look at the other side of the coin. In 1947, total Malayan rice production amounted to 252,000 tons, and the average price of rice per kati was 55 cents, making a total value of about $238 million. Fourteen years later, in 1960, rice production had increased to 560,000 tons, but the price of rice had decreased steadily to 28 cents per kati, making a total value of $245 million. In other words, whilst production had increased by 118 per cent, value in 1960 was actually only 3 per cent higher than in 1947. Indeed, since the general purchasing power of money in 1960 was about 12 per cent lower than in 1947, in terms of real income the 1947 position was in fact far better than the position in 1960. This is a marked contrast with the situation in the rubber sector, where value increased from $539 million in 1947 to $1,709 million in 1960, a rise, in terms of real income, of 179 per cent.

What really matters, in fact, is not just physical productivity, but revenue productivity, or value. And the figures show that in an important sense the story of the Malayan rice sector since

[1] Federation of Malaya: *Final Report of the Rice Committee*. Kuala Lumpur, Government Printer, 1956, p. 25: and *Official Year Book, 1962*. Kuala Lumpur, Government Printer, 1962, p. 149.

the war is one of relative stagnation and increasing relative poverty. The main reason for this has been the steady deterioration in the terms of trade between rice and other products. But even in 1947, when the price of rice was very high, rubber growing was still much more profitable than paddy cultivation. Indeed, even in the Depression years of the 1930's, when the price of rubber dropped to the lowest level in Malaya's history, the same situation had prevailed.

In other words, paddy growing has always been one of the least paying of all the major occupations in Malaya. Generally speaking, in Malaya, to grow nothing but paddy is to ensure relative poverty. This condition is aggravated by the ever-increasing labour/land ratio, which in turn is caused primarily by the failure to enlarge the paddy land frontiers at a pace sufficient to meet the spiralling demand created by population increase.

Institutional defects, such as landlordism, land fragmentation, and credit indebtedness have exacerbated the situation, and accelerated the poverty-generating process. About half to two-thirds of Malaya's rice farmers do not own the land they cultivate. They are tenant farmers, and most of them have to pay a rent of one-third or a half of their crop to the landlord: some even pay as much as three-quarters of their crop in rent. Nor is there any security of land tenure. In Kelantan State, farm tenancies changing hands in a single year have been known to reach a figure of 47 per cent.

The fragmentation of farm holdings arises when a farmer dies and his land is divided amongst his heirs. This process progressively reduces the size of individual holdings, and the plots which make up the whole are often widely scattered. Furthermore, most rice farmers are indebted to money-lenders for the supply of seasonal and other credit. And this frequently obliges them to sell their crops to their creditors, often at a price far below that which they could obtain elsewhere.[1]

Up to the present, however, the Government's role in the rice sector has been mainly confined to the provision of drainage and

[1] For an uncompromising condemnation of the exploitation of farmers by land-lords, money-lenders and shopkeepers, see Ungku A. Aziz, 'The Interdependent Development of Agriculture and other Industries', *Malayan Economic Review*, Vol. IV, No. 1, April 1959, pp. 21–32.

irrigation services, and to giving the rice farmers technical advice.[1] Efforts have been made to deal with landlordism and indebtedness, but these have not been very successful, and the twin evils still persist. Legislation to protect tenant farmers in particular has been half-hearted. For example, not only is the Padi Cultivators (Control of Rent and Security of Tenure) Ordinance of 1955 either ambiguous or defective in a number of important respects, but no real attempt has ever been made to enforce its provisions. The establishment of co-operatives, as a measure to end indebtedness, has met with only limited success; and no action has yet been taken to halt the progressive sub-division and fragmentation of land holdings.

Indeed it is possible to detect a fundamental confusion of thought in the official approach to the problem of rural poverty. After the General Election of 1959, in which control of the two rural States of Kelantan and Trengganu passed to the racially bigoted and religiously fanatical Pan-Malayan Islamic Party, the Government became increasingly aware of the importance of the rural vote. 'Rural Development' became the slogan of the day, in Ministerial speeches, in the Malayan press, and over Radio Malaya. Impressive directives and exhortations to develop the rural economy were promulgated.

But what is 'the rural economy'? War had rightly been declared on rural poverty: but did this mean that the tin mines, the rubber estates, and the palm oil plantations – all of which are in the rural areas – were to be included in the rural development drive? Regrettably, it was even doubtful whether the drive was supposed to cover the hundreds of 'new villages' which had been established under the resettlement schemes carried out at the height of the emergency in 1950 and 1951. It was generally agreed that something must be done: and there was genuine enthusiasm and genuine goodwill among Malayan politicians in this drive to end rural poverty. But it

---

[1] It is noteworthy that these drainage and irrigation facilities have all been designed for the production of one crop a year. Recently, the Government has begun to encourage farmers to plant two rice crops a year, and though the response has been very slow, there are signs that double-cropping will spread more and more widely in time. But double-cropping can only succeed if water supplies are adequate, which means that, in the vast majority of rice fields, the existing drainage and irrigation works will have to be totally reconstructed.

did not seem to be sufficiently understood that the main cause of poverty is not just geographical: the determining factor is not simply where Malayans live, whether in the towns or in the country, but what industrial sector they are in, and what economic and social environment surrounds them. Of particular importance is the fact that rural development must mean the development of the income-earning capacity of the rural population. Unless the rural population can participate actively in the whole development process, they themselves will continue to be left out and to remain poor even though the geographical areas as such may be well developed, as has often been the case in the past. Thus the guiding principle of the Malayan government should be to promote and sustain the income-earning capacity of the rural population (who will know how to spend their extra income when they have earned it) rather than to subsidize expenditure on public development projects as an end in themselves.

Moreover, an economic upsurge cannot be brought about unless the institutional chains that fetter the energies of the rural people are broken, and new ideals and ideas, more conducive to rapid economic and social growth, are substituted in their place. It should also have become increasingly obvious that rural development in Malaya must begin with the eradication of poverty in the rice sector. The Government must act to free the rice farmers from the grip of landlords, money-lenders and shop-keepers: and if the foundation of Malayan society is not to be shaken, and her much valued stability endangered, this policy will have to be carried out without any racial bias or motivation. With the same vigour and non-racial approach, it must concurrently act to stop the process of land fragmentation. Above all it must at the same time act without hesitancy to increase the land/labour ratio in the rice sector, and indeed in the whole of the agricultural industry, including the 'new villages'.

Happily, land is still plentiful in Malaya. Despite what has been achieved this far, about 80 per cent of the country is still virgin jungle, and a large part of this untouched land is suitable for the cultivation of palm oil, coconuts, vegetables and other crops. Rigidity, slowness, reluctance and uncertainty in meeting the needs of a land-hungry peasantry since the early 1930s can undoubtedly be reckoned the major man-made obstacle that retards the progress of the Malayan nation. It is clear that a revolutionary change in land policy, and in the social structure of the countryside, must be brought about in order to permit a greater increase in the land/labour ratio and the generous supply of more land to the landless, and indeed to all those who need land to earn a better livelihood – and the sooner the better. There is no room for conservatism, no room for uncertainty, and in particular no room for the conservation of vast areas of virgin forest or primeval jungle, when so much is at stake. Poverty is a sure road to serfdom.

9

Professor Nurul Islam *is Chairman of the Department of Economics, Dacca University, and also Chairman of the University's Bureau of Economic Research.*

He went to Harvard University in 1951 on a Government of Pakistan scholarship for advanced studies in economics, and obtained the degrees of M.A. in 1953 and Ph.D. in 1955. He was awarded a Nuffield Foundation fellowship for advanced study and research in the UK during 1958–59, and worked at the London School of Economics and the Department of Applied Economics, Cambridge University.

He has served on a number of Pakistan Government Commissions and Committees, and has written numerous books and articles on economic development.

5

PAKISTAN

PAKISTAN as an independent state came into existence in August 1947. The areas now constituting East Pakistan suffered rather severely from the direct and indirect effects of the second world war. Moreover, the partition of the sub-continent was accompanied by widespread communal riots with consequent heavy damage to life and property. Pakistan set out on its future without its due share of assets, proportionate to its population, and with very little in the way of developed resources. The state of the economy at the time of independence is indicated by the fact that *per capita* cereal consumption was around 350 lbs per year and *per capita* steel consumption was 3 lbs in 1949.[1] The total consumption of power was 69,074 kW, and per hundred square miles of area there were only 1·9 miles of railway. The percentage of literacy was only 13·5 per cent, and average life expectation was about 27 years.[2] Even though Pakistan inherited 20 per cent of the population of undivided India, she had in 1947 only 10 per cent of the total manufacturing capacity of the subcontinent consisting of 1,406 establishments.[3] However, she possessed a number of valuable raw materials such as cotton, jute and tea, etc. But in order to exploit them she needed to establish new trade routes, new ports or outlets to sea, new trade contacts overseas, and above all an essential minimum level of banking, insurance and other overhead facilities. In each of these fields a great vacuum was created by the mass exodus of Hindus from Pakistan, which heavily depleted the available technical and professional manpower. The influx of refugees from India who confronted the

[1] Ministry of Finance, Office of the Economic Adviser, *Pakistan – Basic Facts*, Rawalpindi, 1962.
[2] Ministry of Economic Affairs, Government of Pakistan, *Report of the Economic Appraisal Committee*, Karachi, 1953, pp. 70–2.
[3] Ibid, pp. 123 and 126.

Government with huge tasks of rehabilitation could not fill up the vacuum since they lacked the professional and technical background to a commensurate extent. The economic policy as well as the administrative and financial resources of the Government in these early years were devoted towards meeting these basic minimum needs and were strained to the utmost limit to perform such unprecedented functions.

BEGINNINGS OF DEVELOPMENT PLANNING

It was only after these basic needs were met that increasing attention could be diverted to the needs of long-run development. Pakistan inherited at the time of partition a very small number of development projects which were already under way during the pre-independence days, such as irrigation and water development projects in West Pakistan. There was no overall comprehensive plan. It was only in 1950 with the inauguration of the 'Colombo Plan' regional programme of economic development for South and South-East Asia, that the need for a conscious formulation of priorities and objectives of economic policy was recognized.[1] The Planning Commission was established in 1951. A Six-Year Development Programme was formulated as a part of the regional plan, starting in 1951. This marked the beginnings of or first attempts at the formulation of basic objectives and criteria of development planning in Pakistan. A view of some basic considerations weighing with the planners in those early years can be obtained from the following statement in the Six-Year Plan.

... Man does not live on bread alone and a national plan has to take into account not only the production and distribution of goods, but also social services and civilizing activities. The standard of living of a people is a composite whole comprising material, social and cultural amenities. A proper equilibrium amongst these factors probably determines the fullness of life of a people. For the formulation of a national plan, it is necessary to state the norms for the attainment of which the nation must strive. These norms will constitute the measure of the standard of living which, within a specified time, it is desired to achieve. ... Though the social objectives of Pakistan have not been defined, it is certain that they are higher than a mere provision of a standard of living very near the minimum requirements of human life.

[1] The Ministry of Economic Affairs, Government of Pakistan, *Report of the Economic Appraisal Committee 1962*, Karachi, 1963, pp. 68–9, Appendix.

... It will be observed that there is poverty – dire, oppressive poverty – in Pakistan in the midst of a possible plenitude, and one's mind naturally turns to schemes of economic development of the country.... There is a very great deal to be done in every sphere of national life, social services, industries, transport, agriculture and the rest. The Government of Pakistan have, however, decided to follow the good principle that national effort towards social and economic development must be applied first to fundamentals. The first phase of the development programme of Pakistan is proposed to be confined generally to 'basic development', i.e., the development of essential industries and services, e.g., irrigation, mechanization and modernization of agriculture.... The Government of Pakistan are convinced that time is the most important factor in the present situation which confronts not only Pakistan but all the countries in South and South-East Asia. For many centuries religion has been the only solace which has reconciled the peoples of the lands to a life of famine, pestilence and disease, but even faith is now receding from the hearts of the people and the desperation of disbelief accentuates the awareness of their poverty and makes them yearn for any panacea that would cure their many ills or at least bring them relief of oblivion. In such times quacks and knaves do flourish, and such periods of human history are preludes to revolutions.[1]

The Six-Year Plan was formulated in the light of the above objectives. It provided for an investment expenditure of RS2,600 million distributed between the various sectors as follows:[2]

TABLE I SIX-YEAR DEVELOPMENT PROGRAMME (1951–57)

	(Rs Million)	Percentage Distribution
Agriculture and Irrigation	820	31·6
Water, Fuel and Power	490	18·8
Mining and Industry	490	20·4
Transport and Communications	530	18·9
Education and Training	190	7·3
Health	40	1·5
Housing	40	1·5
	2,600	100

(The share of private investment in this total was expected to be about Rs 400 million.)

[1] Ibid, p. 81, Appendix.
[2] Ibid, pp. 72–3, Appendix, and Andruz and Mohammed, *The Economy of Pakistan*, Oxford University Press, London, 1958, Table LXXXI, p. 481.

Before the six-year programme could get into full operation the effects of the Korean War created their own problems and priorities, with the rise in the prices of capital goods and in the costs of projects. These heavily offset the favourable effects of a rise in export earnings owing to war demand. The emergency created by the world crisis led to the formulation of a Two-Year Priority Plan with emphasis on projects based on Pakistan's own resources. This sought self-sufficiency in a few essential consumer goods and speeded up some urgent projects in respect of power and transport. It provided for an expenditure of RS254 million per year, 50 per cent of which was to be on transport, fuel and power and 48 per cent on industry. The onset of the post-Korean commodity recession resulted in a sharp decline in Pakistan's export prices. This coincided with a serious food shortage, resulting in a diversion of shrinking exchange earnings to cereal imports and in a reduction in the capacity to import development goods. The Korean boom, the subsequent depression and its aftermath amply demonstrated how economic developments, in a country dependent on foreign supplies for vital needs, suffer serious setbacks caused by external factors beyond its control, such as war and fluctuations in foreign exchange receipts. The adverse effects were more acutely felt since the role of foreign aid was not important in those days. As a result, increasing attention was paid to projects for which foreign aid had been received or anticipated. Schemes which promised to meet an urgent need or were considered to be highly productive on a short-term basis, with due regard to foreign exchange earnings, were accorded high priority.[1] It was increasingly felt that comprehensive planning necessitated an assessment of overall resources and requirements and a formulation of individual projects in various sectors in the light of overall resources and requirements. Furthermore, individual targets and projects must meet the twin tests of consistency and efficiency so as to fulfil the objectives of a development plan at least cost and with a proper intersectoral balance.

The progress of private and public investment during the years covered by these two plans can be seen in the table on p. 123.

[1] Report of the Economic Appraisal Committee, para 338.

Both private and public investment gradually increased. The annual average of both was higher than was anticipated under the original development programmes. The rise was more remarkable in the field of private investment, the amount of which was considerably under-estimated: as subsequent experience has shown, the achievements of the private sector have consistently exceeded expectations of its performance, although

Investment (Rs Million)

	Public	Private
1949–50	321·9	520
1950–51	304·6	580
1951–52	524·9	700
1952–53	688·5	690
1953–54	710·8	820
1954–55	787·1	676·6

in the years before the development of the system of controls over the amount and direction of private investment, the composition of this investment, with its emphasis mainly upon trade and commercial activity, was not up to expectations.[1] (Private investment contemplated in the Six-Year Plan was only that part of private investment which was included in the plan: the figures quoted above include total private investment in all sectors of the economy, and the definition of investment, especially in the public sector, which has been used in the computation of these figures is broader than that used in the Six-Year Plan.)

FIVE-YEAR PLANS

The First Five-Year Plan (1955–60) was the culmination of successive attempts at integrated economic planning. It had the following objectives: to raise national income by 15 per cent over the plan period, to improve the balance of payments by expanding exports and substituting for imports, to increase employment opportunities, to make steady progress in social

[1] Government of Pakistan Planning Commission, Karachi.

TABLE 2[1] FIRST FIVE-YEAR PLAN (1955–60)

(Million RS)

	Public Sector	Percentage distribution	Private Sector[2]	Total	Percentage distribution
Agriculture	1,505	16·1	(included elsewhere)	1,505	11·9
Water and Power	2,697	28·9		2,697	21·3
Industry, Fuels and Minerals	1,622	17·4	1,750	3,372	26·7
Transport and Communications	1,666	17·8	450	2,116	16·7
Housing and Settlement	861	9·2	800	1,661	13·1
Education and Training	580	6·2			
Heath	288	3·1	300	1,301	10·3
Manpower and Social Welfare	133	1·4	(including agriculture and water and power)		
Expected Short-fall	−1,852			−1,852	
	7,500		3,300	1,0800	

[1] Government of Pakistan, Planning Commission, First Five Year Plan – Preliminary Evaluation Report – Karachi, September, 1959, pp. 2–3.

[2] A major part of investment in agriculture is in the form of non-monetized investment, in the sense that resources originate on and are invested in the self-same farms without the farmers being involved in any monetary transactions. Since planning and development have been considered in terms of monetary investment, this explains the fact that planned investment in the private sector of agriculture is shown as zero. At the same time, the figure of Rs 300 million given for private investment in education, health and manpower was also intended to cover agriculture, water and power, though the figure is only an approximate estimate, and no break-down is available.

services and to accelerate the rate of development in the more underdeveloped regions. The total amount of investment contemplated in the plan, as well as its distribution between different sectors, is given in Table 2 (p. 124).

The First Five-Year Plan postulated an annual investment of RS2,160 million, which represented a substantial increase in total investment over what was contemplated in either the Six-Year Development Plan or in the Two-Year Priority Plan. In contrast with the Six-Year Plan, and reflecting the changed order of priorities, the First Five-Year Plan represented a shift in emphasis towards industry, fuels and minerals and away from agriculture and transport and communications, in terms of the percentage distribution of investment between sectors. There was also a greater emphasis on social services including education, training, manpower, health and housing, etc. In so far as the sectoral allocations of First Five-Year Plan itself are considered, 33 per cent of total investment was to be in agriculture, water and power, 23 per cent in social services, 27 per cent in industry, fuels and minerals and 17 per cent in transport and communication.

The sectoral programmes had specific objectives. For example, the agricultural programme of the First Five-Year Plan was intended to compensate for the slow progress in the past. It was necessary to generate an adequate marketable surplus to provide food for an increasing urban population as well as to provide a wide market for industrial products. So long as agricultural exports tended to predominate, overall exports could be increased in the short run mainly through an expansion of certain agricultural products.[1] The next important sector in the First Plan was the field of manufacturing industry. The industrial programme was intended to save or earn foreign exchange, to provide additional employment opportunities, and to produce certain key commodities considered essential for the successful implementation of the plan, i.e., to prevent bottlenecks in the supply of strategic commodities used by a large number of other industries or other economic activities. The first essential steps in the field of industry were to consolidate past progress, to ensure a fuller use of existing or already

[1] First Five Year Plan, ch. 2, para 67 and ch. 20, Para 2.

installed capacity and to secure a better balance in the development of different industries.[1]

The First Five-Year Plan (1955–60) suffered from serious setbacks in the course of its implementation. The plan did not receive formal government approval until 1957. The financial resources available for development expenditure fell short of expectations owing to (a) a rise in non-development expenditure beyond the level stipulated in the plan, and (b) a shortfall in foreign exchange earnings. The latter was partly caused by a fall in the volume and price of exports as well as a rise in import prices, and partly by shortfalls in arrivals of aid due to administrative and procedural delays in its commitment and utilization.[2] While unfavourable weather conditions adversely affected agricultural output, a substantial rise in prices, both external and internal, upset the cost calculations of the plan. Shortages of key personnel, ineffective co-ordination between Government agencies as well as a failure to observe the discipline of the plan – all contributed to the shortfalls in the implementation of the plan.[3] In financial terms the plan was fulfilled to the extent of about 90 per cent. In real terms, it was much less.

The Second Five-Year Plan started in 1960 and the objectives were substantially the same as in the First Plan especially since shortfalls in various sectors during the First Plan had to be made up during the Second Plan. The main objective of the Second Plan was to increase national income by 20 per cent during 1960–65, a target which has since been raised to 24 per cent. Besides the postulated rate of growth of national income, other important objectives are (a) self-sufficiency in food, (b) improvement in the balance of payments, (c) acceleration of the rate of growth in the relatively less developed areas and (d) expansion of employment opportunities. The sectoral allocation of investment funds has been oriented towards the attainment of the above objectives. As high yields on investment are expected to be obtained in agriculture and industry, they have received large allocations of investment expenditure. According to the Second Plan, the requirements of irrigation, drainage, flood control and power facilities for increasing production in

---

[1] First Five Year Plan, ch. 20, para 22 and para 23–6.
[2] Second Five Year Plan, ch. I, p. 1, para 4.
[3] Second Five Year Plan, ch. I, p. 2, para 6.

agriculture and industry have set the targets for the development of water and power resources. Similarly, attempts have been made to relate transport facilities to the needs of the agricultural and industrial programmes. The programmes for the development of housing, education, health and social welfare services have been determined on the basis of general social considerations.[1]

The proposed sectoral distribution of the Second Plan development expenditure as contrasted with the actual expenditures under the First Plan is shown in Table 3 (p. 128).

The Second Plan lays strong emphasis on (a) agriculture and (b) education, which lagged in the First Plan, and (c) expenditure on further development of infrastructure, the basis of which was already laid in the First Plan, particularly in the fields of water and power, transport and communications. The sectors in which the largest increases are contemplated under the Second Plan are the following: Health, Manpower and Social Welfare, Education and Training, and Agriculture. Investment in education is increasingly recognized as investment in the development of human capital. This is partly a result of shortfalls in the implementation of the targets of the First Five-Year Plan in these various targets. The broad socio-economic objectives of economic development in Pakistan which were initially stated at the beginning of the Six-Year Development Plan run through all the successive plans and policy announcements of the Government in substantially the same vein.[2] The basic objectives of the agricultural programme are substantially the same as in the First Plan. The need to attain self-sufficiency in food production as soon as possible, maintaining as a minimum the present levels of foodgrain consumption for the rapidly

[1] Second Five Year Plan, p. 7.

[2] Both the First and Second Plan reiterate that 'people, at least the vocal sections of the population, desire a rapid economic and social change and that they want eradication of poverty and illiteracy and a reduction in the inequalities of wealth and opportunities'. The second Plan states that 'the awakening aspirations of the people are exerting strong pressures on the existing economic and social order, and no under-developed country today can afford to fall behind in the race for progress without incurring the very grave risk of internal disruption or external intrusion'.

First Five Year Plan, p. 2, para. 6.

Second Five Year Plan Preface, p. xiii.

TABLE 3 DEVELOPMENT EXPENDITURES OF FIRST AND SECOND PLANS

(1960–61 prices)

(Million Rs)

	First Plan Actual Expenditure	Percentage distribution (approx.)	Second Plan Public Expenditure	Second Plan Private Expenditure	Second Five Year Plan (Total)	Percentage distribution	Percentage increase over the First Plan
Agriculture	1,440	10·9	2,520	900	3,420	14·9	138
Water and Power	2,300	17·3	4,330	60	4,390	19·1	91
Industry, Fuels and Minerals	4,100	30·8	2,490	3,630	6,120	26·6	49
Transport and Communications	2,280	17·2	3,140	910	4,050	17·6	78
Housing and Settlements	2,580	19·5	2,280	1,130	3,410	14·8	32
Education and Training	410	3·1	950	105	1,055	4·6	157
Health	140	1·1	490	65	420	1·8	200
Manpower and Social Welfare	50	0·1			135	0·6	170
	13,300	100·0	16,200	6,800	23,000	100·0	73

[1] The expenditure under the First Year Plan was estimated at Rs10,800 million and it actually amounted to Rs13,300 million. The increase is accounted for by conversion of expenditure into 1960–61 prices, increase in physical targets and under-estimation of the cost of some projects.

Economic Adviser to the Government of Pakistan, Ministry of Finance, Highlights on the Second Five Year Plan, 1962, Rawalpindi, pp. 10–11.

Second Five Year Plan, Revised Estimates, 1961

growing population, has been emphasized.[1] As in the First Plan, so also in the Second Plan the income-creating and employment-providing effects of industrialization are emphasized. Persistent adverse movements in terms of trade as well as the relatively slow expansion and fluctuations in the volume and value of traditional exports provide an added incentive for the diversification of the economy in the direction of industrialization. However, it was soon realized that the objective of self-sufficiency in food production is not realizable within the plan period. Nor is it necessarily desirable to aim at self-sufficiency in food grains without an analysis of costs and benefits of alternative crop-patterns. It is, nonetheless, recognized that in view of a stagnation in export earnings, the replacement of imports by domestic production assumes a great urgency.

MAGNITUDE AND PATTERN OF ECONOMIC GROWTH

The national income of Pakistan over the past twelve or thirteen years has recorded only a very moderate increase, the average rate of growth being about 2·28 per cent per annum over the whole period 1949–50 to 1960–61. The growth in *per capita* income was much less, and in some years an actual decline was registered. Over the whole period, the average annual rate of growth in *per capita* income appears to have been even less than 0·5 per cent. The reason for this was the high rate of increase of population, which is estimated at 2 per cent–2·2 per cent per annum.[2]

The various sectors of the economy have grown at unequal rates. For example, the average annual rate of growth of income derived from the manufacturing sector has been around 9·3 per cent over the period 1949–50 to 1960–61. This is considerably higher than the rates of growth in either agriculture or

---

[1] Second Five Year Plan, p. 127. Renewed attention was paid to the raising of dietary standards through increased supplies of fish, fruits and vegetables. The expansion of the output of jute, cotton, tea and forest products to the maximum possible extent was contemplated in order to work towards a favourable export position.

[2] Government of Pakistan, Ministry of Finance, Office of the Economic Adviser, Pakistan—*Basic Facts*, Rawalpindi, 1962, p. 100.

commerce, which were 1·58 per cent and 2·72 per cent respectively.[1] The higher rate of growth of industrial income is partly due to the very small size of the manufacturing sector in the initial years. The differences in the rates of increases in average levels of sectoral incomes during the First Five-Year Plan (1955–60) over the levels of the preceding quinquennium, i.e. 1950–51 to 1954–55 are shown below.[2]

TABLE 4 PERCENTAGE INCREASE BETWEEN
TWO QUINQUENNIUMS

In Sectoral Incomes

	Percentage
1. Agriculture	6·8
2. Manufacturing:	58
(a) Large Scale	142·8
(b) Small Scale	10·5
3. Wholesale and Retail Trade	13·6
4. Total National Income	10·5
5. *Per Capita* Income	0·3

The highest rate of growth was in the field of large scale industry, and the agricultural sector recorded the smallest increase. But the considerable rise in industrial production has not made a commensurate difference to the growth of overall national income because the industrial sector still continues to contribute relatively a very small proportion of total income. Even though there was a decrease in the share of agriculture in national income from an average of 60 per cent during the years 1949–50 to 1953–54 to 50 per cent during the years 1956–57 to 1960–61, agriculture's contribution is still substantial. During the same period the share of manufacturing industry only rose from an average of 7 per cent of national income to an average of 12·3 per cent.[3]

It is remarkable that the growth of overall income has been so small in view of the large investments which have taken place, particularly in more recent years. The average ratio of gross

[1] Ministry of Finance, *Basic Facts*, p. 100.
[2] Ibid.
[3] Ibid.

investment to national income has been around 8·8 per cent during the period 1954–55 to 1959–60.[1] While industrial investments have yielded comparative largely increases in income, investments in other sectors, including agriculture, have not yielded commensurate returns. This is due partly to the fact that many of the projects in the field of water, power and agriculture, etc., have long gestation periods and take time to show results. Moreover, the great preponderance of the agricultural sector means that any reverses in this field caused for example by weather conditions, are reflected in the aggregate, i.e. they more than offset any increases which may take place in other sectors. Even in the non-agricultural sectors there are time-lags of varying duration between investments and increases in income, so that investments in one plan period often result in increases in output and income in subsequent periods.

It may be worthwhile to investigate in greater detail why development efforts have not borne much fruit in the field of agriculture. Agriculture in Pakistan continues to be dependent on weather conditions. Recurrent floods in East Pakistan and water-logging and salinity in West Pakistan have serious adverse effects on agricultural production. Floods not only destroy crops, i.e. the farmers' current income: they also destroy agricultural capital, including farmers' homesteads. The result is a diversion of resources to the replacement of capital-stock and a diminution in the capacity for net investment on the part of the farmers. Similarly, as a result of the menace of water-logging and salinity, vast tracts of lands in West Pakistan regularly go out of cultivation and many others lose their fertility, with a consequent decline in their yields unless offset by commensurate investments in land reclamation and conservation. The crucial role which vagaries of nature play in determining the annual levels of agricultural production places the farmers under great uncertainty regarding their future income from investments of either labour or capital on land. This acts as a serious disincentive to efforts on the part of farmers to increase agricultural production. The past decade, however, has not been marked by any significant alleviation of this important limiting factor.

The basic problem in agricultural development is how to

[1] Government of Pakistan, Planning Commission, Karachi.

influence the behaviour and actions of a multitude of small farmers spread over a wide area in both the regions, whose decisions in the last analysis determine the volume of agricultural production. But the introduction of land reforms in East Pakistan has led to the abolition of intermediary rights in land without any concomitant changes in agricultural organization such as uneconomic sizes of holdings, supply of credit and marketing arrangements, etc. The land reform measures in West Pakistan have been mainly oriented towards greater equity in the distribution of land in so far as the top 5 per cent of the landlords have been obliged to dispose of their surplus lands. However, the upper limit fixed to the size of holdings is too high. Neither does it altogether abolish intermediary rights or non-cultivating interests such as share-cropping. In both wings of Pakistan such reforms as have been legislated are still in the process of implementation and their effects on agricultural production are yet to be felt. Another related handicap in the field of agricultural development arises from an instability – which is often considerable – in the prices of agricultural commodities. This adds to the uncertainty, created by natural calamities, regarding the income to be derived from agricultural output and thus acts as a further disincentive. The dispersal of agricultural production over innumerable small farms, run by individuals of small means, raises difficult problems of organization not merely of producers themselves but also for the provision of supplies and technical guidance to them. The past history of co-operatives has been a sad one and attempts at revival have not been very successful. Experiments are being worked out with village co-operatives in selected areas, but it is still too early to pass judgment on the results of this experience with any degree of assurance, or to be able to formulate rules for their successful future operation.

As the Report of the Food and Agriculture Commission[1] rightly points out, while measures for increasing agricultural production are broadly well known, the main problem is how to implement these measures. Semi-autonomous Agricultural Development Corporations have been established in both the wings of Pakistan to undertake the production, procure-

[1] Ministry of Food and Agriculture, Government of Pakistan, Karachi, 1960.

ment, transportation and distribution of seeds, fertilizers, plant protection materials, and farm implements throughout the country. These organizations have yet to get off to a successful start. In order to fulfil their objectives they have to overcome the slowness with which millions of small cultivators can be educated and induced to accept the change in their attitudes and values which is involved in a departure from traditional agricultural methods. Even when fertilizers are available in sufficient quantity, there is a limit to the amount agriculturists can absorb in a given period, say a five-year plan period, partly because a continuing education campaign will need time to bear results and partly because the adoption of improved methods spreads slowly among the farmers, as the successful pioneers are gradually imitated by their neighbours. Even when irrigation facilities are ready there have been bottlenecks in respect of financial and administrative arrangements for the distribution of water to individual farmers or for the settlement of land among farmers. However, it is expected that with the strengthening of the Agricultural Development Corporations as well as with the increased efforts of the Water and Power Development Authorities in the field of flood control and of extension of irrigation facilities, the stage has been set for achieving substantial results in the field of agriculture in the future.

In the field of manufacturing industry more encouraging developments have been due to a great extent to the leading part played by the Pakistan Industrial Development Corporation – an autonomous public corporation established by the Government to initiate and develop manufacturing industries either alone or in combination with private enterprise.[1] The P.I.D.C. was established in 1952, the whole of the initial capital being provided by the government. Finance for individual projects is derived from annual grants from the central government budget, private capital, and foreign aid and loans. The PIDC projects have served as an important medium for the joint participation of private and public capital. Private industrialists have felt induced to invest in PIDC-sponsored enterprises because these have greater access to the foreign and domestic loan market, as well as having the support of the financial and

---

[1] M. Ayub, 'The Role of Private and Public Enterprise in the Industrial Development of Pakistan', P.I.D.C., Karachi, 1958.

133

technical resources at the disposal of the government. The relative share of public and private investment in the PIDC enterprises is as follows :[1]

Period	Total investment in P.I.D.C. projects (Rs million)	P.I.D.C. investment	Private investment
To 1955	157·06	128·18	128·88
To 1962 (February)	1,721·5	1,367·5	354·0

During the Second Five-Year Plan, more than 89 per cent of the total public investment in large scale industry is expected to be undertaken by the PIDC either in its own factories or in enterprises with a private participation.[2] The main objectives of PIDC are to promote and establish industrial undertakings in those fields in which private enterprise is either wholly unable or unwilling to come forward or does so to an inadequate extent. The PIDC in its original charter is entrusted with the responsibility of developing the following industries: jute, paper, heavy engineering including iron and steel, ship building, heavy chemicals, sugar, cement, textiles, natural gas, chemicals, pharmaceuticals and dyestuff and development of power from Sui natural gas. The PIDC has not only taken the initiative in establishing pioneering ventures in almost all these fields of production; it has also supplemented private enterprises wherever possible and to the extent its resources permitted. It has devoted special attention to industries which (a) require a heavy initial investment, (b) take a long time to be constructed and to mature and (c) require a great deal of technical knowledge and operating experience.

The pattern of total PIDC investment in the projects sponsored by it either wholly or in co-operation with private capital is as follows: 22·3 per cent in paper and paper products, 15·2 per cent in gas transmission and distribution, 15 per cent in

[1] P.I.D.C. Annual Report, 1955–56, pp. 12–16, and Government of Pakistan, Ministry of Finance, Economic Survey, 1961–62, p. 39.
[2] Second Plan, pp. 244–5.

134

chemicals, 14·2 per cent in ship and dockyards, 11 per cent in jute, 9·4 per cent in sugar and 8 per cent in cement.[1] It has borne the initial risks and high costs in the early years of experimentation in hitherto untested fields of enterprise. The total industrial assets under the aegis of both the PIDC and private enterprises increased from RS580 million in 1948 to RS5,020 million in 1959.[2] Many of the enterprises initially started by the PIDC have been sold out to private industrialists either partially or completely. By 1958, eighteen out of thirty-seven PIDC projects had already been transferred to private management and control.[3] The resources of the PIDC thus serve as a sort of revolving fund for initiating new and difficult ventures in fields where private initiative is not forthcoming. The process of disinvestment by PIDC confirms the Government's policy of encouraging private enterprise whenever the latter is willing and able to take over.

As has already been explained, the pattern of overall industrialization, both public and private, was initially based on the utilization of domestic raw materials and on the replacement of imports of manufactured goods. Rapid developments have taken place in light manufacturing or consumer goods industries. In 1958, the cotton, jute, silk and woollen textiles contributed about 51 per cent of total industrial production, whereas food and beverage industries contributed 18 per cent. The heavy and intermediate goods industries, such as basic metals, electrical products, transport and other equipment, paper and cement, etc., accounted for only 9 per cent of total industrial output.[4]

But in spite of remarkable achievements, the industrial base of the economy of Pakistan remains very small. The important obstacles to progress in this field are the scarcity of capital, especially of foreign exchange, and of skill at all levels of operation and of management. Pakistan has developed over the past years a small entrepreneural class, and from indirect evidence

[1] M. Ayub, 'Public Industrial Enterprises in Pakistan 1960', Karachi, 1960, Annexure, pp. 1–32.

[2] G. Papanek, 'The Development of Entrepreneurship'. Papers and Proceedings of the American Economic Association, May 1962, pp. 8–10.

[3] Ayub, op. cit., pp. 6–16, P.I.D.C. Annual Report, 1957–58.

[4] Central Statistical Office, 'Census of Manufacturing Industries 1958', Karachi, 1961, Table I, pp. 3.

it appears that in recent years potential demand for private industrial investment may not have been fully met owing to a shortage of foreign exchange.[1] There does not seem to be a dearth of enterprise or of desire to improve one's material welfare and to earn profit among those, for example, who are engaged in trade, in construction, in money lending and even in small scale industries. It is precisely from the trading classes, among whom a vigorous pursuit of the profit motive is only too evident, that many of the leaders of industrial enterprises have come. The history of private industrial investment in Pakistan can be traced from the days of the Korean boom when abnormal trading profits provided substantial funds for investment. The drastic curtailment of imports in the subsequent depression, combined with the very small scale of indigenous production, created an acute scarcity of goods and enhanced the opportunities for profit. However, private enterprise in industry has not been widespread among a large numbers of investors. In common with other under-developed countries, Pakistan has a comparatively small middle class which cannot mobilize capital and organize production in any degree comparable with industrially advanced societies. This is partly because many potential investors lack adequate technical knowledge or expert guidance in formulating schemes for industrial investments. Widespread provision of competent industrial and technical advisory services to help private entrepreneurs formulate sound projects would enlarge the flow of technically and financially sound investments. Moreover, smaller private entrepreneurs lack sufficient financial resources to undertake large scale enterprises in fields in which large units are technically desirable for ensuring efficient and economic operation. A lack of social overhead capital, of credit institutions and money markets, and an unfamiliarity with and distrust of the corporate forms of organization, further inhibit the development of large scale industrial enterprises. The tendency to go in for those industrial enterprises which bring in the largest short-run profits with the minimum risk is naturally strong among private entrepreneurs with a commercial background. This brings us to the relative role of

[1] It is generally recognized how potential investors applied pressure, offered bribes and were willing to pay a legal surcharge of over 100% to import machinery. See Dr. Papanek, op. cit.

private and public enterprises in the economic development of Pakistan.

PUBLIC AND PRIVATE ENTERPRISE

The major emphasis in the economic policy of Pakistan is on the promotion of private initiative and enterprise. However, in view of the great need for development, it is recognized that there is ample room for both private and public enterprises and that both are desirable agencies for development. The first statement of government policy in 1948 postulated that main communications and transport services such as posts, telegraphs, telephones, wireless, broadcasting, railways and air transport should be owned and operated by the Government. In road and river transport the prospect of the eventual nationalization of the then existing private enterprises was not ruled out. Excepting three other specific fields of activity, namely (a) arms and ammunitions of war, (b) generation of hydro-electric power and (c) manufacture of railway wagons, telephones, telegraph and wireless apparatus, private enterprise was left free to operate in any other field. However, the government reserved the right to 'take over or participate in any other industry vital to the security or economic well-being of the State'. Moreover, it was decided that if in any particular industry of national importance adequate private capital did not come forward, the government might set up 'a limited number of standard units more as a measure of attracting private enterprise than for any other object'.[1] In the restatement of industrial policy made in 1959, greater emphasis is placed upon private enterprise.[2] The fields reserved for public enterprise remain broadly the same, i.e. (a) arms and ammunitions, (b) railways, air transport and tele-communications and (c) production of atomic energy, although the generation of hydro-electric power is no longer specifically reserved for public enterprise. River transport is left free for private enterprise without any threat of nationalization. Road transport is to continue to have both private and state enter-prises. In all other fields, the maximum scope is to be provided

[1] Government of Pakistan, Statement of Industrial Policy, April 2, 1948.
[2] New Industrial Policy, April 1953, pp. 10–12. Pakistan Trade, January 1959, pp. 8–12.

to private enterprise, and the general provision that the government may take over any industry considered essential or vital has been removed. Where private enterprise is inactive, the government intends to establish such industries as are essential to the life of the community through specially constituted corporations which are to be transferred to private enterprises as circumstances permit. The Second Plan reiterates the basic economic philosophy in the following words.

No doctrinaire assumptions underlie the plan, and neither an exclusively capitalist nor an exclusively socialist economy is postulated. The approach throughout is pragmatic. The fundamental problem is how, under severely limiting conditions, to find some way towards the liberation of the people from the crushing burden of poverty. . . . Progress must, however, be sought mainly through inducement, less through direction. The creative energies of the people can be best harnessed to the needs of development, if policies of economic liberalism are pursued. . . . Controls which have a strangulating effect on private initiative will need to be relaxed, and replaced progressively by fiscal and monetary measures and operation of the market mechanism.[1]

The relative importance of public investment has considerably increased in the last decade, so much so that by 1957–58 it exceeded the amount of private investment. Between 1951–52 and 1961–62, public investment increased almost four-fold, from RS525 million to RS2,052 million, while during the same period private investment barely doubled, from RS700 million to RS1,350 million.[2]

The government seeks to regulate the amount and direction of private investment in various sectors so as to conform as far as possible to the sectoral targets laid down in the Five-Year Plans. While in some sectors there is an excess demand, i.e. a willingness on the part of private entrepreneurs to invest in excess of targets fixed by the government, in some others demand falls short of predetermined targets. But then the private investment resources which cannot be utilized in the former sectors because they exceed planned targets, do not necessarily flow to

[1] The Second Five Year Plan (1955–60), June 1960, pp. xiii-xiv.
[2] Planning Commission, Government of Pakistan and Second Five Year Plan, op. cit., Table I, p. 26. Private investment figures given above include only investments in the monetized sector of the economy and exclude real investment resources which originate and are reinvested in the self-same farms without entering into the market mechanism. Government of Pakistan, Planning Commission, Mid-Plan Review, Karachi, October 1962, p. 49.

other alternative sectors. Thus a scarcity of foreign exchange resources which puts a limit to overall industrial investment may cause a relative under-utilization of domestic investment funds, if the latter are not forthcoming in the specified sectors in predetermined amounts. In such cases public enterprise attempts to fill the gap. Moreover, the government, in order to achieve targets of private investment in desired amounts and directions, undertakes various measures of inducement and assistance to private enterprise such as the supply of finance through a number of State sponsored financial institutions,[1] the establishment of industrial estates and the provision of tax incentives – all designed to encourage investment in the private sector. Small scale and cottage industries have been the recipients of special financial and technical assistance provided through the medium of a number of 'Small Scale Industries Corporations'.

The government also exercises a large number of controls designed to regulate the private sector. They extend over the allocation of foreign exchange, the licensing of imports, the location of industry and the allocation of materials in short supply as well as over the prices and production of specific commodities. The existence of various kinds of controls coupled with the limited size of the market implies that free entry, as conceived in the theoretical model of competition, does not exist. Moreover, controls have developed in a haphazard manner and on an *ad hoc* basis, often in response to the immediate and compelling demands of particular situations in isolation,[2] and this has resulted in over-lapping and duplication. They have undergone frequent changes, with a resultant uncertainty in the minds of businessmen, and have discouraged long term commitments. Many controls have been only partially effective owing to inadequate enforcement. The administration of controls affecting considerable business fortunes has concentrated great powers in the hands of public officials, whose individual incomes can seldom compare favourably with large business gains, and this has opened the door to temptation and consequent corruption.

[1] Government of Pakistan, Ministry of Finance, Government sponsored Corporations, 1959.

[2] Government of Pakistan, Ministry of Industries, Economic Controls Manual, 1954 and 1959.

The recent tendency is to rationalize and relax the system of controls, and, if possible, to replace direct controls by taxes and subsidies as regulatory weapons.

IMPACT OF EXTERNAL FACTORS

Foreign aid, loans and investment[1] have played an important role in Pakistan. Total foreign aid up to December 1961 was RS6,205·57 million and total foreign loans were RS2,632·03 million. The total amount of aid utilized up to 1960 was distributed as follows: 18·6 per cent in project aid, 78·4 per cent in commodity aid and 3 per cent in technical assistance. The overwhelming proportion of this came from the U.S.A., accounting for 88 per cent of the total, whereas only 7·5 per cent was from Canada, 2·5 per cent from the rest of the Commonwealth, 1·82 per cent from West Germany and the remainder was from Japan and the UN agencies, etc. Foreign loans have been granted mainly by US (53·5 per cent) IBRD (23 per cent), UK (9 per cent), and Japan (3·2 per cent).[2] During the First Five-Year Plan foreign resources constituted 47 per cent of the total investment. Similarly, during the Second Five-Year Plan foreign aid, loans and foreign private investment are expected to constitute about 48 per cent of total planned investment and to meet the entire foreign exchange component of the plan.[3] Pakistan's own foreign exchange earnings are at present not even adequate to meet her current import needs on account of consumer goods, raw materials and spare parts. During the Second Five-Year Plan a part of these 'maintenance imports', as they are called, is also to be met from foreign aid.

As for the distribution between aid and loans of the total

---

[1] In this section, a clear distinction is made between *aid* which is an outright grant, and *loans* which are repayable and carry a rate of interest. Foreign private *investment* involves either the establishment of subsidiaries of private foreign companies, or the purchase of a share in Pakistani enterprises by private persons or institutions abroad.

[2] The figures for aid and loans refer to utilization and not to commitment. Commitment usually exceeds utilization owing to delays in finalization of agreements on specific projects and delays in the delivery of goods and services committed under aid. Government of Pakistan, Ministry of Finance, 'A Review o Foreign Economic Aid to Pakistan', Rawalpindi, 1962, pp. 110–11, and p. 114.

[3] Revised Second Plan, p. 17. This excludes aid under PL 480 and also excludes works programme from the total amount of contemplated investment.

foreign capital inflow, excluding foreign private investment, there has been an increase in recent years in the proportion of loans to aid.[1] This is due to an increased preference in favour of loans rather than outright grants on the part of foreign governments and aid-giving agencies. While loans may induce a greater economy in the use of funds or the choice of projects, in the present stage of development in Pakistan they deplete resources available for further investment by the amount of debt service payments. This is specially important when the past growth of national income has been so small. A rise in the ratio of loans to aid has the effect of increasing the burden of debt service payments on our own foreign exchange resources. Moreover, interest and amortisation payments introduce an element of inflexibility in Pakistan's foreign payments. This is of a special concern in view of the considerable fluctuations in Pakistan's export earnings. Foreign direct investment, on the other hand, has been of much less quantitative significance than foreign loans or aid. Total private investment up to 1960 was RS1,752 million and the average annual inflow in the four years 1957–60 amounted to RS80·1 million.[2] The country-wise distribution of the total inflow of foreign private investment during 1957–60 is as follows: 50 per cent from the UK, 9 per cent from the USA and 41 per cent from the rest of the world. The major portion of investment (i.e. 65 per cent) is in commerce and mining and the rest is in miscellaneous industries.[3]

The total debt service payments in 1962 amounted to 12·1 per cent of Pakistan's foreign exchange earnings. The current level of remittances of profits and dividends represents an average return of 8 per cent to 9 per cent on foreign private investment whereas the rates of interest on loans average between 5 per cent and 6 per cent.[4] Thus the burden of private investment appears to be higher than that of loans. But the former has two redeeming features. Whereas foreign loans create firm commitments for interest and principal repayments, irrespective of the success or failure of the projects financed by loans, dividends on direct

[1] 'A Review of Foreign Economic Aid', op. cit.
[2] State Bank of Pakistan, Foreign Liabilities and Assets and Foreign Investments in Pakistan, Karachi, 1962, Statement No. 1, p. 22 and pp. 15–17.
[3] Ibid.
[4] Government of Pakistan, Ministry of Finance, Proceedings of the First Meeting of the Panel of Economists, Rawalpindi, 1962, pp. 14–15.

investments are remitted only when the latter are profitable. Secondly, while private investments seldom involve a net repatriation on a large scale, foreign loans involve certain and full repayment in a relatively short period. Moreover, foreign private enterprise provides access to patented techniques developed elsewhere and brings in managerial and technical skill as well as creating opportunities for the training of local personnel. The employment of foreign consultants and technicians cannot always reproduce all the characteristics of a modern enterprise of the kind with which the Pakistani industries have eventually to compete abroad. Insofar as foreign private investment takes place in the private sector and foreign loans finance the public or semi-public sector programmes, they supplement rather than compete with each other.

At present remittances of profits and dividends on account of private foreign investment exceed the current inflow of private investment. This reinforces the need for greater private foreign investment. The government policy towards private foreign investment is a liberal one. With the exception of a few industries such as defence industries, railways and air transport, and tele-communications, private foreign enterprise is welcome in any field. The government places no restrictions on the remittance of current profits or on the repatriation of capital from industries established after 1954. It assures fair compensation in case 'circumstances or emergency' necessitates nationalization and provides for relief from double taxation. There is no rigidity about the participation of local capital in foreign enterprises, though the government expects that 'required local expenditure will be met from local equity capital' and that 'progressive employment and training facilities' will be offered for Pakistanis.[1] However, the government seeks to attract foreign capital specially in those fields which involve large investments and complicated processes such as heavy engineering, heavy chemicals, synthetic distillation of coal and gas, pharmaceuticals, antibiotics, mining, refining, and manufacturing of producer goods and spare parts.[2]

The dependence on foreign economic assistance in Pakistan

[1] Government of Pakistan, The Statement of Industrial Policy, February 1959.
[2] A. M. Ghouse, *The Economy of Pakistan*—A Review Businessmen's Seminar, Lahore, 1961, pp. 89–90.

assumes a critical significance in view of a declining trend in the terms of trade and a state of relative stagnation in export earnings. The relative stagnation in export earnings is evident from the fact that the average annual value of commodity exports which was RS1,631 million during 1950–55 was only RS1,572 million during 1955–60. The average annual commodity imports, on the other hand, recorded a 50 per cent increase between the same periods. The average annual net deficit on account of both goods and services increased seven times between the two quinquenniums.[1] The widening deficit is the result of the foreign exchange requirements of an increasing development programme in recent years. The stagnation in export earnings is partly the result of the increasing domestic absorption of such export commodities as raw jute, jute manufactures, cotton, tea and hides and skins. The development of new exports of manufactured goods or of different and new raw materials has been very slow and inadequate. But under the impact of the export bonus scheme, there have been substantial gains in the exports of manufactured goods, i.e., processed cotton and jute since 1959, even though these items still contribute a very minor fraction of total export earnings.[2] Under the export bonus scheme the exporters of these commodities get titles to foreign exchange equal to a certain percentage of their total exports. These 'bonus vouchers' are sold in the free market at a rate much higher than the official exchange rate, so that the exporters receive an indirect subsidy to compensate them for any loss incurred in selling abroad below cost or below domestic price.[3] However, the stimulating effect of this indirect subsidy on the exports of these two important items of manufactured goods has been limited by (a) an inadequate domestic production of raw materials and (b) by an increase in the domestic demand for finished products.

A continuous deterioration in the terms of trade has also adversely affected the availability of foreign exchange resources. The index of the terms of trade declined from an average of 80

[1] State Bank of Pakistan, Pakistan's Balance of Payments, July 1948–June 1959 and 1959–60 and 1960–61.

[2] H. J. Bruton and S. R. Bose, 'The Export Bonus Scheme—A Preliminary Report', Pakistan Development Review, Summer 1962, Vol. II, No. 2. (Raw cotton and raw jute are *not* covered by the export bonus scheme.)

[3] Ibid.

during 1952–56 to an average of 62 during 1957–61, primarily owing to a rise in the index of import prices. The latter increased continuously from 79·4 in 1949–50 to 163·0 in 1960–61.[1] The phenomenon of 'tied' loans or grants has the effect of increasing the import price of aid-commodities by doing away with international competition in their supply. As a result the purchasing power of exports in terms of imports fell continuously from RS2,114 million in 1951–52 to RS855 in 1959–60 and recorded an increase to RS1,104 million in 1960–61 under the impact of the export bonus scheme. The value of exports in 1960–61 was RS1,799 million whereas their real purchasing power in terms of 1948–49 import prices amounted to RS1,104 million. Thus the decline in the purchasing power of exports by RS695 million was not even offset by foreign aid and loans which amounted to RS500 million[2] during 1960–61.

HUMAN FACTORS IN DEVELOPMENT

Human, social and cultural factors contribute to the complexity of the problems facing a developing economy in its efforts to raise the standard and quality of living. Pakistan faces the problem of a large and increasing population, which was 90 million strong in 1961, and is growing at the rate of approximately 2·2 per cent per annum.[3] The government has adopted a policy of encouraging family planning by means of educational publicity and by the establishment of advisory clinics, mainly in urban areas. The popularization of family planning measures is partly a matter of education of the masses in the adoption of a rational attitude towards the size of a family, and partly a matter of the knowledge and of availability of the means, given the will, to control the size of a family. The social and religious attitudes which discourage family planning can be changed only slowly. The higher income groups, with a higher education, are increasingly inclined to control the size of a family and often tend to make favourable reinterpretations of religious injunc-

[1] Central Statistical Office, Monthly Statistical Bulletin, December 1960 and October 1962.
[2] Government of Pakistan, Planning Commission, Mid-Plan Review, October 1962, op. cit., p. 82.
[3] Government of Pakistan, Ministry of Home Affairs, Population Census of Pakistan 1961, Census Bulletin, No. 2, pp. 10–12.

tions, but their number is too small to make any appreciable impact on the overall situation. Past experience suggests that a spread of general education, an improvement in the standard of living and specially a change in the social status of women may create a more favourable environment.

Pakistan faces the paradoxical situation of a chronic surplus of manpower coupled with critical scarcities of skills in occupations of crucial importance for development. There is a great imbalance between supply and demand in terms of different levels of skill and occupations. The most serious bottleneck is in the intermediate range of skilled labour, like artisans, masons, supervisors, sub-engineers and craftsman, where an adequate supply is essential if highly skilled professional experts are to put their skill and knowledge to effective use. The performance recorded during the First Five-Year Plan in the field of education and training, specially that of technical education, was very disappointing. Unfortunately no comprehensive survey of manpower requirements for major sectors has been undertaken. Efforts at improvement in the field of manpower training take time to bear fruit and consequently necessitate long term planning. A number of organizational changes have taken place recently to co-ordinate and administer the various forms and branches of technical education. It is only recently that two new engineering universities and two new agricultural universities have been established under the Second Plan.

The provision of universal primary education as soon as possible is considered a desirable social objective. However, the impact of primary education on productivity and income is not expected to be either direct or immediate. Its indirect benefits in terms of a widening of horizons, a greater receptivity to changes in techniques and organization, production, and in ways of living, an eagerness for modernization and for material advance are felt only slowly. We are faced with a pressing shortage of funds and an immediate need to increase physical output; and it is worth serious consideration whether we should not now place less emphasis during the next two Five-Year Plans on primary education and much greater emphasis, for example, on the training of technical manpower which has an immediate impact on increased productivity in industry and agriculture. The choice here is politically a difficult and delicate one, since political and social forces have aroused expectations of a rapid expansion of universal primary education. Because of the sheer numbers involved, the rush for the fastest possible extension of primary education necessitates huge expenditure, and speed in this direction militates against the quality and the content of education. Moreover, the increase in the numbers of the intellectual proletariat, caused by the shortage of opportunities for employment for non-technical personnel, and by conservative social values discouraging manual work for school-educated persons, may tend to create a critical social problem.

FUTURE PROSPECTS

It is expected that the achievement of the targets laid down in the Second Plan will lay the basis for accelerated growth in the future. But the stagnation in agricultural production poses a major problem. It is now widely recognized that concerted efforts have to be made in this sector and the stage has now been set for significant progress in measures for flood control, irrigation, and the prevention of water-logging as well as in the supply to cultivators of the ingredients of efficient production in agriculture. In the industrial field greater attention must now be paid to the improvement of technical efficiency and the quality of products. This will increase the competitive strength of industries in Pakistan, progress in respect of which has been hindered by the growth of monopolies in a sheltered market. This re-emphasises the great urgency of the need to achieve rapid progress in the field of technical education at all levels. The Third Five-Year Plan, now in the making, must accord a very high priority to this field if large investment programmes in the future are to yield commensurate results. The intensification of geological surveys, etc., now being pursued, may enlarge the resources-base of the economy, as exemplified by recent discoveries of gas in East and oil in West Pakistan. The possibility of developing nuclear power in the face of paucity of oil, gas and coal may point to new horizons.

There has been an increase in the rate of growth of income in the past two years during which period national income increased by 11·4 per cent (in 1959–60 prices). From the point of view of availability of resources, future growth depends upon the success of measures adopted for mobilizing domestic savings and upon a continuance of foreign economic assistance. The average gross propensity to save increased from 6·2 per cent in 1959–60 to 7·3 per cent and 8·3 per cent respectively in 1960–61 and 1961–62.[1] If this trend continues, the percentage of income saved may show significant improvements in the future. An evaluation of the effectiveness of various alternative monetary and fiscal measures in increasing the supply of domestic saving is imperative. The recent successes with high interest-bearing savings certificates as well as prize bonds indicate a greater scope for higher financial incentives as a method of mobilizing savings.

The amount of necessary external assistance will in all probability continue to be substantial in the next 10 or 15 years. A recent exercise in long term projections of the economic growth of Pakistan puts the requirements of capital inflow around $1,733 million even as late as 1971.[2] The planners in Pakistan are at present engaged in visualizing prospects of development in a long run perspective. The broad aim seems to be to double *per capita* income in 25 years' time. To accomplish this it is necessary to achieve a rate of investment of 25 per cent of GNP by 1985, assuming a productivity of capital which is implied in the capital–output ratio of 3:1 – i.e. three rupees' worth of investment would generate in general an increase in income worth one rupee in this period. Foreign aid in such a model serves the dual function of a supplement to domestic savings as well as to foreign exchange earnings. Pakistan's traditional exports of raw materials, such as jute, cotton, tea, hides and skin, etc., do not respond appreciably to increases in income abroad owing either to increasing economy in the industrial use of raw materials or to the development of substitutes. (In the case of tea, the major factor in the recent fall of exports has been increasing consumption of the product in Pakistan.) Nor do they respond easily to price decreases. The majority of the developing countries are actively promoting such light manufacturing industries or consumer goods as

[1] Mid-Plan Review, op. cit. This is in constant prices of 1959–60.

[2] P. N. Rosenstein-Rodan, International Aid for underdeveloped countries. Review of Economics and Statistics, May 1961, pp. 107–37. This projection assumes doubling of national income by the fourth plan, capital–output ratio of 3:1, and an average saving rate increasing from 7·8% to 11·2% by 1971.

textiles and leather goods, etc., so that Pakistan cannot look to them for an expanding market overseas. This is specially true in the field of cotton textiles, where competition among developing countries in each other's markets, as well as in third markets, is severe. The expansion of Pakistan's exports of cotton manufactures under the impact of the export loans scheme took place at the expense of competing countries. Even so, expansion occurred mainly in respect of cotton yarn, where the value added in manufacture is slight, so that foreign exchange earnings are little higher than those from exports of raw cotton. Moreover, as a result of increased domestic consumption of cotton yarn, the export bonus scheme has only succeeded in diverting output from the domestic market. In the case of jute textiles, the long-term prospect is clouded by competition from substitutes. The main emphasis should be on exports of new manufactured goods, which are as yet insignificant, and where, again, competition among developing countries may become acute, except where Pakistan may have special advantages – as, for example, with fisheries and some specific forest products.

From all indications it appears that a subsidization of exports of manufactured goods will continue to be necessary in the next few years to enable the latter to face world competition. Progress in this respect is expected to be slow and insufficient. Under these circumstances, if aid is not to continue indefinitely, the need for considerably enlarging the domestic supply of intermediate and capital goods assumes critical importance. Considering the extent of known mineral or metallurgical resources within Pakistan, a substantial expansion of heavy industries does not seem to be likely without recourse to considerable imports of raw materials. This makes the problem more difficult than in a country like India. A proper choice of new industries is necessary to ensure that there is a net saving of foreign exchange and that it does not permanently raise the cost structure of other industries using their products.

The future of Pakistan's economy depends not only on the availability of financial and technical resources but also on an efficient administrative and political set up. As the Second Plan document itself points out :[1]

[1] Second Plan, op. cit., p. xv.

Faith, vision and courage of a high order will be needed to meet the challenge of the coming years. Success will depend upon the initiative, vigour and administrative competence which the instruments and agencies of the Government, under energetic leadership, are able to develop and apply to the task (of development in the future). But success will depend much more on the extent to which the mass of the people come to have a passionate awareness of the urgency of economic and social progress of this country, and are committed to do their part in a spirit of high dedication.

II

DR PUEY UNGPHAKORN *was born in 1916, and graduated from the University of Moral and Political Sciences in Bangkok in 1937. He was awarded a Thai Government scholarship to the London School of Economics, where he obtained the degree of B.Sc. (Econ.) in 1941, and Ph.D. in 1949. From 1942 to 1945 he was on military service.*

Since 1949, Dr Puey Ungphakorn has served the Thai Government as a Senior Economist in the Ministry of Finance, as Deputy Governor of the Bank of Thailand, as Economic and Financial Counsellor at the Royal Thai Embassy in London, and as Budget Director in the Prime Minister's Office. In 1959, he was appointed Governor of the Bank of Thailand. He is also a member of the National Economic Development Board of Thailand.

Dr Puey Ungphakorn was assisted in the preparation of his study by Mrs Suparb Yossundara, Director of the Department of Economic Research, Bank of Thailand, and by Mr Chavalit Thanachanan, an economist in the International Trade and Payments Section of the same Department.

6

THAILAND

INTRODUCTION

THAILAND has a total area of approximately 200,000 square miles and a population, according to the census taken in 1960, of 26·3 million.

Agriculture occupies over 80 per cent of the working population, and, together with a few extractive industries such as tin-mining, lumbering and fishing, forms the essential foundation of the economic structure. Other economic activities in the country are confined to handicrafts, processing of agricultural and forestry products, and a few light manufacturing and service industries. Most of Thailand's cultivated area is devoted to rice, and because of favourable climatic conditions and a low population density, rice production not only provides for domestic needs but also furnishes, at present, almost two-fifths of the total export earnings.

The economy of Thailand is heavily dependent on foreign trade. The annual value of exports as well as that of imports usually amounts to between 18 and 20 per cent of the gross national product. Among the commodities that are exported, rice is the most important. Other principal export commodities include rubber, tin, teak and, since 1960, maize, kenaf and tapioca. Imports consist mainly of manufactured goods, machinery and petroleum products.

SITUATION AT THE END OF THE SECOND WORLD WAR

Although agricultural production, as a whole, was little affected by the war, Thailand was nevertheless confronted with several problems in 1946. First, there was the need to restore foreign trade and exchange. Secondly, there was the problem of ful-filling the obligations imposed by the Allies for making available quantities of rice free-of-charge and subsequently at low prices. Thirdly, there was the urgent need to repair the damage in-flicted upon power facilities, the port of Bangkok, the railway system and other means of communication. Overriding all these problems was the inflationary pressure which gathered strength during the war through the heavy financing of Japanese military expenditure in Thailand, and which became aggravated by heavy government budget deficits.

There follows a brief discussion of the main measures taken by the Government to meet these problems in the immediate post-war period.

Exchange System

The Baht was at first tentatively fixed at Baht 60 to the Pound Sterling but subsequently changed to the rate of Baht 40. To safeguard the depleted gold and foreign exchange reserves by using them only for payment of essential consumption goods, the demand for which had been kept unsatisfied during the war years, the government decided to impose a system of compre-hensive exchange control. The entire proceeds of all exports had to be turned over to the Bank of Thailand at the official rate, and exchange was sold only for approved imports. This system proved ineffective, however, and consequently was replaced by a multiple exchange rate system in early 1947. Under the new system exporters of the main products, namely, rice, rubber, tin and teak, were required to surrender, in some cases the whole, and in others part, of their foreign exchange receipts at the official rate. Importers generally had to buy the needed foreign exchange in the free market at a much higher rate. Govern-ment imports and a few essential payment items such as hospital supplies and students' expenses abroad were permitted the cheaper official rate. Beginning in March 1948, some foreign exchange was sold by the Bank of Thailand for imports at rates slightly below those of the open-market. The profit which accrued from these transactions was then placed in a Stabiliza-tion Account at the Bank of Thailand. This exchange profit, amounting to about Baht 515 million in 1949, served to counter the inflationary effect of the Government budget.

Rice

To fulfil international obligations and to keep the internal price of rice lower than that prevailing in the world market, the Government assumed a monopoly of the rice export trade in 1946. Minimum prices for paddy and milled rice at all levels of distribution were fixed and rice was bought from the mills by the Rice Office at a price which was well below the Baht equivalent of the export price. The difference between the export price calculated at the official rate of exchange and the internal buying price, less taxes, resulted in the Rice Monopoly gaining a handsome profit, the greater part of which was turned over to the Treasury.

Despite the fact that these measures were deflationary in effect, money supply after 1947 continued to show an increase. This was partly due to the heavy world demand for Thailand's exports, particularly rice and rubber, which resulted in a growing trade surplus from 1948 until the end of the Korean boom in 1951. Another major factor accounting for the rise in the volume of money during this period was the big increase in budget spending.

DEVELOPMENT MEASURES

Financial and Fiscal Reform[1]

During the period 1947–55, when a multiple exchange rate system was in effect, the government was relying on exchange rate policy to combat inflation. The official rate for government imports served as a means of lowering the cost to the government of imported goods, and the profits earned from the sale of exchange at higher rates also helped to finance government deficits. On the other hand, the penalty rates of exchange for the country's main exports served indirectly as anti-inflationary taxes. However, during the world trade recession immediately following the Korean boom, a sharp deterioration in tin and rubber prices set in. The rice market also changed from a seller's to a buyer's market. By 1953, the usual trade surplus had

---

[1] See S. C. Yang, *A Multiple Exchange Rate System – An Appraisal of Thailand's Experience 1946–1955*. The University of Wisconsin Press, Madison, 1957.

turned into a sizeable deficit. The country was also rapidly losing reserves as a result of the official appreciation of the Baht against sterling for imports in 1952. The purchasing power absorbed from the private sector as a result of exchange operations was placed back in the market through government deficit spending at an average annual rate of over fifteen hundred million Baht during 1952–4.

The government soon realized that to rely on exchange policy to finance this huge government deficit was something which could not go on in view of conditions prevailing in the world market for Thai exports. Some drastic financial reform was needed. Measures to improve government revenue and to bring about more orderly allocation of government resources were clearly essential. The government therefore decided in 1955 to abolish multiple exchange practices and to unify the exchange rate. The Rice Monopoly was disbanded, and export taxes – on sliding scale bases – were imposed on rice, rubber and tin exports, to replace the former partial surrender of export proceeds at the official rate. In the case of rice, the tax imposed to replace the Rice Monopoly profits was called an 'export premium', the rate of which could be changed according to world market conditions, and used as an instrument for preserving rice supplies for domestic consumption at low prices.

All exchange transactions have since then taken place in the free market, with rates determined by market forces. The Currency Reserves were officially revalued from the rate of Baht 12·50 to the US dollar to Baht 20·00. An Exchange Equalization Fund was set up from the surplus accruing in this revaluation, with the purpose of evening out short term fluctuations in the exchange rate.

In 1957, the government undertook several measures which were to prepare the ground for more conscious and orderly planning of expenditure, especially for development in the 1960s. In this year, the World Bank was asked to send a mission to make a general survey of the country and draw up a public development programme. Their recommendations resulted in the establishment of the National Economic Development Board in 1959. In the meantime, a Public Administration Service Team, which had been brought in a few years earlier with the aid of the US Government, drew up a scheme of reform for budget procedure and the government accounting system. Their recommendation resulted in the enactment of a new Budget Procedures Act in 1959.

Besides more orderly planning of expenditure, several measures were also taken to increase revenue. The Customs Tariff Code was revised, so that classification of items now follows the Brussels nomenclature. A new method of collecting the business tax was introduced in 1961. The government also abandoned the system of borrowing from the central bank by means of an overdraft. It also tried to mobilize more savings from the private sector by raising the interest rate on long-term government bonds to 8 per cent in 1956, as well as declaring the interest tax free and making the bonds resaleable to the government on demand.

These financial reforms have considerably strengthened the government's fiscal position since then. By 1958 the government cash deficit was reduced to less than Baht 500 million, and direct borrowing from the Bank of Thailand to less than Baht 250 million.

Provision of Basic Facilities

It was becoming evident by 1949 that the government would have to make a determined effort to provide the necessary basic facilities before the private sector could grow. A larger portion of government expenditure was still taken up by current expenditure – especially on the pay of civil servants, and defence. To accelerate the rate of spending on development, and at the same time to avoid inflationary pressures, foreign capital had to be sought.

In 1950, the government was able to obtain three loans from the International Bank for Reconstruction and Development, US $18 million for an irrigation project in the Chao Phya area, US $4·4 million for development of the Bangkok Port, and US $3 million for rehabilitation of the railways. A second Port loan for US $3·4 million was obtained in 1951, and a second Railway loan for US $12 million in 1955. The Yanhee Hydroelectric Loan for US $66 million, signed in 1957, is designed to provide both power and irrigation benefits. In 1950 the Thai Government signed an Economic and Technical Co-operation Agreement with the Government of the United States. During the period 1951-4, economic aid in various forms averaged more than US $6 million annually, but since 1955 the total of grants and loans from the US Government has averaged nearly US $30 million per year. In addition Thai Government Agencies have also been able to obtain financing from the US Export-Import Bank, or the Development Loan Fund. Assistance, both financial and technical, has also been received from the United Nations and other foreign governments both directly and through the Colombo Plan.

The Second World War left Bangkok, the capital, with an acute shortage of electricity. With US aid and loans from the US Export-Import Bank and the Development Loan Fund, Bangkok now has a generating capacity of nearly 170,000 kW. Another power station, with a capacity of 75,000 kW financed by the US Export-Import Bank, is due to be set up and will come into operation in 1963.

Development in transport and communication has also helped to open up the country, and pave the way for the growth of exports in more recent years. The Friendship Highway, primarily built for military purposes, has contributed much in forming a fast and direct means of transporting such crops as maize and kenaf, grown in the north-east of Thailand, to the Bangkok port.

Efforts at Industrialization

In the past decade, the Government made several attempts to lead the country towards more industrialization. A few pilot plants were set up with the purpose of showing the private sector what could be done. Instances of these are the paper umbrellas, paper clips, metal cabinets, and ceramics plants. Many factories were also set up under the aegis of the Ministry of Defence with the primary aim of supplying the Armed Forces, examples being the glass, pharmaceutical, and battery plants. An oil refinery was set up at Fang, 950 kilometres north of Bangkok, in a fairly inaccessible area, where the amount of probable oil reserves has not yet been quite established. A company, with part of the shares held privately, was set up to produce cement needed by the Irrigation Department in its construction work.

Another conspicuous example of government activity in the

field of industry is the National Economic Development Corporation (NEDCOL). This Corporation was established in 1954 with shares partly owned by many members of the government of the day. It was able to obtain a $10 million loan from a private foreign bank and bought plant from abroad with supplier's credit, all with Government guarantee. Listed among its holdings are a gunny bag factory, two modern sugar mills, and a paper mill using rice straw as raw material. Most of the machinery was bought at exorbitantly high prices, and the projects indeed lacked planning from the beginning. Within a little while it became evident that the government would have to bear the brunt of the debt burden, and now ownership of the Corporation has totally reverted to the government. With protection for the gunny bag and sugar industries in force, two of its plants are paying their way. The second sugar plant (at Supanburi, 192 kilometres north-west of Bangkok, where cane growing is only in an experimental stage) has yet to run at full capacity, with adequate cane supply, before recovering. The paper mill has yet to start operation. Meanwhile the Government is paying the last instalment of debt service on behalf of the Corporation in the current fiscal year.

In the meantime the Government has taken several measures to promote industry. In 1954, an Industrial Promotion Act was passed. In this Act, the Government declared its policy of non-interference where private initiative was present. Several benefits were offered to industries which were announced as eligible for promotion. This Act has been amended and revised from time to time to offer more attraction to private investors as well as ensuring the practicability and speedy implementation of the provisions. The principles of promotion in the Industrial Promotion Act of 1962 include exemptions from duty on exported products, exemption from tax on profits for a prescribed number of years, and special immigration quotas for technical and managerial personnel and their families. Facilities have long been granted to foreign investors under the Exchange Control law for the remittance of profits and repatriation of capital, even prior to the enactment of the Industrial Promotion Act.

In 1959, the government reorganized the old Industrial Bank. The Industrial Finance Corporation was formed with private capital, subscribed by Thai and foreign commercial banks, and the Corporation took over the assets of the old Bank. A loan, three times the amount of the initial paid-up share capital, was obtained interest free from the US Government. The main objectives of the Corporation are (1) to assist in the establishment, expansion or modernization of private industrial enterprises, and (2) to encourage the participation of private capital, domestic and foreign, in such enterprises.

The Corporation was faced with several difficulties at the initial stage of operation – a lack of capital and inadequate staff at its disposal, and poor management and accounting on the part of the loan applicants. In 1962, a drastic reform took place in the organization and management, and the Corporation is showing signs of being able to function effectively. Additional resources have been and are about to be made available from its own increase in share capital, from government loans at nominal interest rate, from the Federal German Government and the International Bank for Reconstruction and Development and the Industrial Finance Corporation.

Health and Education

Vast improvements have taken place in the field of health since the Second World War. Here again foreign assistance has played an important role. Technical and financial aid have been received from the World Health Organization, the UN Children's Emergency Fund and the US Government. Recorded deaths from malaria have substantially decreased, and cases of smallpox have become rare. No outbreak of plague has been recorded since 1952. Cholera is believed to have been eradicated, although there was an outbreak in Bangkok and Dhonburi in 1958.

Tuberculosis still presents a large problem, although BCG treatments have been instituted, and expansions have been made at the Nondbhuri tuberculosis hospital and lung operations can now be performed. Projects for the control of leprosy and yaws have also been started.

Maternity and child care schemes have been enlarged, special attention having been given to the increase of facilities in the rural area. Efforts are still being made to increase the number of doctors, nurses and dentists. A new medical school has been set up at Chingmai, in the North of Thailand, to supplement facilities for clinical work now afforded by the two main teaching hospitals in the metropolitan area. At present the ratio of doctors to inhabitants stands at 1 per 7,700 as compared with 1 per 13,600 in 1947.

A compulsory elementary education system has been in force in Thailand for more than thirty years. Government expenditure on education now accounts for around 21 per cent of total annual expenditure and ranks top of the list, exceeding expenses for economic services and defence. From the end of World War II to 1960, the number of school pupils increased by about 50 per cent, while budget appropriations for education increased by seventeen times. The Government subsidizes education even up to the University level where students are asked to pay very nominal fees. Most parents aim at giving an academic type of education to their children, but every year nearly two out of three of the aspiring candidates have to be turned down, due to the lack of space in the Universities, while at the same time there is a feeling that jobs cannot be created readily to receive graduates of all branches. The Government in more recent years have made an effort to expand technical schools to build up the more specialized skills required by a developing economy.

In general, the education programme seems to have so far achieved satisfactory results on the quantity side but not so much on quality, which is attributed to the lack of qualified teachers and up-to-date equipment.

Planned Development

In the 1950s in spite of efforts to bring about some order in the allocation of government resources, public development effort was unbalanced, unco-ordinated and indicative of a total lack of scientific planning. An economic planning committee was set up in the National Economic Council, to comprise a group of technicians who tried to work out development expenditure budgets for various ministries and state enterprises. The work was, however, purely of an advisory nature. The final job of trimming down requests was that of the Ministry of Finance, which at that time also lacked the necessary personnel to carry out a proper evaluation of projects. The outcome was that expenditure was mainly decided by arbitrary negotiations and by yielding to the strongest pull.

In 1959, as a result of one of the major recommendations of the World Bank Survey Mission,[1] the National Economic Council was reorganized into a National Economic Development Board to function as a Central Planning body. The present constitution of the Board is not, however, of the form envisaged in the Mission's recommendation. Instead of being composed of Cabinet Ministers directly concerned with economic matters, it consists of forty-five members, drawn from various walks of life, but mostly from the Armed Forces and the civil service, while all the Cabinet Ministers are advisers. An executive committee of ten members deals with the day-to-day problems, and the Secretariat is administratively under the Prime Minister's Office.

A Six-Year Development Plan covering the fiscal years 1961–66, was promulgated by a Royal Decree. Some specific targets were indicated, but due to the lack of the types of statistics which are needed for scientific planning, the document should be viewed more as a general outline of Government policy on economic development, and a programme of public development expenditure. Emphasis is laid on agricultural development, and the provision of such basic facilities as irrigation, power, transport, and communications.[2]

GROWTH AND STRUCTURAL CHANGES SINCE 1951

National Product

Thailand's gross domestic product, i.e. the value of the production of the nation, is estimated to have doubled during the 1951–61 period. After allowing for price increases, the real rate of growth was 70 per cent for the entire period or about 5·5 per cent annually. During the same period the annual growth of population has been slightly above 3 per cent. Consequently, real output *per capita* has increased on the average by almost 2·5 per cent a year.

---

[1] See *A Public Development Program for Thailand.* Johns Hopkins Press, Baltimore, 1959.
[2] See Section on the Six-Year Plan, below.

It will be seen from Table 1 that the growth in this period has been predominantly in public utilities, construction and transport. Agriculture, which is the largest item, increased by 52 per cent and manufacturing by only 50 per cent. Other items which registered a smaller increase than that of the total are mining and quarrying, wholesale and retail trade, and

TABLE I GROSS DOMESTIC PRODUCT OF THAILAND, 1951 AND 1961[1]

(In million baht at 1956 prices)

	1951	1961	Percentage increase during 1951–1961
Agriculture	13,731	20,099	52
Mining and quarrying	557	764	53
Manufacturing	3,949	5,721	50
Construction	924	2,568	248
Electricity and water supply	43	169	307
Communication and transportation	1,203	3,857	246
Wholesale and retail trade	5,927	9,393	57
Banking and finance	1,565	2,494	64
Services	3,302	5,815	80
Total	31,199	50,881	70

banking and finance. The relative importance of these industries also declined in the period under consideration while that of the remainder showed a rising trend.

Agricultural Production

In the decade 1951–61 agricultural production increased on the average by about 4·4 per cent annually. The increase is attributed principally to the increase in the production of the main commercial crops other than rice, and to a smaller extent, to the expansion in the output of rubber. The last three years of

[1] Source: National Income Division. Office of the National Economic Development Board.

this decade are indicative of the process of diversification which has been going on in the agricultural sector.

Rice – Production of paddy, which is by far the most important crop, varied during this period between 5·7 million metric tons and 8·3 million metric tons. The acreage under cultivation has shown little change while average yields have slightly improved from 203 kg per rai[1] in the crop year 1950–51 to 232 kg per rai in 1961–62. Total output increased on the average at the rate of about 2 per cent annually. With the completion of the main canals under the Chao Phya Project in 1962, it is expected that considerably more land will be brought under cultivation thereby resulting in a much larger output than at present.

Other main crops – Apart from rice the main commercial crops are sugar cane, tobacco and cotton for the fast-growing domestic processing industries, and maize and kenaf, chiefly for export. Under the stimulus provided by the expansion in world demand, output of the two latter crops has increased spectacularly during recent years: from 1956 to 1961, production of maize rose from 115,000 metric tons to 600,000 metric tons and that of kenaf from 17,000 metric tons to 150,000 metric tons. Output of other crops such as cassava, soya-bean, ground nut and castor seeds also increased during the period with the result that the production index of non-rice crops (1953 = 100) rose from 88 in 1951 to 322 in 1961.

Rubber – Rubber output in 1961 amounted to 186,000 metric tons. This compares with about 99,000 metric tons in 1951. However, it should be noted that a large proportion of rubber trees in production are over-age, and the government has been concerned about the prospects for Thai rubber. In order to help rubber growers to meet competition from more efficient producers of natural rubber and synthetic rubber, the government in December 1960 enacted the Rubber Plantation Aid Fund Act. Under this Act, aid will be provided from the fund, which is composed of contributions from rubber exporters, to the planters for the improvement of rubber trees and replanting.

Forest Products – Production of teak, the most important timber product of Thailand, has shown a steady decline from about 560,000 cubic metres in 1953 to 105,000 cubic metres in 1961, mainly due to the decreased stock of mature trees. However, the

[1] One rai = 1,600 sq. metres.

government has already undertaken a teak reafforestation programme as part of an extensive forest conservation programme. Under an initial three-year plan, which began in 1961, about 2,000 acres were to be planted with teak seedlings annually. For the second three-year period this target will be renewed.

Industrial Production

Manufacturing – Industrial expansion has proceeded gradually in Thailand, though since 1958 there has been a noticeable acceleration. Manufacturing now contributes, at current prices, about 12 per cent of the gross national product compared with 10 per cent in 1951. Most of these industries are light industries producing mainly for the domestic market. The major industries are cotton textiles, gunny bags, cement, sugar, paper and tobacco. During the five years 1957–61, the output of the first three more than doubled, while that of paper and tobacco also increased although at much lower rates. In the case of sugar, production in 1961 even rose in excess of domestic demand and means had to be found for exporting the surplus.

Development of Thai industry has been hindered mainly by the lack of sufficient electric power capacity. However, this problem is being partially met by long-range development of hydroelectric potential and by building lignite thermal power plants. Other principal bottlenecks to industrial development are the high speculative prices of industrial sites, shortage of skilled labour and management, poor communications and high transportation costs. In addition, private entrepreneurs in the past have had to face competition from state-owned enterprises in a number of fields.

Mining – Production of tin ore during the period 1950–55 was steady at about 14,000 tons, but thereafter increased to about 19,000 tons in 1957 which, however, was still far below the peak prewar record. In 1958 when control under the International Agreement came into full force, production had to be cut by nearly 45 per cent. Consequently, production of tin ore in 1958 and 1959 amounted to only 10,892 tons and 13,446 tons respectively. However, as a result of the recent rise in tin prices and the lifting of export quotas since the third quarter of 1960, production of tin has again risen to 16,756 tons in 1960 and 18,402 tons in 1961.

Other minerals which have been mined include tungsten, lead, antimony, manganese and iron but none of them has much significance in Thailand at present – in 1961 production of tungsten ore was only 472 metric tons and that of manganese ore only 532 metric tons.

Electric Power – In 1951 the total installed capacity of electric generators in Thailand was about 33 MW, of which total about 25 MW, or almost 80 per cent, was confined to the Bangkok and Dhonburi area. Since then there has been a considerable expansion. In 1961, total installed capacity was 264·47 MW of which 168·19 MW or approximately 64 per cent belonged to Bangkok and Dhonburi area and total generation of electricity amounted to 601·82 million kWh. In addition, there are three power development projects, two steam and one hydro-electric, now under construction which, when completed, would add about 675 MW to the present installed capacity.

Foreign Trade and Payments

Expansion of Trade – In the decade 1951–62, in terms of dollars, Thailand's exports increased from $367 million to $462 million

TABLE 2 PERCENTAGE SHARE OF EXPORTS, 1951–1962[1]

	Rice	Rubber	Tin	Others	Total Export Value (US $Million)
1951	54·0	26·6	6·6	12·8	367
1952	65·7	15·2	6·9	12·2	329
1953	66·2	11·6	6·3	15·2	323
1954	51·4	15·5	6·3	26·8	283
1955	44·2	25·1	6·2	24·6	335
1956	41·3	22·1	7·3	29·3	335
1957	48·0	18·7	7·1	26·2	365
1958	46·1	20·6	3·9	29·4	309
1959	34·1	30·8	5·7	29·4	359
1960	29·8	29·9	4·2	36·1	408
1961	35·9	21·3	6·2	36·6	477
1962[2]	34·3	22·0	7·2	36·5	461

[1] Source: Department of Customs.   [2] Estimate.

while imports increased from $272 million to $550 million, reflecting an increase of 26 per cent and 102 per cent respectively.

During the period the annual value of exports varied considerably depending mainly on the world market prices and the production of the three main export commodities, namely, rice, rubber and tin. On the whole the importance of these three commodities has shown a steady downward trend in relation to the total value of other exports, as may be seen from Table 2 (opposite). It is also significant that for the last three years, the

TABLE 3 PERCENTAGE DISTRIBUTION OF IMPORTS BY

MAIN CATEGORIES, 1951 AND 1962[1]

	1951	1962[2]
Food	13·4	6·6
Beverages and tobacco	2·6	1·3
Crude materials	1·7	1·8
Mineral fuels and lubricants	7·2	10·6
Animal and vegetable oils and fats	0·4	0·2
Chemicals	6·1	10·3
Manufactured goods	41·8	33·4
Machinery and transport equipment	15·6	27·4
Miscellaneous manufactured articles	10·4	4·9
Miscellaneous transactions and other commodities	0·8	3·2
Total value in $ million	272	549

value of exports of goods other than rice, rubber and tin for the first time in Thailand's history exceeded that of rice exports. This was due mainly to the spectacular rise in the exports of jute and kenaf, maize and tapioca products which together in 1961 and 1962 accounted for about 16–17 pr cent of the total exports compared with only about one per cent in 1951.

On the import side, it is also significant that imports of capital goods and raw materials together have risen from about 48 per cent of the total import value to slightly over 64 per cent in 1962. Chemicals and petroleum products showed the largest

[1] Source: Department of Customs.　　　[2] Estimate.

165

12

increase, while crude material and machinery and transport equipment also increased substantially.

Table 3 (p. 165) gives the percentage distribution of imports by main categories for 1951 and 1962.

Terms of Trade – From Table 4 it will be noted that on the whole export prices fluctuated considerably, whereas import prices show steady increases, with the exception of 1957–58 and 1961–62.

TABLE 4 TRADE INDICES AND TERMS OF TRADE[1]

(1953 = 100)

	Unit Value		Terms of Trade
	Exports	*Imports*	
1953	100	100	100
1954	111	105	106
1955	109	106	103
1956	100	106	95
1957	99	109	91
1958	102	105	97
1959	108	104	104
1960	111	106	105
1961	108	107	101
1962	107	101	107

Bearing in mind that the base year 1953 was a depression year, this table does not represent a true perspective from a long-term viewpoint. It does show, however, that during the bad years of 1956–58, the terms of trade moved sharply against primary products.

Balance of Payments – Table 5 gives a summary balance of payments of Thailand for the years 1951 to 1962. With the exception of 1951 and 1961 Thailand always had a deficit on current account. Despite these deficits, however, gold and foreign exchange reserves increased in eight years out of the total twelve, due mainly to the fact that a large proportion of imports was

[1] Source: Bank of Thailand.

TABLE 5 THAILAND'S BALANCE OF PAYMENTS, 1951–1962[1]

(Millions of US $)

	1951	1952	1953	1954	1955	1956	1957	1958	1959	1960	1961	1962 Preliminary
Current Account												
Exports, f.o.b.	367·1	329·4	322·6	283·4	334·9	361·5	390·1	307·0	357·4	405·0	473·3	457·2
Imports, c.i.f.	−272·3	−304·4	−330·4	−311·7	−321·1	−358·5	−404·7	−385·5	−424·4	−447·4	−479·9	−535·0
Trade balance	94·8	25·0	−7·8	−28·3	13·8	3·0	14·6	−78·5	−67·0	−42·4	−6·6	−77·8
Other items	−39·4	−42·1	−50·7	−40·5	−37·5	−27·2	−31·0	−1·5	—	4·9	13·9	24·8
Balance on goods and services	55·4	−17·1	−58·5	−68·8	−23·7	−24·2	−45·6	−80·0	−66·9	−37·5	7·3	−53·0
Official Donations	0·4	3·0	4·5	6·4	14·1	27·1	35·0	25·3	41·3	34·1	21·4	25·1
Capital Account												
Medium and Long-term Capital	3·2	7·3	6·8	0·3	19·4	14·9	23·4	14·7	20·9	19·1	40·2	75·3
Changes in International Reserves (increase +)	83·6	−22·3	−46·0	−21·6	28·8	14·4	7·7	−19·4	6·2	44·9	78·5	62·3

Source: Bank of Thailand.
[1] In this table the item 'errors and omissions' is not shown.

financed by foreign aid and loans, especially grants from the US and loans from the World Bank. At the end of 1962, the total value of reserves amounted to about twelve months' imports.

The National Economic Development Board produced in mid-1960 Thailand's first economic plan covering a six-year period from 1961 to 1966. The plan is divided into two phases: 1961–63 and 1964–66, with the intention of making it a 'rolling' plan, i.e. subject to constant revision and addition. In the next few paragraphs, we present a summary of the targets and the estimated amount of total development expenditure during the period, including the sources of financing.

Targets

For the first phase, 1961–63, a number of specific physical targets have been established. These targets take account of the estimated impact on the general economy of public sector (Government) activities, such as 'infrastructural' improvements: irrigation, road, port, rail, power, etc. Regarding agricultural production, rice is expected to increase by 1·3 per cent annually, rubber by at least 6 per cent during the three-year period, and maize by 100 per cent in three years.

The relative contribution of industry to national income is expected to be raised during the first phase of the Plan by about 12 per cent annually. Among industrial production during 1961–63, the following increases are expected: 400 per cent for paper, 300 per cent for both lignite and gypsum, 100 per cent for textiles, and 50 per cent each for gunny bags, tobacco, and cement. Other development goals for the first three years include an increase in electric power capacity from 138,000 kW to 370,000 kW, an additional 1,000 km of highways, improvement in railway services and beginning of tele-communication facilities. Further expansion of trade is also expected.

Development Finance

For 1961, the total development plan expenditure financed through the annual budget was estimated at Baht 1,600 million or 19·5 per cent of the estimated total government expenditure.

For each of the following years the increase in development expenditure is estimated to be about Baht 300 million as against an estimated annual increase of Baht 500 million in total government expenditure. Thus development expenditure for 1966 would amount to about Baht 3,100 million or 28·7 per cent of total government expenditure and, for the six-year period covered by the Plan, to Baht 13,900 million with the following distribution:

TABLE 6 SUMMARY OF DEVELOPMENT PLAN EXPENDITURE, 1961–1966[1]

	Baht million	*Percentage of total*
Agriculture	4,000	28·8
Industry	1,100	7·8
Communications	4,400	31·7
Social services	2,600	18·7
Miscellaneous	1,800	13·0
Total	13,900	100

In order to give special attention and different emphasis to different regional needs, the development programmes for the north-east, the north and the south have been entrusted to three special committees, each headed by a prominent member of the Cabinet. Co-ordination among the three regional programmes, and between each programme and the overall plan is done through the National Economic Development Board Secretariat.

For the fiscal years 1961[2] and 1962 actual development expenditure for items included under the Six-Year Plan were respectively Baht 1,322 million and Baht 1,701 million as against Baht 1,388 million and Baht 1,900 million originally envisaged. Comparable figures of original Plan targets, budget allocations and actual expenditure for these two years are presented in Table 7 (p. 170).

With regard to the financing of the Plan, additional resources

[1] Source: Office of the National Economic Development Board.
[2] Fiscal year 1961 covered only nine months i.e. from January to September.

TABLE 7 DEVELOPMENT EXPENDITURE, 1961 AND 1962[1]
(Millions of Baht)

	Fiscal Year 1961			Fiscal Year 1962		
	Plan	Budget	Actual Expenditure	Plan	Budget	Estimated Actual Expenditure
Agricultural Development	438	386	354	541	567	548
Industrial Development	422	471	448	268	391	378
Industry	(238)	(248)	(230)	(106)	(258)	(252)
Power	(119)	(164)	(164)	(82)	(93)	(84)
Water	(64)	(59)	(54)	(79)	(40)	(42)
Communications and Transport Development	319	466	352	618	524	516
Commercial Development	7	—	—	8	—	—
Social Development	202	169	168	346	308	260
Contingencies	—	—	—	120	—	—

are expected from an annual increase of 5 per cent in tax revenue as a result of the growth of national income and improved methods of collection. Also, new taxes are to be introduced as necessary during the Plan period, and net domestic borrowing is expected to rise by about Baht 50 million annually. State enterprises are expected to contribute a further Baht 500 million throughout the period. Foreign grants and loans needed will be about Baht 7,000 million.

At the moment of writing (end 1962/beginning 1963), the National Economic Development Board Secretariat is in the process of evaluating the progress of the first three years and filling in the details of the second three-year plan.

CONCLUDING REMARKS — PROBLEMS AND PROSPECTS

Concluding Remarks

In this study, attention has been mainly focused on the facts relating to production and trade. Space and time do not allow

[1] Source: Office of the National Economic Development Board.

more than passing mention of such matters as the development of the banking systems and other financial institutions, the successful savings mobilization through the Government Savings Bank and commercial banks which has resulted in a considerable increase in investment in Government bonds and bills, the absence of any tax reform until recently when a beginning has just been made, the extent of foreign aid and loans in economic and social investment, the problems of manpower and skill, the relationship between educational planning and economic planning, administrative changes during recent years, etc. For these subjects, the reader is referred to other studies,[1] some of which have yet to be published. In spite of this fact, it is hoped that the present study has provided sufficient information for drawing certain conclusions, some of which may be of general use. The writer's main conclusions are as follows:

1. Among many prerequisites to economic development in countries like Thailand, the two most important are peace on the political side, and monetary stability on the economic side. There must be peace, both external and internal. Regarding internal politics, government may change perhaps frequently; but as long as there is no actual fighting, or if *coups d'état* are, as in Thailand, bloodless, the general atmosphere may remain peaceful enough for economic progress.[2]

Stable currency is essential for development as long as human actions are motivated, to a large extent at least, by monetary incentives. Savers and investors, both domestic and foreign, can be seriously discouraged by the weakness of the currency. It is much more difficult to prepare Government budgets while prices and wages are violently fluctuating. Rising cost of production and cost of living also add to the problems of trade and payments.

2. During the years under study, there were two periods of trade-depression centring around 1953 and 1958. In the latter period the difficulties were fewer and less intense than in the former period, and recovery swifter. The explanation lies mainly in the fact that there was a drastic reform in financial management in 1955: exchange reform, abolition of rice monopoly,

[1] For instance: Annual Reports and Monthly Reports of the Bank of Thailand.
[2] Government instability is, of course, adverse to administrative reforms, particularly taxation reforms, which require courage and self-confidence.

more liberal trading policy, etc. This reformed economic management indeed is generally considered to be the basis of the progress in 1960–62. Again, the government from 1960 onwards has been able to increase its spending both on current and capital accounts, following a drastic improvement in its accounting and budgetary system. These reforms, which required both wisdom and courage, have proved amply rewarding.

3. In countries like Thailand, good luck and good management still do not earn sufficient resources for development. Grants and loans are needed from international bodies and from other governments. Foreign private investment is also necessary. The figures in the previous section of this essay show the extent to which the Six-Year Plan depends upon foreign resources. Technical skill of all sorts must also be borrowed or imported. More important still, a project approved for loans by an international lender or a friendly foreign government usually has the benefit of a second opinion and its soundness is normally assured.

4. In a country where much land is still unutilized, investment in communication – roads, railways, waterways – normally brings rapid, and sometimes unforeseen, results. The 'Friendship' highway, built with American aid, from Saraburi to Korat, is a case in point. The big increase in the production and export of maize and kenaf in recent years was made possible by it. A road which at first sight is built for administrative or military reasons may have incalculable economic potential, which cannot be realized before the event.

5. Industrialization has not to date been successful in Thailand. The NEDCOL experiment (p. 157) should provide a lesson against hastiness and wishful thinking. One serious defect of NEDCOL operations, more marked at the initial stages, is its secrecy. Not only may it shelter irregularities, it may also hide simple illnesses which could have been remedied if discovered in time. Another conclusion to be drawn is perhaps that an enterprise owned by influential politicians tends to combine both the defects of private enterprise and the defects of government enterprise.

Problems and Prospects

Although Thailand has achieved a fairly satisfactory rate of growth in real income *per capita*, and at the moment is enjoying a period of prosperity, there are considerable problems lying ahead. The diversification in the export economy has provided some measure of protection against fluctuations in total income. Concern is, however, felt over the fact that the recent increase in income has been too concentrated in Bangkok and has resulted in bigger investment in construction, especially of apartment houses and shopping areas, and not enough has gone into the rural areas and provincial towns in order to increase the productive potential in agriculture and industry to a more satisfactory level.

Each year the Government spends considerable sums on irrigation and highway development, yet no appreciable improvement in the farmers' standard of living or farming methods has been noticed. It is true that the irrigation canal network of the Chao Phya project is not yet completed but measures have to be taken to see that farmers are ready to take advantage of the expansion in irrigated area and proper water control. It is essential that the income of the farm population be improved if markets for the growing industrial products are to be found. Prices which farmers receive for their products and perhaps the crop marketing system need to be thoroughly reviewed. At present the government relies on the rice export premium for 10–12 per cent of its total revenue. If rice premiums are the main cause of farmers' income remaining too low, other sources of government revenue should be explored.

Under the present tax system, tax on foreign trade accounts for about one half of total government revenue while income tax constitutes less than 10 per cent. There is no property tax, and the rate of land tax is relatively low compared with that in neighbouring countries. Professional incomes remain practically untouched. This heavy reliance on foreign trade for revenue makes government resources for development expenditure highly vulnerable to fluctuations in world trade.

In the past the Government has relied on foreign aid and loans to a substantial extent in financing the country's development. There are however limits to borrowing from abroad, as the country cannot afford to see its future foreign exchange income always siphoned away in debt service. The recent tendency to use medium term suppliers credit in financing long term projects also means that repayments are generally due before the projects bear fruit. Nor can export income be expected to increase at such a spectacular rate as it has in the past three or four years.

The movement towards more conscious planning is to be welcomed. It is too early yet to assess the results of the first three-year phase of formal planning. Whatever these results turn out to be, Thailand, having begun in 1963 with a creditable financial system, a sound international reserve, an economy much more diversified than ever before, is in a favourable position to move forward at greater speed. Whether she will do so depends on how successfully she solves the above mentioned problems: increase in the income of the common man, increase in government resources, and wisdom in the choice of government spending.

PART II

A Comparative Analysis

THE six countries covered by the studies in Part I of this book have a total population of some six hundred million people. Together, India, Pakistan, Ceylon, Burma, Thailand and Malaya account for about half the population of the less developed world outside Communist control; and though each country may have special problems of its own, it is true to say that they have many major economic, political and social problems in common, and that many of these are very similar to those that arise elsewhere in the less developed world. For this reason, the experience of these countries in the field of economic development is of general application and importance, not only for other individual countries in Africa or Latin America which are facing similar problems, but also for the more developed nations who are so closely concerned, both economically and politically, with the future progress of the less developed world.

At the same time, and as the studies themselves reveal, the less developed world is not a homogeneous and stagnant mass, though it is often written and spoken of as such. Within this area of Asia there are wide diversities in population density and growth, in political and social institutions, in rates of progress, in the economic qualities of the population and in many other respects. Much of India, Pakistan and Ceylon is densely populated; in Burma and Thailand the population is relatively sparse. The societies of India and Pakistan are traditional and highly stratified, while in Malaya particularly the social structure is very much more fluid. These diversities are reflected not only between individual countries, but also within each of them. Again, though all less developed countries are by definition poor, there are substantial differences in the actual degrees of poverty. For example, the *per capita* income in Malaya in 1961 was nearly five times greater than that in Pakistan and Burma, and more than three times greater than in India.[1]

Nor is it correct to suppose that because a country is under-developed, its economy is or has been stagnant. Here, out of the six countries under consideration, the most striking example is undoubtedly Malaya. Since the end of the nineteenth century, Malaya has been completely transformed. In the 1890s, it was a thinly populated region of hamlets and fishing villages, where tribal warfare was recurrent and malaria endemic, with no central government and a rudimentary system of communications. By the 1930s, law and order had been established, and malaria very largely suppressed; the population had increased greatly, both through immigration and natural growth, and there had emerged a number of thriving and populous cities, linked by good communications. At the turn of the century there was practically no rubber production in Malaya; today, Malaya's rubber exports total about 750,000 tons a year.

Malaya's example may be considered an extreme one. But Ceylon's case is comparable; and over the same period there had been appreciable material progress throughout the region, chiefly as a result of the establishment and expansion of contacts with the developed countries, and the inflow of resources from more advanced areas. Even in India and Pakistan, where material progress is generally thought to have been slow, there is ample evidence of substantial advance in the comparative volume of industrial production, the increase in the literacy rate, the reduction in famine and disease, the fall in the infant mortality rate and other indicators. And most of this advance had already occurred before the outbreak of the Second World War; this is particularly clear in the case of Malaya, but it is also true of the region as a whole.

It must also be remembered that in this area, as elsewhere in the less developed world, there have been great increases of

[1] *Per capita* G.D.P. at factor cost, 1961 (in $US).

Federation of Malaya	— 242	These figures are very low by Western
Ceylon	— 128	standards, even though the gap be-
Thailand	— 93	tween Asian poverty and Western
India	— 73	prosperity is not quite as wide as
Pakistan	— 56	conventional comparisons suggest.
Burma	— 55	

(Yearbook of National Accounts Statistics, 1962, Department of Economic and Social Affairs, UN, New York, 1963.)

population in recent decades. Since 1900, the combined population of India and Pakistan has almost doubled, from about 280 million to about 560 million; over the same period, the population of Ceylon has grown from about $3\frac{1}{2}$ million to almost $10\frac{1}{2}$ million. These increases are in themselves evidence of economic advance, since they reflect a fall in death rates resulting from the elimination or reduction of famine and disease, as well as the improvement of communications and the development of the exchange economy. But they also tend to obscure the realities of economic progress where this is measured purely in *per capita* terms. The fact is that there was a considerable increase, in the years before national independence, in the total volume of production and consumption throughout the area, and that much, but not all, of this was taken out in the form of an increased population.

These preliminary points have to be made in order to clear the way for the consideration of the individual studies of Part 1. Naturally enough, these studies reflect both the different approach of each author and the degree of national diversity in the area. Nevertheless, they clearly show that these economies do have certain common features, and that they are faced by certain common problems; and since the purpose of this analysis is to examine how these problems have been tackled, and with what success, and to draw conclusions that can form a basis for future action, it might seem that the simple solution is to compare the results actually achieved by the six countries under consideration over the period covered by the studies. But this is only possible in the most superficial sense, since any attempts to draw valid or valuable comparisons of depth immediately run into almost insuperable difficulties. These include fundamental problems of measurement, with regard to both base and accuracy – it is questionable, for instance, whether Indian population statistics can be accepted as accurate to the nearest ten million – and equally fundamental problems of causation and proof. Thus, so wide are the circumstantial differences between India and Malaya that it may not even be safe to conclude that, because Malaya's gross domestic product was doubled between 1947 and 1960, and India's was not, the Malayan approach to economic development is much superior to the Indian.

However, there are certain conclusions which can be drawn, and even though those may be negative, rather than positive, they are by no means valueless. For instance, there were obvious similarities in the pattern and extent of economic development in Ceylon and Malaya in the prewar period, and the striking contrasts in the subsequent performance of these two countries are certainly suggestive. Again, there is ample evidence in the studies of Mr Lim and Dr Ungphakorn to suggest very strongly that the approach to economic policy and planning adopted in Malaya and Thailand is consistent with rapid economic progress and with the preservation of individual liberty, and therefore that the type of planning and policy epitomized in the Indian Second Five-Year Plan is not an indispensable condition of economic advance.

This same broad conclusion gains further support from Professor Rao's own indirect comparison between India's First and Second Five-Year Plans. In his own words, the first was 'modest and moderate', and scarcely a 'plan in the orthodox sense' (see pp. 72–3). It did not cause a serious drain on reserves. It did not create a balance of payments problem. The bulk of the finance was found from domestic resources, and foreign aid was only a marginal factor. In spite of the fact that some of the subsidiary objectives were not achieved – the modest industrial target was not reached, land reform measures ran into legal difficulties, and the community development programme was a disappointment – the overall targets were in fact substantially exceeded.[1] The Second Plan, on the other hand – and this plan was certainly much less 'modest and moderate', and much more 'orthodox' – created a critical situation with regard to government reserves and to the balance of payments. It relied very heavily on external finance, its overall targets were not achieved, and at the same time it was accompanied by greatly increasing taxation and severe restrictions upon the individual range of choice resulting from extensive licensing.

This brief juxtaposition suggests that it may well be legitimate to draw some conclusions from the experience through time of a

[1] To quote Professor Rao's own figures, during the plan period national income rose by 17·5 per cent, as against a target of 11 per cent, while *per capita* income increased by 10·5 per cent instead of the planned 5·5 per cent (see p. 72).

single country, to supplement the more tentative conclusions drawn from international comparisons. However, any useful assessment of this evidence, and of relevant official policies, still requires an examination of the main assumptions involved and of the results of the policies which have been based upon them. It is therefore necessary in this analysis to isolate and examine the major theoretical assumptions on which the development approach of the various governments appears to have been based, and where these are advocated on economic grounds, to judge them by economic reasoning and standards. On the evidence of the studies in Part 1, these major assumptions include the following: that progress is impossible without planning; that economic advance depends upon investment; that the development of heavy industry is indispensable to economic progress; that public investment is not competitive with private enterprise; that economic independence is a desirable condition; that a decline of traditional exports is inevitable; that general material advance is impossible without agricultural development; that agricultural progress depends upon land reform; that social factors are of minor importance and that foreign aid is indispensable. All these assumptions are contained, explicitly or inferentially, in one or other of the six studies in Part 1. Some of them may be consistent, but others are clearly contradictory and mutually incompatible. If any or all of them are to continue to serve as bearings for future policy, it is clearly of some importance that they should be carefully re-examined.

DEVELOPMENT PLANNING

In considering the place of planning in the process of economic advance, the first and most important point that emerges is not so much economic as political. Development planning has become a major preoccupation of government in many less developed countries. But no government can determine its approach to economic development without first answering, whether consciously or unconsciously, the question: 'What is our proper function? Is it to administer, or to plan?' The differing answers that may be given to this crucial question are well illustrated in the various studies in Part 1. On the one hand, there is the Indian view, exemplified in Professor Rao's study, that the proper function of government is to control and direct, in a large measure, all but the subsistence sector of the economy – a view which, as U Tun Wai shows, is also shared in Burma. On the other hand there is the Malayan view, set out by Mr Lim, that the primary function of government, in the economic sphere, should be to construct and maintain the framework within which the individual members of society pursue their activities with the minimum of official interference. This approach has also broadly prevailed in Thailand, whereas Ceylon and Pakistan lie much nearer the official Indian position than the Malayan. But since, for comparative purposes, it is the extremes that are most useful, much of what follows will deal with the fundamental contrast between the Indian view and the Malayan.

The true extent of this contrast is all too often obscured by imprecise definitions and confusing terminology. No doubt Professor Rao would agree with Mr Lim that this is the age of planning (see p. 106). But the word 'planning' is susceptible to widely different interpretations. It may simply mean that, to prevent waste and duplication, the plans of different government departments are co-ordinated over a number of years ahead, as is the pattern in Malaya. On the other hand, it may imply that all sectors of the economy except small-scale agriculture are officially directed and regulated, as is the case in modern India. The difference between these two interpretations of 'planning' is so wide that it seems scarcely reasonable to use the same word in each case.

At the same time, this is not just a matter of economic semantics. The determining choice is political. It depends upon the attitude of government to a number of factors, by no means all of which are strictly economic, in the sense of being primarily concerned with general material progress. The fact that there are widely divergent interpretations of the meaning of 'planning', which are influenced in each case by political considerations, is by no means peculiar to the less developed world. But it has a special importance in countries which, because they are underdeveloped economically, are also underdeveloped administratively.

There are a number of functions which the government of

every country should try to perform, and which cannot normally be delegated to or performed on an adequate scale by any other agency within the community. These include the management of external contacts to the best advantage of the nation; the provision of national defence; the maintenance of internal law and order; the creation and preservation of a stable currency; the provision of basic education, health and welfare services; and the development of an adequate system of communications and public utilities.

This list should be extensive enough to show that the prime functions of government are sufficient to exhaust, if not to exceed, the governmental resources, in terms of trained personnel, of all less developed countries. This becomes even more significant when it is understood that although the efficient performance of these functions must be conducive to economic advance, none of them necessarily demands that government should also exercise direct control over large sectors of the national economy: whilst the administrative effort involved in attempting the comprehensive direction of the economy can only involve the diversion of scarce resources from the performance of the essential governmental functions. Professor Rao recognizes this fact in his study, when he states that the Indian administration was 'already overstrained' in 1950, and unable to stand the much greater strain that would have been involved 'in any large extension of public ownership and operation of economic activity (see p. 71). Five years later, in spite of official efforts to strengthen this civil service, the situation was little improved; yet the decision was then taken that the administration should bear precisely this additional strain.

This can only have been a political decision; and it has led some critics to charge the Indian government with being more interested in the political results of its planning policies, in the shape of the consequent extension of the powers of government, than in their economic effects. It could be argued in defence of this that the performance of official economic policy, like that of any other official policy, is always subject, in a democracy, to the political judgment of the electorate – though the validity of such a defence clearly depends, in part, upon the ability of the electorate to understand the issues involved, and upon the extent to which they can isolate the various components of the package of party policy. And it might seem that if it is accepted that any decision on 'how to plan' and 'how much to plan' is basically political, it should follow that the success or failure of whatever form of planning is adopted must ultimately be assessed in political, and not economic, terms. This may well be a view that is shared by many planners. But when economic arguments are adduced in support of political decisions for or against particular forms of planning policy, it is both legitimate and important that these should be examined on the same economic basis. Comprehensive planning, on the Indian pattern, does not simply mean the co-ordination of public investment: it extends to close control over the whole economy, to the point where the use of resources is determined by the government rather than by individual consumers. This inevitably involves the over-riding of individual preferences. It is argued that the economy will progress more rapidly if the composition of economic activity is laid down by the government. But if development is to make sense as a desirable process, it can only be defined as a process which increases the supply of goods and services which determine living standards. The more individual choice is ignored, and the more consumer preference is over-ridden, the more meaningless 'development' becomes. Moreover, it is not clear why government determination of the composition of economic activity should be necessary for the promotion of economic development. Nevertheless, this is very frequently assumed to be axiomatic, in spite of the failure of comprehensive planning to raise general living standards, and regardless of the evidence that growth can take place in the absence of comprehensive planning.

In practice, much of the uncertainty of economic life is actually enhanced by the impact of comprehensive planning, particularly in countries such as these. Planning authorities have to react to changes in the world around them. But these reactions are in themselves unpredictable both in timing and extent. Moreover, the further element of compulsion which they introduce into economic activity is inevitably applied both violently and discontinuously. This adds to the uncertainty confronting the participants in economic life, which is likely to inhibit development. The relevance of these points is illustrated by Mr Lim's comment that, 'in Malaya, as elsewhere, formal planning is meaningless unless the planners know, or succeed in estimating, what the main changes in the economy are going to be during the Plan period : and the longer the Plan period, the more difficult it is to form a correct estimate of such changes' (see pp. 107–8). This magnifies the effect of the administrative failings and deficiencies' which Professor Rao calls 'inevitable in planning the economic development of such a vast country as India' (see p. 89), and which are familiar causes of initial miscalculations and faulty implementation of planning policies.

INVESTMENT AND GROWTH

The alleged necessity for comprehensive planning is also based on various other economic arguments, though these are seldom presented in a consistent or systematic form. In India's case, two main themes are the need for increasing investment, and the need to develop heavy industry, both of which are emphasized in Professor Rao's contribution. However, there are a number of reasons why neither of these arguments provides an obvious justification for comprehensive development planning. In the first place, it should be clear that it is possible to achieve an increase in investment expenditure without comprehensive planning. Various fiscal measures, such as budget surpluses, can be used to promote both public and private investment, as also can depreciation allowances which provide preferential encouragement for investment expenditure.

Even so, it is by no means evident that an increase in investment expenditure, especially on the part of government, is either a necessary or sufficient condition of economic advance. To begin with, the definition of investment is largely arbitrary. It has become fashionable to term as 'investment' all forms of expenditure other than expenditure on current consumption. But it is clear that expenditure does not become productive simply by being classified as 'investment' :[1] and whatever the exact relation between investment and growth, it should also be obvious that the growth of income depends upon the productivity of investment and not simply upon its volume. The

---

[1] It is noteworthy that the meaning of investment is nowhere explicitly defined by any of the contributors, although it would be unfair to suggest that they are alone in this.

practical effects of investment expenditure must therefore depend upon such factors as the availability of complementary skills, and the extent of the market for the end product.

Nevertheless, it is now widely assumed that any increase in expenditure labelled 'investment' will promote economic development. There have certainly been instances where other conditions of rapid advance have been present and only an injection of additional capital has been required for their mobilization, the classic case being the postwar experience of Western Europe under the impact of Marshall Aid. A similar situation, on a smaller scale, seems to have existed in Burma during the early postwar period (see p. 14). In recent years, however, these special cases have been extended into a general proposition which has been applied indiscriminately to the development problems of all economies, even though an increase in the money expenditure classified as investment does not by any means always represent the best possible deployment of resources. A massive increase in investment expenditure normally requires the imposition of heavy taxation as well as the introduction of restrictions on the production and import of consumer goods: both these courses are likely to retard or even prevent advance from subsistence production to production for sale in the agricultural sector. Preoccupation with investment expenditure also diverts attention from such major obstacles to economic progress as adverse social or institutional factors, not the least of which is a general lack of interest in material advance.

The issues have been further confused by a widespread tendency to disregard the cost of investment expenditure, both in terms of the alternative use of funds (that is, to think of investment expenditure as a net addition to resources rather than as a diversion of funds) and also in terms of the repercussions of the costs of collection, such as the possible disincentive effects of additional taxation and of the imposition of controls. Scepticism about the value of investment as a specific for development problems must be enhanced when, as is often the case, particularly in India, investment is regarded uncritically as the key to all economic advance and indeed virtually as an end in itself. Indeed, unless governments undertake massive investment expenditure, they are accused of neglecting their duty to promote development. Even private investment expenditure is not invariably or necessarily productive, but the probability of waste and its likely scale are clearly much greater in the case of public investment. Where investment expenditure takes place in the public sector, the test of an economic return is much more difficult to establish. There is an obvious distinction between those who have to bear the cost of such expenditure, and those who receive the return from it. The politicians and civil servants who are responsible for the outlay do not themselves bear the cost, nor do the vast majority of the population, in any sense that they can directly appreciate. (As Dr Corea comments, 'in the context of an electoral system based on universal franchise, the small size of the investing class implies the virtual non-representation of the direct taxpayer in parliament'.) (See p. 51.) The direction of government expenditure is all too likely to be determined by considerations of electoral expediency, national prestige or sheer self-advertisement, all of which have little connection with material advance. In Burma, for instance, 'projects were at times included for political considerations such as obtaining votes in an election or because of the personal preferences of one or more ministers' (see p. 16): and even in Thailand, the history of the National Economic Development Corporation provides a reminder of the possible pitfalls (see p. 157).

The habit of regarding all investment expenditure as productive by definition not only encourages and spuriously justifies expenditure which is in fact wasteful: it also diverts attention and effort from the performance of the essential functions of government, which tend to be correspondingly neglected. Meanwhile, the investment cult has become so widespread that there are few to question its validity. Professor Nurul Islam does note that 'it is remarkable that the growth of overall income has been so small in view of the large investments which have taken place, particularly in more recent years' (see p. 130); but, like Professor Rao, he seems prepared to explain away the contradiction partly on the grounds that it must take time for expenditure to fructify. Professor Rao, again, concedes that 'the inevitable lengthening of the period between investment and output has had an adverse effect on the growth of national income in the short term' (see p. 81). But when he adds that 'this is an inevitable accompaniment of *any type of planned*

development that aims at the long-term growth of the economy'
(ibid), (my italics) this implies that long-term growth is
incompatible with short-term growth, which is plainly not so.
Indeed, there is evidence from Ceylon's case that in certain
circumstances the real incompatibles are investment and
growth, and that growth may take place in spite of investment,
not because of it (see p. 52 et seq).

DEVELOPMENT OF HEAVY INDUSTRY

Within the field of investment policy, the development of heavy
industry has acquired a special place, both quantitatively and
qualitatively. Such development has become a major component of investment expenditure, and the supposed need for it
is widely adduced as the main justification for increasing investment, as well as another major argument in favour of comprehensive planning. Though 'heavy industry' is seldom exactly
defined, in practice it comprises a wide range of capital goods
and intermediate products – to quote Professor Rao, for example, 'steel, cement, coal, power and oil . . . and machine
tools, machine building, heavy engineering and heavy chemicals . . .' (see p. 73). All these, like any other particular
economic activity, could of course be promoted without the
introduction of comprehensive planning; possible alternative
measures in this case include government subsidies or tariff
protection. But in considering the desirability of heavy industry
as such in the context of economic development, India provides
both the most important and the best documented case.

Professor Rao himself explains the shift of emphasis to heavy
industrial development in India's Second Five-Year Plan on the
basis that it is such development that gives a country 'its growth
potential in the physical sense and will set it on the road to self-
sustaining and self-accelerating economic development' (see
p. 73). This was, and is, the official argument, and it deserves
to be quoted at length because of its explicit nature as well as its
extensive influence.

'The expansion of the iron and steel industry has obviously
the highest priority since, more than any other industrial product, the levels of production in these materials determine the
tempo of progress of the economy as a whole.

'. . . Heavy engineering industries are a natural corollary of iron and steel works. The high priority accorded to them arises both on this account and from the fact they will provide from within the country a whole range of industrial machinery and capital equipment, such as locomotives for railways and power plants for the generation of electricity. In the absence of facilities for their manufacture, a developing economy has to depend on foreign sources of supply with attendant difficulties and uncertainties. To facilitate the production of a wide range of items going into the manufacture of plants intended to turn out a product like steel, diverse types of fabricating facilities have to be created in a large number of establishments. In other words, heavy engineering industries and workshops in the country have to be generally strengthened for undertaking such tasks as the construction of steel plants, fertilizer factories, etc. In this context the creation of basic facilities such as the establishment of heavy foundries, forges and structural shops is absolutely necessary. It is therefore proposed that the establishment of these facilities, which constitute an essential and primary phase of development for the manufacture of heavy industrial machinery in the country, should be undertaken at an early date. These developments have a priority second only to that of expansion of the steel industry.'[1]

Lest it be thought that these extracts from the Second Five-Year Plan are quoted out of context, there is no lack of other evidence to show the pervasive nature of this influence over Indian economic thought. It can be seen, for example, in a paper by Professor P. C. Mahalanobis[1] which was officially published at about the same time as the Second Five-Year Plan.

'In the long run,' the paper states, 'the rate of industrialization and the growth of national economy would depend on the increasing production of coal, electricity, iron and steel, heavy machinery, heavy chemicals, and the heavy industries generally, which would increase the capacity for capital formation. One important aim is to make India independent, as quickly as possible, of foreign imports of producer goods so that the accumulation of capital would not be hampered by difficulties

[1] Second Five-Year Plan, p. 394.
[2] Professor Mahalanobis was the statistical adviser to the Prime Minister, and very close to Mr Nehru.

189

in securing supplies of essential producer goods from other countries. The heavy industries must, therefore, be expanded with all possible speed.'[1]

There are a number of points of special interest in these quotations. In the first place, and this point is striking, they contain no reference either to costs, prices or prospective demand. Second, they reflect an obsession with the concept of economic independence. Third, and most important, they are based on an obvious *non-sequitur*. For if it were true that the existence of heavy industry is the pre-requisite of economic development, then no economic development would ever have been possible. Nor is it even true that the rate of economic growth is determined by the development of specific types of heavy industry. There are indeed highly developed countries with practically no heavy industry at all, as for instance Denmark and New Zealand. Moreover, in Asia, both Malaya and Hong Kong are obvious examples of rapid development without heavy industry.[2]

The Indian emphasis on heavy industries, and the simultaneous neglect of costs, of demand, and of consumer preference, is reminiscent of Soviet planning. It is of interest that Professor Rao takes pains to rebut this comparison in his study, though he confines the rebuttal to India's First Five-Year Plan, and does not extend it to the Second Plan (see p. 70). Many observers have noted the similarity of emphasis between the Second Indian Plan and Soviet planning. At the same time, there are certain important differences between the conditions prevailing in each country, so that even by Soviet standards, and quite apart from any questions of the merits of Soviet-style planning as a method of promoting economic advance, India cannot be said to have offered the best prospects for success. These differences include, first, the relatively much greater abundance of land in the Soviet Union: second, the sizeable agricultural surplus, in terms of excess of output over subsistence requirements, which existed in Russia in the 1920s,

[1] Second Plan Papers, p. 43.

[2] The only exceptions, more apparent than real, are one or two countries, notably Kuwait and Venezuela, which have taken a short cut to riches through the exploitation of their natural resources of oil. However, the existence of this industry is obviously not synonymous with development and in many ways, including the living standards of the majority, both Kuwait and Venezuela are still underdeveloped.)

and which was certainly lacking in India in the 1950s: and third, the fact that not only was the literacy rate in the USSR already far higher in the 1920s than it is in India even now, but Soviet planning also placed much greater emphasis on the importance of educational development.

A fourth major difference is that India's economic infra-structure was much less highly developed than that of European Russia. Mention of this point at once raises yet another problem of definition. It is usually accepted that a nation's 'infrastruc-ture' comprises its basic social services, as well as its system of communications and public utilities. On this hypothesis, there seems at first no reason to dissent from Professor Rao's statement that 'to bring about an all-round increase in the tempo of economic activity pre-supposes an adequate build-up of social and economic overheads' (see p. 69), although it might strictly be more accurate to state that this build-up must take place in the course of economic advance, since it cannot well precede it. But it subsequently becomes clear that Professor Rao includes in his definition of economic overheads, or infra-structure, '. . . not only transport, power and irrigation, but also *minerals, steel, (and) basic industries* . . .' (my italics) (see p. 81). This is certainly in line with Soviet thinking. But if the argu-ment is followed to its logical conclusion, it must mean that any part of the economy which is thought to contribute to economic growth should also be included within the definition – in other words, not only heavy industry, but also light industry, com-merce and agriculture: so that, in this view, virtually the whole national economy has to be classified as 'infrastructure', and the term itself ceases to have any useful meaning.

THE PRIVATE SECTOR

The public investment programme in India has been openly based on the twin assumptions that there are certain things that must be done if economic growth is to be achieved, and that these things cannot be done by private investment. It is not only taken as axiomatic that the nation requires more steel capacity and expanded oil output: it is also assumed, as Professor Rao explicitly states, that these would not have come into existence if they had been left to private enterprise (see p. 82). But there is certainly evidence to suggest that private finance could have been found for at least one steel plant, while the international oil companies could, and no doubt would, have financed the expansion of India's oil industry if the government had taken the political decision to allow them to do so. Private industry has been excluded from these activities by official policy, which has thus obstructed the movement of capital into this sphere of industry, as well as the flow of foreign private capital into India. This is so regardless of any contribution that the development of these particular sectors of industry may or may not make to economic development.

Close controls over the private sector are an integral part of planning in India, as in other countries in this region. In India, there are specific controls over capital issues, the allocation of raw materials, imports, exports, and exchange transactions with all foreign countries including those within the sterling area. In Pakistan, controls cover the allocation of foreign exchange, import licensing, the location of industry and the supply of raw materials, as well as the levels of prices and production of specified commodities (see p. 139). In Burma and Ceylon, large sectors of the economy are completely socialized, and in both countries the private sector is very closely controlled.

Some of these controls have benefited important sections of private industry, at least for a time. Professor Rao points out, for instance, that the private sector in India has been stimulated by the closed economy that has accompanied planning, with its severe restrictions on imports of consumer goods, and the more or less guaranteed domestic market that this has created 'has acted as a tonic to private industry' (see p. 83). This is true in the sense that official policy has made it possible for some parts of private industry to reap large profits with comparatively little effort. But it has not necessarily led to the most efficient deployment of economic resources: as Professor Nurul Islam shows, the competitive strength of industries in Pakistan 'has been hindered by the growth of monopolies in a sheltered market' (see p. 146). Thus the tonic has scarcely been a healthy one for the economy as a whole. Once again, consumer demand and costs are both ignored. The compulsory limitation of competing imports suggests that cheaper supplies could have been obtained from abroad. Controls have also inhibited competition within the country, which tends to raise costs as well as to inflict hardship on those compulsorily excluded from the regulated activities and to prevent the fullest mobilization of private capital (see p. 138). Moreover, the benefit to the sheltered industries and firms is often short-lived. They may well be affected adversely by the general retardation of development; and in a closely controlled economy, private enterprise becomes progressively more vulnerable to political pressure for its expropriation, as Burmese experience shows. In the long run, the relatively effortless profits that accrue to firms in the private sector under these conditions must act as a magnet for penal taxation or total expropriation.

There are other instances where official policy definitely and specifically restricts progress through private enterprise. To cite only one of several possible examples, cottage industry in India is being assisted on a large scale both by direct subsidies financed out of general taxation, and by heavy protection in the form of severe restrictions on the private factory production of competing products. The cash subsidies divert resources from other directions. Probably more important, the restrictions on manufacture raise the price of the commodities produced competitively by factory and cottage industry, which include important articles of mass consumption, such as textiles, shoes, soap and matches. The main consumers of these products are the agricultural population, and the higher prices and reduced supplies of these goods are likely to act as a substantial disincentive to agricultural production for sale. Even if assistance to cottage industry is regarded simply as a politically expedient rural dole, it should still be noted that this is granted by means which obstruct the development of the economy as a whole.

The cumulative effect of Indian official policy towards the private sector is summed up by Professor Rao as follows: 'The incentives which have been strengthened are mainly monetary reward and economic betterment of the individual entrepreneur, rather than the kind of social and community-centred motivation that goes with a socialist pattern of society' (see p. 86). This may seem a somewhat subjective judgment, since the Indian government's powers over the private sector are so extensive that private firms virtually exist on official sufferance. If private industry's response is to be stigmatized as 'antisocial', it must be recognized that the outlets for individual enterprise have been extensively, if not wholly, determined by official policy. Professor Nurul Islam's contribution effectively illustrates some of the adverse effects of the system of controls and restrictions, that has existed in Pakistan (see p. 189), and he also notes the resultant economic uncertainty. His conclusions are equally applicable to India and Ceylon. But what has happened in these countries certainly does not prove that private industry cannot contribute to general economic development if it is given the chance to do so. It is only necessary to reflect that the private sector is predominant in both Malaya and Thailand, where the most striking progress has been registered, in order to see that conditions in which the private sector remains free to cater for individual choice and consumer preference are likely to be conducive to overall economic advance, as well as to the development of responsible private enterprise. As U Tun Wai comments, 'economic development is not only concerned with the economics of the government sector; it covers the private sector as well. Therefore, unless the efforts of all the people can be directed at achieving economic development, the rate of growth must be unsatisfactory' (see p. 26 and also p. 51).

ECONOMIC INDEPENDENCE

The preoccupation with the concept of 'economic independence' that is a prominent feature in India's Second Five-Year Plan has already been noted. The fashionable arguments in favour of 'economic independence' – or, to express the concept differently, against 'neo-colonialism' – are not difficult to trace in outline. They run roughly as follows; it is desirable that a colonial territory should achieve the condition of independence: the first step to this end is the attainment of political self-government – but experience shows that the exclusion of foreign political influence does not necessarily result in the exclusion of all foreign influence: foreign economic influence still subsists: and since complete independence, which is absolutely desirable, cannot be said to have been achieved until all foreign influence has been eliminated, steps must be taken to remove foreign economic influence.

The concept of political independence – which can be defined as the situation wherein the government of the country concerned is free to make decisions and to act upon them without reference to any external authority, except in so far as it may be bound by agreements freely contracted with other governments of equal status – is generally understood, and generally supported. But the same is by no means true of the concept of economic independence: nor is it either necessary or desirable that the latter should be accepted as an essential and logical extension of the former. If it is capable of precise definition, 'economic independence' ought to mean a state of affairs in which a country is unaffected by external economic conditions: and clearly such a state can only be achieved if external economic contacts are reduced to an absolute minimum.

It should, however, be equally clear that this state of affairs does not promote material progress. Only subsistence producers are completely independent in the sense of having no external economic contacts, and subsistence producers are generally the most backward of all economic communities. Throughout this region, and notably in India, the poorest and least developed areas are those with the fewest contacts with the world around them. What is true within the national unit is equally applicable at the international level. In the past, it was the external contacts made possible by the colonial system that were instrumental in drawing the individual parts of the less developed world into a wider sphere of international economic life. Through these external contacts, the peoples of Asia were able to draw upon the capital resources and the technical skills of the more developed countries, and their economies were thus raised and maintained above the level of subsistence production. The evidence of this is to be seen throughout the region, and Malaya has already been cited as the outstanding example: but as is shown by Thailand's case, it is equally possible for valuable external economic contacts to be developed without the external political domination of a colonial regime.

The attainment of self-government, and the elimination of objectionable political overtones, should have made these external economic contacts more, not less, desirable, and the case for economic interdependence stronger, rather than weaker. As U Tun Wai says, 'The hard facts of economic life are the same for colonies and independent nations' (see p. 14). This has been acknowledged in Malaya, but elsewhere a number of forces have combined to obstruct the recognition of the facts of economic life. It is this interaction of political and economic forces, the chief of which are socialism, nationalism and xenophobia, which explains the popularity of 'economic independence' as a major policy objective in most of the less developed world.

The concept of economic independence is naturally attractive to the socialist, because the achievement of his political objectives depends upon the creation of a controlled economy: and the most easily controlled economy is the one which is least dependent upon external factors. The objectives of the nationalist are not necessarily identical with those of the socialist: but they correspond to the extent that both are anxious to see all foreign influences eliminated from the economy, whilst the xenophobe is simply opposed to any form of foreign influence, whether political, economic, religious or cultural. Of the three, the socialist is undoubtedly the most important, because he is best able to provide a political justification for his approach and its consequences.

Burma is a country which has adopted a thorough-going socialist attitude to economic development, although there has been 'no official economic rationalization for this approach'. The decisive factors, as U Tun Wai shows, have been a combination of political theory and general feeling that though prewar economic growth might have been satisfactory in its pace, it had been wrongly orientated and that the Burmans themselves had not been allowed to play a sufficiently active role (see p. 15). Therefore, after independence in 1948 both socialist and nationalist pressures favoured the reduction of foreign economic influence and the 'Burmanisation' of the economy.

It was recognized that this step could prove disadvantageous economically, and would imply a sacrifice in terms of efficiency, since the reduction or exclusion of foreign business activities must involve the loss of essential expertize in commerce and industry. It was accepted that this loss could not be made good by Burmese private enterprise, since the Burmans, as individuals, lacked just this same expertise as well as the necessary capital resources. But it was argued by the socialists, and accepted by the nationalists, that this state of affairs provided a further justification for governmental intervention – in other words, that Burmanization must be achieved through nationalization. This line of reasoning is certainly not peculiar to Burma, and at first sight it may appear perfectly logical. In fact it rests upon an obvious fallacy, which U Tun Wai exposes. For it is illogical to suppose that individuals who, as private citizens, are deficient in commercial or industrial expertise can somehow acquire these qualities by the simple process of becoming civil servants (see p. 15).

If the concept of economic independence demands the exclusion of foreign economic influence, and the technical skills associated with it, this end can only be attained at a cost which cannot be made good by the adoption of a socialist approach. Moreover, the loss involved is one for which external financial assistance on a government-to-government basis, and the employment of foreign technical advisers, can only provide partial compensation. Such technicians differ from personnel associated with foreign private investment in several important respects. Their employment is not necessarily dependent upon the profitability of the ventures in which they are engaged: they are not empowered to make important decisions; and they are not free to take risks, or to instruct others in risk-taking. For these and other reasons it is important to accept Professor Nurul Islam's conclusion that the employment of foreign consultants and technicians does not provide an adequate substitute for foreign private investment (see p. 142).

Nor, indeed, is it easy to see how a country whose official economic policies depend upon massive external financial and technical assistance can claim, in any real sense, to have attained a state of economic independence. On the contrary, such a situation actually postulates an extension of political dependence, since the continued availability of this assistance is conditional upon external political decisions. And there is great force in the argument that the economic policies pursued by the Indian government since the mid-1950s have made the country much more dependent on external factors than ever before. This is still so even when such assistance is multi-lateral in origin, and channelled through United Nations agencies, or organizations like the Colombo Plan: though the degree of

14

dependence upon individual external factors is diffused to some extent in the process, the continuation of such programmes still depends ultimately upon the political attitudes and financial policies of a small number of major donor countries.

But even if the concept of economic independence is limited to the achievement of self-sufficiency in certain sectors of the economy, the desirability of this end is still far from absolute. For example, Professor Mahalanobis, in the passage already quoted, states that 'one important aim' of the Second Five-Year Plan was 'to make India independent, as quickly as possible, of foreign imports of producer goods', so that difficulties in acquiring such goods should not hamper the accumulation of capital. The assumption that the rate of economic growth is in fact dependent upon this special factor has already been questioned. But even if it could be shown that this assumption is correct, it still would not follow that there is an economic justification for the establishment of a self-sufficient sector within the national economy, to ensure the availability of these essential goods, irrespective of the cost. There may be certain sectors, in any economy, where self-sufficiency is considered to be desirable for reasons that are not economic, but political. But where this is so, such a decision should be justified on political grounds.

Meanwhile, it is economic interdependence, in the sense of the existence of a wealth and variety of contacts with the outside world, that conduces to economic progress, not economic independence, in the sense of self-sufficient isolation. There are inherent hazards in this. It may still be true, as Mr Lim says, that every time America sneezes, Malaya catches influenza (see p. 109), though the danger of this can be greatly reduced by the creation of budgetary surpluses and foreign exchange reserves in times of prosperity. But the value of external economic contacts must be manifest. These are the channels through which human and material resources, skills and capital from more developed countries reach the less developed world. They open up new markets and sources of supply, and they bring new commodities and techniques to the notice of the local population. And they undermine the traditional customs and attitudes which obstruct material advance: for it is aroused expectations, and dissatisfaction with existing circumstances, that are the first condition of progress, whether economic or political.

This is particularly important in the modern world, where highly developed communications give less developed countries much readier access to the fruits of scientific and technical progress elsewhere than was ever the case in the past. Although external contacts by themselves are not sufficient to ensure progress, their value today, and the dangers of the retrograde concept of economic independence, can scarcely be exaggerated. In practical terms, this means that less developed countries must pay special attention to such problems as the encouragement of foreign private investment, and to the effects of official policies upon export prospects.

FOREIGN PRIVATE INVESTMENT

In principle, all the governments in this area appear to have recognized, at some stage, the importance of foreign private investment as a means of providing managerial skills and new techniques, as well as fresh capital. But in practice, their success in attracting such investment has varied greatly. The extreme example is to be seen in Burma, where official measures to encourage foreign private investment proved of little or no effect, and where the door has now been closed against such investment, as U Tun Wai notes (see p. 23). So far as the measures themselves are concerned, these do not seem to have differed very significantly from those introduced with more success in Thailand or Pakistan. The important point that emerges from experience in Burma, as in Ceylon, is that in conditions where the world demand for private capital far exceeds the supply, the potential investor naturally judges the opportunities open to him with particular care.

In the formation of such judgments, the various incentives offered may have some weight. But much more significant factors must be the general economic climate and the political stability of the country where investment is envisaged. Foreign private investment requires the expectation of an economic return, which depends in part upon the presence of complementary factors and upon a market for the output. To some extent, therefore, the prospects of a return can be influenced by official incentives such as tax concessions or franchises. But where there is extensive government intervention in economic activity, this is found to affect the decisions of potential foreign investors, whose assessment of a worthwhile return must also be governed by the likelihood of long-term security of tenure and by the extent of their freedom to dispose of profits. This is not unreasonable: but the legitimate requirements of foreign private enterprise inevitably conflict with the aims of the comprehensive planners, who are correspondingly prone to disparage foreign investment. It is sometimes argued, for instance, that the burden of foreign private investment is greater than that of official loans. However, as Professor Nurul Islam points out, 'whereas foreign loans create firm commitments for interest and principal repayments, irrespective of the success or failure of the projects financed in this way, dividends on direct investments are remitted only when the latter are profitable. Secondly while private investments seldom involve a net repatriation on a large scale, foreign loans involve certain and full repayment in a relatively short period' (see pp. 141–2). Security of tenure must also depend upon political stability. Here the government's treatment of the existing private sector is certain to be relevant. In Burma, the attitude of successive governments towards private enterprise, whether domestic or foreign, has been highly confused and inconsistent, and there have been frequent changes of policy (see pp. 16–18). The deterrent effect of this is probably more important than the mere fact that the regime itself has been unstable. Power may have changed hands fairly frequently in Thailand since 1945: but the relatively bloodless coups in Bangkok have not disturbed the generally peaceful atmosphere (see p. 171). In Thailand, and even more so in Malaya, the extent of foreign private investment can be taken as the measure of real economic progress: in Burma and Ceylon, the lack of response to official measures of inducement is evidence that conditions of economic stagnation prevail, and are likely to continue to do so.

EXPORT POLICY

Problems of external trade are considered in most of the studies in Part 1. Of the six countries concerned, Malaya undoubtedly has the most export-oriented economy, but exports have been a major feature of the economies of the other five, and they are still of vital importance. What is notable is that three of the six contributors judge the export experience of their countries in recent years as disappointing on grounds which are, by implication, outside their government's control. Professor Nurul Islam comments upon the set-backs suffered by Pakistan's traditional exports, Dr Corea comments similarly upon Ceylon's experience and Professor Rao notes that a large proportion of Indian exports of traditional goods is facing increasingly effective competition in foreign markets.

It is true that there is a good deal of variety in the nature of the exports from this area, and correspondingly in the demand for them. Some countries have been better placed by circumstances than others: as Mr Lim points out, the impact of the Korean War on international trade was much more beneficial to Malaya than to most other primary producers (see p. 100), although Thailand, Burma and Ceylon also benefited substantially in this period. Nevertheless, there is no evidence that the overall experience of primary exporters in the postwar years compares unfavourably with experience in the 1920s and 1930s; indeed, the evidence is to the contrary (see p. 23). It is therefore very difficult to accept some of the pessimistic or defeatist arguments that have been advanced in the field of export policy.

The factors determining the volume of exports are complex, and total world demand for a particular product is certainly not the only or even the major factor. There may be extreme cases where a single country has enjoyed a virtual monopoly of world supply, and where the exhaustion of resources or the collapse of demand brings the export trade to an end. But where individual exports represent only a part of total world exports, the volume of the former does not necessarily bear any relation to the total world demand. Even where total demand has declined, the volume of individual exports may still increase, since this depends principally upon the relative prices at which the product concerned is available from different sources of supply. For instance, Professor Nurul Islam notes the stagnation or decline of jute exports from Pakistan over the period (see p. 143). Over the same period, there has been a 'spectacular rise' in jute exports from Thailand (see p. 165). This is only one example of the familiar phenomenon whereby an absolute or relative decline in exports from one country coincides with the increase of exports from another: a second, and more obvious, example, can be found in the contrasting trends of rubber exports from Malaya and Ceylon, and there are many others.

Export prices depend largely upon the cost of production, currency exchange rates, and domestic demand. These in turn are substantially affected by fiscal and monetary policy. In most of the countries in this region, official policy has retarded the expansion of primary production for sale, and thus for export, in a variety of ways, which include restricting the supply of incentive goods, depressing the prices received by the farmer through heavy taxation, or failing to maintain law and order and efficient administration. Thus the volume of exports is much affected by internal factors, many of which can be substantially influenced by government action. Though Malaya's record is good, and so is Thailand's, Burma provides a clear case of the adverse effects of official action and inaction. Rice production and exports have been seriously retarded both by the extremely severe taxation of producers, and also by the unsettled conditions in the countryside resulting from failure to maintain law and order. In India, exports have been hit by various measures of official policy, and notably by the over-valuation of the rupee as a result of massive deficit financing. In Ceylon, again, even though improved production techniques have resulted in larger yields of export commodities, repeated tax increases designed to finance the social services and the food subsidy, as well as other government expenditure, have inevitably forced up export prices and thus largely offset the competitive gains that should otherwise have occurred. And in several of these six countries, if not in all, resources have been diverted from production for export to production for the home market by increases in population, higher living standards or domestic inflation.

This situation in itself has helped to create an additional threat to export volumes, in the development of substitute synthetic products. The production of synthetics, particularly rubber, is to some extent due to strategic considerations, and is thus not wholly governed by the cost factor. But the emergence of synthetic products as a threat to primary exports has occurred at least partly, and probably largely, as the result of the rise in costs and the diversion to home consumption in the exporting countries. Malaya's experience clearly shows that provided primary prices can be kept competitive, the emergence of synthetics does not create an insuperable barrier to the expansion of exports: but in meeting this threat, enlightened domestic policies must play a powerful part.

It should be clear, therefore, that whilst it can seldom, if ever, lie wholly within the power of an exporting country to dictate to the market, many of the disabilities experienced by primary exporters are of their own making, and that a solution to them can be found in more enlightened domestic policies. At the same time, some of the conventional solutions are likely to make matters worse rather than better. A case in point is the encouragement of industrial diversification which has taken place in Pakistan and elsewhere.

This policy is usually justified on two grounds; first that, since traditional primary exports have declined, processed products must be exported in their place, and second, that where there is also a home market for these products, diversification will help to improve trade balances by bringing about a reduction of imports. There are certain superficial attractions in such a policy. It appears likely to fill the export gap, and to lead to a saving of foreign exchange. It satisfies the urge for industrialization. It may be justified on the grounds that it provides additional employment opportunities. Furthermore, it is likely to be encouraged by the more developed countries, as a means of stimulating machinery exports, and it will probably be favoured by domestic private enterprise, where private participation is allowed, since it must depend for success upon the creation of a captive home market.

But in fact such a policy has serious drawbacks. Such diversification is apt to lead to the promotion of uneconomic activities which divert resources from other more valuable uses, and correspondingly retard the rise of living standards. Even though particular employment opportunities may increase, the overall result of an uneconomic deployment of scarce resources is likely to be a reduction in the aggregate volume of employment opportunities. Similarly, any benefits derived from a saving of foreign exchange are likely to prove illusory. Not only may the reduction of certain types of imports be offset by a fall in exports, but this may also create an expansion of demand for other imports, besides obstructing a rise in living standards.

Some of these points are brought out explicitly by Professor Nurul Islam (see p. 148) who stresses the importance of a correct calculation of costs, to ensure that there is a net saving of foreign exchange, and to prevent a permanent rise in domestic consumer prices. Moreover, as Professor Nurul Islam adds, most less developed countries are actively promoting the manufacture of identical light industrial products, for which the export market is therefore likely to become progressively more competitive.

This is not to say, however, that all diversification is intrinsically undesirable. Both Thailand and Malaya provide important examples of successful diversification in the primary field, in the development of new crops for export (see pp. 162 and 104), But in these cases success has been due to the fact that normal economic forces have been encouraged to operate by liberal official policies. This, indeed, is the situation which is most likely to promote trade in both directions, though it may well be that exporters in Malaya and Thailand would not have derived so much advantage from such policies if their export rivals had not had to contend with policies which adversely affected their competitive position. Ultimately, a degree of diversification in the secondary field is also likely to be desirable, where it is warranted by costs and market considerations: but failing these, diversification is premature and must be wasteful. Conventional policies serve only to confuse cause and effect, and this confusion is greatly intensified by the fact that many of the present barriers to the expansion of trade are strengthened by the economic policies of the developed countries of the West.

THE AGRICULTURAL SECTOR

The critical importance of the agricultural sector is recognized by all the contributors. There are, of course, differences in their approach to its problems, but basically all are in agreement. As Professor Rao writes, at one point, 'Without a substantial improvement in the productivity of agriculture, and in that of small industry and commerce, it will not be possible to bring about a substantial increase in domestic output within a short period' (see p. 79). This may sound a far cry from the view expressed by the authors of the Second Plan, that it is the amount of investment in heavy industry that pre-eminently determines the tempo of progress of the economy as a whole. Nevertheless, it represents recognition of the fact that in India, as in all the other countries under review, agriculture is over-whelmingly the biggest sector of the economy, and that over 80 per cent of the population lives in the rural areas.

Without agricultural advance, the markets for industrial products, the sources of manpower for industry and ancillary services, and the sources of government revenue are likely to be inadequate for any real and sustained national progress. Generally speaking, the obstacles to such advance are very diverse. They include the influences of climate: the scarcity of fertile land: the low level of capital, technical knowledge and communications: social and religious attitudes which act as a barrier to higher productivity: the absence or restricted supply of consumer goods: defective systems of land tenure: and the heavy incidence of taxation, direct or indirect. The existence and importance of most of these in Pakistan is analysed by Professor Nurul Islam (see pp. 131–3).

Some of these obstacles are clearly more susceptible to governmental action than others. For instance, the levels of taxation are obviously determined wholly by the government: but equally obviously, government's ability to compensate for, or to counteract, the influences of climate is strictly limited. Thus it is evidently wrong at the outset to assume that the pace of agricultural advance depends entirely upon the extent of direct government intervention in the sector, just as it is also wrong to assume that direct intervention, in the form of legislation or investment in the name of agricultural progress, will necessarily prove more efficacious than the indirect benefits conferred upon agriculture, as on other sectors of the economy, by the adequate performance of what have already been listed as the essential functions of government.

The existence of defective systems of land tenure is cited by Mr Lim (p. 114) as well as by Professor Nurul Islam (p. 132), as a major obstacle to agricultural progress: and no doubt the prevailing structure of landlordism has political critics in both Malaya and Pakistan, where, as in India, there is considerable agitation for land reform in the sense of the expropriation of many medium or large land-holdings and the abolition of tenancy. But the existence of the prosperous tenant farmer in the agricultural communities of the West is proof that the landlord system is not incompatible with farming progress. Nor is it clear why landlordism, that is to say, the separation of ownership and management in the cultivation of agricultural property, should be reckoned any more undesirable or inhibiting than the same separation in the case of commerce or industry.

Agricultural land should clearly be occupied and farmed on an economically viable basis: but this is a question of distribution as between holdings rather than one of ownership or intermediary rights. Meanwhile, measures which are basically political in their motivation and aims will not necessarily produce any economic benefit. For example, the enforcement of land nationalization in Burma appears to have had little if any effect in raising agricultural production. Conversely, it is clear from Professor Rao's study that it is possible to register progress in the agricultural sector without major reforms of the legal system of land tenure. This is shown by the fact that under India's First Five-Year Plan, agricultural targets were actually exceeded in spite of failures to implement the land reform programme (see pp. 72–3).

Nevertheless, the rack-renting of tenant farmers and the chronic indebtedness of small proprietors are habitually interpreted as evidence that landlordism and moneylending constitute 'twin evils' (see p. 115). This interpretation ignores the real causes of the situation. If the terms of agricultural activity, as expressed in rents, appear to be harsh, it is because they reflect the underlying factor of a low level of the supply of fertile land as against a large and poorly skilled labour force. If private interest rates are high in rural areas, it is because they reflect the scarcity of capital, the high administrative cost of small loans, and the risk of default. In these circumstances it is to be expected that the price commanded by such capital and land should be relatively high. It does not reflect a monopoly situation, since no part of the available supply is being withheld to secure higher returns on the remainder. Thus while legislation to scale down or eliminate the payment of rent or interest charges may appear to yield a short-term economic benefit, the long-term results are by no means sure to be beneficial. Indeed, legislation aimed at landlordism and indebtedness, like many other measures taken in the name of progress, may well obstruct advance and not promote it. However politically popular such action may be, there is no economic advantage in the victimization of these particular groups of capitalists; and even if the precedent thus created does not have an unsettling and harmful effect upon private investors in general, potential investors in land will certainly be deterred if they are not altogether barred. The same will apply to potential suppliers of credit, and the resultant reduction in the supply of agricultural finance must also curtail output.

These probabilities are implicitly recognized in the common tendency for land reform legislation to be accompanied by measures to establish state-supported agricultural co-operatives. Such co-operatives have long been a feature of agricultural policy in India, and further encouragement has been given to them in recent years. Similar experiments have also been mounted in both Pakistan and Malaya, though with little success in either case (see pp. 132 and 115). Indeed, the uneconomic nature of the Indian co-operatives is tacitly acknowledged by official admissions that the movement will have to continue to be supported from public funds for the foreseeable future. This situation should not be unexpected, for although there are familiar political reasons why the establishment of state-sponsored co-operatives may be favoured – for instance, as a means of bringing the rural population into a position where their lives and activities are subject to close governmental control – there is no inherent economic advantage in supplying credit or marketing facilities through this particular form of organization rather than through the agency of private institutions, or by means of direct departmental assistance to the individual producer.

The use of co-operatives to subsidize agriculture cannot be said to amount to more than a recognition of the backwardness of the sector as a whole. Even if it is accepted that the supply of capital to farmers should be increased by diverting it from other uses, and thus reducing the rate of interest in this sector at the cost of raising it elsewhere, the co-operatives are clearly not the only means of doing so. It is often argued that co-operatives will ultimately become financially self-sufficient, and that there can be no objection to providing such state assistance as is necessary to enable them to overcome their early difficulties. This view is scarcely tenable in the face of actual experience in India and elsewhere, which shows that after years of official subsidization the co-operatives are more dependent than ever on government support. But even if it were true that these co-operatives can eventually become self-supporting, there is still no special economic or social reason why this particular form of economic organization should be massively subsidized at the expense of the rest of the community.

It should therefore be clear that the solution to the basic problems of agriculture must be sought elsewhere. Even if the introduction of legislation to penalize landlords and money-lenders, or the establishment of state-sponsored co-operatives, may be well intended, in practice such measures are little more than palliatives, which may suppress the symptoms, but cannot cure the disease. The fundamental causes, which remain untouched, are the low level of capital, fertile land, skills and knowledge, and the inadequacy of communications and markets.

The importance of the alienation and opening up of the greatest possible acreage of 'new' land is powerfully and rightly stressed by Mr Lim (pp. 116–17). Various measures can be taken to the same end. Virgin jungle may be cleared for cultivation. Irrigation schemes may make arable land of what was once desert. The introduction of new crops or new strains may make it possible to bring waste land into full cultivation. New roads may bring hitherto unused areas within reach of markets and thus make them worth farming. As Dr Puey Ungphakorn notes, 'in a country where much land is still unutilized, investment in communications normally brings rapid results' (see p. 172): and his study provides a striking illustration of the way in which agriculture can benefit from the side-effects of other government policy, in the case of the new military road which has opened up fresh farming areas for the production of the new crops which now contribute substantially to Thailand's exports (see p. 156). By the same token, protective measures against flooding and salinity such as those taken in Pakistan must have a valuable effect in increasing the supply of land in full use.

It might seem, indeed, that investment in such projects as irrigation schemes, improved communications and agricultural education provides the real key to agricultural progress. This must, after all, be the way to bring forward latent resources into productive use. But, to quote Dr. Puey Ungphakorn again, 'each year the government spends considerable sums on irrigation and highway development, yet no appreciable improvement in the farmers' standard of living or farming methods has been noticed' (see p. 173). This conclusion is not necessarily unexpected, however, since the expansion of agricultural production and prosperity depends upon many other factors besides an increase in the area available for cultivation and in expenditure on development projects. These other factors include the ability and willingness of the producer to take advantage of opportunities, the level of communications, and the existence of a ready market for the product at a remunerative price.

The level of output is also influenced by the extent and incidence of taxation and the operation of controls. In both India and Burma, taxation bears very heavily on farmers. This is sometimes justified by the argument that the proceeds of such taxes are used to stimulate agricultural progress, although in fact they are very largely diverted elsewhere. As U Tun Wai shows, the main burden of Burma's official investment programme has fallen on the agricultural sector, in the form of the monopoly profits garnered by the State Agricultural Marketing Board from the sale of rice for export. It is certainly no accident that total rice production and the acreage under rice in Burma, where the internal price of the crop has been fixed at the same level since 1948 in spite of the general rise in other prices, were still, in 1962, well below the prewar figures, whereas there had been marked increases in the production of other crops which were not subject to price control (see p. 18). Even the Thai government relies, for some 10 per cent of its total revenue, upon the rice export levy, and there is much force in Dr Puey Ungphakorn's comment that if it is 'the main cause of farmers' income remaining too low, other sources of government revenue should be explored' (see p. 173).

Direct controls which eliminate or greatly restrict the supply of consumer goods, such as those in operation in India, Pakistan, Ceylon and Burma, also obstruct agricultural progress, as they reduce the incentive to produce for the market. Separately and *a fortiori* in conjunction, controls and taxation can, and do, constitute formidable obstacles to agricultural advance. It may seem some consolation that the importance of agriculture as a factor in development is recognized by Professor Rao, both in the passage already quoted (p. 205, above), and particularly in his comment that 'increase in agricultural production constitutes the key factor in India's plans for economic development' (see p. 89). But it must still be said that there is a direct conflict between the interests of agriculture and the essential elements of Indian development policy, for the controls and taxation that obstruct agricultural progress in India are the direct result of official insistence on the massive development of heavy industry. This is a fundamental contradiction, and it cannot be resolved by such devices as patriotic appeals for sacrifice or sweat and toil. U Tun Wai rightly points out that the value of public exhortation as a stimulus to progress is strictly limited, and that in time its effect may become positively discouraging, as the promised 'rain of silver and gold' fails to materialize (see p. 15). Nor does it often happen that the burdens of sacrifice are borne by those whose policies have made them necessary.

Both Professor Rao and Professor Nurul Islam draw attention to the inherent difficulty of dealing with a sector which consists of a myriad small units, and it is often argued that this is the reason why the agricultural sector remains basically poor. Peasant farmers, it is said, do not respond to economic opportunity because they do not recognize it, and the sector is in any case so fragmented that the stimulus of the market-place is irrelevant. This is plainly not so. The values and objectives which determine the extent of the response may differ widely, but the general validity of such a stimulus is certainly acknowledged by the common practice of subsidizing commodities whose production a government wishes to encourage. Specific examples of the response by farmers to the development of new markets have already been cited from both Thailand and Burma. A further notable instance of the same readiness to respond, and the additional ability to take a long view, can be found in the development of the smallholding section of the Malayan rubber industry, where large numbers of small proprietors have proved that they are both willing and able to acquire skills and to invest capital and labour in a form of cultivation from which they can expect no return for a period of at least five years, but which will thereafter greatly increase their incomes. The same applies in Malaya again to the small-holders' response to the government's rubber replanting and land development programmes (see pp. 102–3).

Agricultural advance is of paramount importance throughout the region. The prospects of success, and thus of wider economic progress, depend in part upon official attitudes to the economic factors which have already been outlined: but they also depend to a large extent upon governmental willingness to recognize and to tackle a variety of social factors which have yet to be considered.

SOCIAL FACTORS

'An economic upsurge cannot be brought about unless the institutional chains that fetter the energies of the rural people are broken and new ideals and ideas, more conducive to rapid economic and social growth, are substituted in their place' (see p. 116). 'Human, social and cultural factors contribute to complexity of the problems facing a developing economy . . .' (see p. 144). Other contributors also touch upon the importance of such factors: for instance, Dr Corea's study contains some very interesting reflections on the influence of socio-political factors upon development policy in Ceylon. But even allowing for the limitations of space, it is questionable whether the nature and relevance of all these factors is adequately examined in any of the studies in Part 1. These factors are certainly complex and extremely diverse. However, it is possible to isolate some of the most important of them. The most obvious is, perhaps, the growth of population, to which Dr Corea and Professor Nurul Islam draw particular attention, and which is a major factor in all the countries under consideration. Problems of formal education policy are also cited by both Professor Nurul Islam and Dr Corea: but scarcely less significant are other factors of religious origin which are not dealt with by any of the contributors, although they are present to some extent in every one of the six countries covered here.

The population growth which has occurred within the last fifty years in this area, as elsewhere, is originally due to economic advance as well as to medical progress. The discovery and dissemination, through external contacts, of new curative and preventive methods has greatly reduced both infant and adult mortality rates, while improved communications and increased food supplies have virtually eliminated famine in the classical sense. Much of this advance has taken place since the Second World War: as Mr Lim notes, the crude mortality rate in Malaya has fallen by about 50 per cent since 1947 (see p. 112), and Ceylon's experience has been similar (see p. 42). But the relationship between population increase and economic growth is not simple. An increase in population is likely to retard the growth of income per head if it adds to the burden of dependency (that is, to the proportion of the population outside the productive age groups), or if it increases the demand for schools, houses, hospitals and the like, thereby diverting capital from more directly productive uses. The practical importance of this lies in its effect upon development policy.

Malaya provides a striking example of a country that has been able to absorb the impact of a rapidly expanding population, whilst still achieving a high rate of overall growth. Here, as in Thailand, government expenditure on education is the main item of expenditure in the annual budget: and in both countries health expenditure has registered almost equally dramatic advance in the postwar period (see pp. 105 and 158). In India, by contrast, development expenditure on elementary education under the Second Five-Year Plan was allocated about half as much finance as the cost of each of the three steel plants planned in the public sector: and it is questionable whether education in India is even keeping pace with population growth, let alone making any significant progress towards the raising of literacy levels. Yet the rate of population growth in Malaya has, if anything, been rather greater than that in India or in Pakistan.

From this it can be seen that the severity of population pressure really depends upon the rate of economic progress.

Where this rate is slow, population growth can have a doubly inhibiting effect. In the first place, the widest possible diffusion of new and improved skills and techniques is essential to the promotion of material advance and to the breakdown of social attitudes which militate against the acceptance of change. Success in this, in the less developed world, depends very largely upon an improvement in the general level of literacy. Yet in India primary education is being curtailed because it is considered that expenditure in other directions will be more effective in meeting the immediate need to increase physical output: and Professor Nurul Islam seems to be inclining towards the same view when he writes 'it is worth serious consideration whether we should not now place less emphasis, during the next two Five-Year Plans, on primary education, and much greater emphasis, for example, on the training of technical manpower which has an immediate impact on increased productivity in industry and agriculture' (see p. 145).

As Professor Nurul Islam goes on to add, any such decision must be politically difficult where popular expectations have already been aroused. But from the economic standpoint, the arguments against such a course are very strong. It is by no means self-evident that an increased supply of technically-qualified manpower is either the best or the only means of achieving increased productivity, since an equal or greater impact should certainly be attainable through straightforward fiscal measures and through the relaxation of controls. Nor does the available evidence suggest that the present pattern of higher education in many of these countries, notably Ceylon (see pp. 55–6) and Burma, is always producing the kind of trained manpower that is most needed. In too many instances, university education is regarded as a symbol of status, and little thought appears to be given to the ultimate employability of graduates, with the result that there is considerable misdirection and waste of expenditure in this field.

The second inhibiting effect of population growth can be seen in Dr Corea's statement that in Ceylon substantial resources that would otherwise have been available for development have been directed to the social services as the direct result of political pressures (see p. 47). These pressures are the product of the expectations and demands which Professor Nurul

Islam has also cited: but where they create, as in Ceylon, a demand for subsidies on food, the effect on development prospects is potentially very serious. To finance such expenditure government is forced to increase taxation: the main burden falls upon private industry and commerce, a fact which is unlikely to concern the majority of the electorate: the result is the stifling of economic progress in the private sector, and thus throughout the economy as a whole. To quote Dr Corea again, 'the inadequacy of development generates conflicts and antagonisms that in turn make difficult the attainment of an adequate rate of development' (see p. 50).

Many of the causes of mass poverty in this area stem from roots which can broadly be described as religious. For example, in both India and Burma relatively recent legislation has prohibited the slaughter of cattle. In Burma's case, the ostensible reason for this legislation was the shortage of plough animals created by the Japanese occupation. But although there is now, as U Tun Wai indicates, a surplus of such cattle, the legislation remains in force (see pp. 19–20). This is undoubtedly due to the Buddhist aversion to the taking of any form of life. The situation in India is similar but even more extreme. For though no such cattle shortage has existed there, and although the universally familiar Hindu veneration of the cow might be thought to make such measures redundant, legislation has been introduced in several of the largest Indian states within the last few years to prohibit the slaughter of all cattle and the sale of beef products in any form. Such legislation has three significant results. First, it provides stautory reinforcement for traditional attitudes: second, it forces members of other religions, and Moslems in particular, either to go without meat or else to buy more expensive mutton or goat meat, thus inflicting either nutritional hardship or economic hardship upon them: and third, it perpetuates an enormous waste of scarce grazing resources and thus greatly retards agricultural progress. The significance of this situation can be judged from the fact that although India supports about a quarter of the world's entire cattle population, the great majority of the human population of the country suffer from a deficiency of protein in their diet.

Similar objections apply to the legal prohibition of the consumption of alcohol. This is also religious in origin, but it has the practical effect of restricting the supply of an important incentive product, as well as diminishing government revenues from excise duty. Other customary factors of religious origin may not have the same formal sanction in law, but they are nevertheless important. In India again, the continued prevalence of the caste system is a major obstacle to advance. At a conservative estimate, the Scheduled Castes still account for at least 15 per cent of the whole population, and a high proportion of this total is to be found in the rural areas. This perpetuation of outdated social and economic distinctions has various damaging effects on material progress. The caste system prevents very large numbers of people from taking up more productive employment, and thus causes a serious waste of talent. It enforces uneconomic divisions of labour, by narrowly restricting the tasks that may be performed by members of particular castes. It requires the otherwise unnecessary duplication of equipment, including simple tools, and facilities such as wells. Even where its effect has weakened, there still lingers a disdain for manual labour, and even skilled work, among members of the higher castes. Although the central government has made some attempt to break the hold of caste by education and propaganda, the effort has been very limited, and natural forces which should make for the disintegration of the system are meanwhile obstructed by the operation of the various official controls on trading and industrial activity which severely restrict occupational mobility.

Other retarding factors that could be cited include the encouragement of beggary by both Hinduism and Islam, the Moslem prejudice against the pig, which considerably curtails the exploitation of agricultural opportunity in Pakistan and elsewhere, and the Buddhist's habit of expending much of his wealth in devotional displays which often take a conspicuously wasteful form, and which generally inhibit saving and capital formation. Religious forces are also responsible, in part at least, for the non-acceptance of birth control measures: for the adoption of retrograde linguistic policies, which create further obstacles to efficient administration, notably in Ceylon (see p. 49) : for the inflammation of communal tensions: and for the fatalistic outlook of large sectors of the population of the area, which depresses interest in material progress and thus

215

constitutes a very powerful obstacle to economic development.

No doubt there are extremely strong political reasons why little sustained effort has been made to break down these attitudes. Indeed, some governments have been willing, as in India, to enact legislation that is specifically designed to appease traditional forces as a means of securing their support for other official policies. There is also a general reluctance on the part of both Asian authorities and Western commentators even to consider the relevance of the problems which such factors create. It may well be that to draw attention to these factors in Asia is to court unpopularity or worse. It may be that to mention them in the West is to run the risk of creating a less favourable climate for the provision of aid. But it is still right that the retarding effect of social and religious factors in the underdeveloped world should be recognized and assessed, not only in the countries directly concerned, but also in the West. And where the impact of these factors can be shown to be of major significance, as it is for example in the agricultural sector in India, it is as well that the extent to which they can and do frustrate other efforts to promote progress should be critically examined.

FOREIGN AID

'With luck, a more massive domestic effort on our part, and a more understanding and more generous policy of aid by our foreign friends, the Indian economy will not only help to preserve our independence, but is also sure to reach the take-off stage by the end of the current decade, though it will still continue to be faced by balance of payments problems' (see p. 91). So Professor Rao sums up the future prospects of India's economic development towards the target of 'self-sustaining and elf-accelerating growth', and the emphasis he places upon the importance of foreign aid is echoed by Professor Nurul Islam, who judges that 'the amount of necessary external assistance will in all probability continue to be substantial in the next ten or fifteen years' (see p. 147) and by Dr Puey Ungphakorn, who writes that 'good luck and good management still do not earn sufficient resources for development. Grants and loans are needed from international bodies and from other governments' (see p. 172).

The term 'Foreign Aid' is customarily used to cover a variety of inter-governmental transactions, including financial grants and loans, the extension of credit, and the provision of personnel. These transactions may be bilateral or multi-lateral in character. But in so far as there is any discussion in individual studies of the problems of foreign aid, this is almost entirely confined to questions of detail, rather than of principle. The fundamental purpose of such aid is not examined by any of the contributors. It seems important, therefore, to try to establish at the outset what this purpose should be, and to what extent it is being fulfilled in practice.

In strictly economic terms, the first object of any governmental aid programme should clearly be to promote economic development in the recipient countries by providing resources which are essential to progress, and which are not otherwise available. The mere fact that economic development is necessary and desirable does not by itself constitute a *prima facie* case for the provision of governmental aid, since the purpose of aid should be to supplement other resources, whether internal or external. Resources for development can be generated internally, by various fiscal means, or externally, through the expansion of trade and by attracting foreign private investment, and the justification of aid must depend largely upon the reasons why these other resources are proving inadequate.

Capital is a scarce resource, in urgent demand throughout the world. Its productivity is often greater in donor than in recipient countries, because industrial techniques are more advanced, technical progress is more rapid, and skilled workers, technicians and administrators are more plentiful in the former than in the latter. Indiscriminate transfers of large aggregates of capital from rich to poor countries on a government-to-government basis are therefore likely to lead to its less effective use, especially where the supplier of capital has no control over its utilization. The belief that development depends upon capital investment, and that any expenditure that is classified as investment is necessarily productive, greatly increases the probability that large scale government-to-government capital transfers through foreign aid programmes will result in the uneconomic deployment of this scarce resource. The provision of aid in this form frequently serves to obscure the need for more far-reaching social, economic and structural changes in both rich and poor countries. Moreover, it also serves to diminish the need, both apparent and real, for private capital transfers; and at the same time it reduces the amount available for this purpose, both because of the effects of taxation, and because governmental aid tends to absorb a significant share of the capital resources which the authorities are prepared to see transferred.

Foreign aid thus leads to an uneconomic use of a very scarce resource. Quite often, it is even more likely to obstruct the material advance of the less developed countries than to promote it. However, the importance of these considerations is often obscured by the intrusion of political or emotional arguments to the effect that aid is an essential weapon of foreign policy, or that the richer countries have a moral obligation to provide poorer nations with a share in their own prosperity.

Though these arguments are not necessarily compatible, if either of them is accepted as valid it might well seem that any discussion of the economic aspects of aid must become largely pointless. In fact, the moral argument is essentially a misleading one. Because governmental aid is entirely financed from taxation, it lacks the moral element that is present in voluntary charity. The contributor to charity surrenders a part of his own resources of his own free will. But taxes are by definition compulsory, and have to be paid even by those who are unaware of, or totally opposed to, the particular uses to which the product will be put. It is irrelevant that the payment of tax may be made marginally more agreeable, in some cases, by humanitarian sentiment. Foreign aid is still wholly different from voluntary charity: and this difference is certainly sensed by its recipients, who tend to become progressively more suspicious of claims that aid is disinterested the more they are told that this is so. Nor is foreign aid analogous to redistributive taxation, whatever the merits of the latter. Many of those who benefit from foreign aid are richer than many of the taxpayers in donor countries; and the poorest people in the recipient countries often do not benefit from foreign aid at all.

The most that can be said with regard to any moral aspect is that because aid represents money compulsorily collected from taxpayers, there is a moral obligation upon the taxing government to exercise the closest and most careful control over its allocation and use. Such control is notoriously difficult to maintain in the case of governmental aid.[1]

The political argument may be harder to answer, since politics have the power to override economics. But this argument can only be said to apply if the purported political objectives are being achieved, or are capable of being achieved, by this means, and if there are no other means through which they could be attained. A detached survey of the international scene reveals few, if any, cases where it can be said that the political influence of a major donor country has noticeably increased as the direct result of its programme of economic aid. Indeed it is notable, to take a specific instance, that in spite of the very large foreign subventions which both India and Pakistan have received, the Kashmir dispute still remains unresolved. This is no doubt due in part to the fact that aid has become available from a number of different sources, so that political influences are balanced and so cancel each other out. But it is also directly attributable to the fashionable notion that aid should be given and received with no 'strings' attached.

As a general principle, the concept of aid without strings is extremely questionable. Not only does it make aid nugatory, as an instrument of political policy: it also rules out any element of economic reciprocity, or mutual benefit, and reduces aid transactions to the level of the blank cheque. The practical effects of this are very significant. If aid is regarded as self-justifying, its extent is potentially unlimited. Because an impression exists that this is in fact so, a state of something approaching aid-addiction has been allowed to emerge in certain countries, notably India. Evidence of this can be seen in an interesting contrast between Professor Rao's approach and that of Dr Puey Ungphakorn. The latter, in considering the burden of loan repayments, comments that 'the country cannot afford to see its future foreign exchange income always

---

[1] This raises an interesting constitutional point concerning the aid programme of the United Kingdom government. It was, until recently, a rigid policy that financial aid from Britain must be confined to dependent territories for whose administration H.M.G. remained ultimately accountable to Parliament. Grants of aid to independent countries, albeit within the Commonwealth, are scarcely compatible with the principle of parliamentary control, particularly where the premise of 'no strings' is explicitly involved.

syphoned away in debt service' (see p. 173). Professor Rao expresses similar anxieties (see p. 88): but where Dr Puey Ungphakorn concludes that there must therefore be a limit to borrowing from abroad, Professor Rao calls instead for 'a more understanding and more generous policy of aid by our foreign friends' (see p. 91). In fact, if foreign loans are used efficiently, and enlarge productive capacity correspondingly, there should be no cause for anxiety, because they will either promote additional exports or replace import requirements without extra cost. Where such problems have arisen, as in India, it has been because lending governments, applying the doctrine of 'no strings', have chosen to ignore the fact that the investment policy of the recipient government is not concerned with productivity.

The concept of 'no strings' is thus directly responsible for some of the current economic problems of the less developed world. At the same time, certain forms of aid, whilst not conditional in principle, are nevertheless conditional in practice. These are still open to various criticisms. Professor Nurul Islam points out, for example, that 'the phenomenon of 'tied' loans or grants has the effect of increasing the import-price of aid commodities by doing away with international competition in their supply' (see p. 144). The same point is made by Professor Rao. However, it is not difficult to see that the device of tying aid to the purchase of goods of a specific character and origin represents an attempt on the part of the donor country to ensure that even if no political advantage is going to accrue, and even if the recipient is denied the maximum economic benefit, some domestic advantage will still result. 'Tied' aid is thus partly a subvention to the recipient country, and partly a subsidy to domestic industry in the donor country. This last element lends plausibility to the criticism that foreign aid is only given as a means of ridding the more developed countries of unmarketable surpluses, or of exporting their unemployment. Such criticism is reinforced where, as often happens, 'tied' aid is accompanied by action in the donor countries to restrict or deny a market to the products of the recipients of their aid.

The harmful effects of 'tied' aid are reproduced, with much greater intensity, in the sort of barter agreements with Soviet

Bloc countries to which U Tun Wai refers (see p. 25). It is open to question whether such transactions are strictly 'stringless': what is certain, however, is that these agreements can have the double disadvantage of denying the less developed partner the opportunity to sell in the highest market, as well as making it impossible to buy from the cheapest supplier. A further, and equally specific, criticism is applicable to United States commodity aid under the aegis of Public Law 480 (the Agricultural Trade Development and Assistance Act of 1954). The distribution of American agricultural surpluses to the underdeveloped world under PL480 is usually justified on the grounds that it serves to alleviate immediate and urgent needs by augmenting food supplies and curbing inflation in the recipient countries. In the short term, it may well have this effect (see p. 89): but in the long run, the availability of such external food resources undoubtedly enables recipient governments to ignore the fundamental problems of their own agricultural sector. PL480 thus acts as an insulator against change, and it therefore retards development, both at home and abroad.

Some attempts have certainly been made to correct the most obvious abuses of foreign aid. These are reflected, for instance, in the detailed feasability studies that are undertaken by agencies such as the World Bank. But though it may be true in Thailand, and elsewhere, that 'a project approved for loans by an international lender or a friendly foreign government usually has the benefit of a second opinion, and its soundness is usually assured' (see p. 172), the general value of such safeguards is very slight. They may prevent the financing through aid of projects which are in themselves relatively or absolutely uneconomic, and they may reduce the dangers of waste through inefficiency or corruption. But in the context of foreign aid as a whole, it is the overall economic policy of the recipient governments that matters, and not the viability of individual projects. This becomes clear once it is understood that the provision of external aid for particular development purposes, however intrinsically desirable these may be, in no way prevents the recipient government from devoting its own resources to other projects and policies which may be not merely wasteful but positively harmful to development prospects. Indeed, experience suggests that the availability of aid makes the adoption of such policies more rather than less likely: there can be little doubt, for example, that without the underwriting effect of massive foreign resources, the Indian government would have been quite unable to pursue the course that it has followed since 1956.

There are now signs that influential opinion in some donor countries, particularly the USA, is becoming much more critical towards conventional attitudes to foreign aid programmes. Although this is welcome as recognition of the fact that the provision of aid should be conditional upon the interest of the donor as well as the recipient, it is still essential that any reappraisal should concentrate upon the real issues involved. If this is to happen, there are two further points that must be taken into account: first, that aid programmes inevitably increase the importance of the public sector in the recipient country; and second, that there is no such thing as 'self-sustaining and self-accelerating growth'.

The transfer of resources on a government-to-government basis increases the importance of the public sector in two ways. First, it obviously enlarges the resources of government in relation to the private sector of the economy. Second, preferential treatment is given, in practice, to those governments which engage in comprehensive development planning, so that government determination of the composition of economic activity virtually becomes a condition for the grant of aid. Since aid is often provided with the implicit aim of underpinning an existing regime, there may appear to be a positive political advantage in enabling and encouraging the state to extend its economic powers. But however friendly a regime may be, its economic policies may still not conduce to genuine economic progress, and there is therefore no inherent advantage in the extension of official control of economic activity, unless there is some respect in which the essential functions of government are being neglected. Thailand provides a case in point. There is certainly evidence in Dr Puey Ungphakorn's contribution of a connection between increased governmental efficiency and the increased volume of US aid. This is not in itself objectionable: but where the effect of aid is to make government more powerful, rather than more efficient, there are obvious economic objections.

In India, as in Ceylon, foreign aid has certainly encouraged government to assume greater economic powers, to embark upon policies of comprehensive planning, and to impose controls and restrictions upon the economy, with detrimental results to development performance: it has also tended to remove the need for, and thus to discourage, foreign private investment, in defiance of the principle that aid should be a supplementary source of development resources. It is possible to detect a political paradox in the fact that the creation of a socialist state in India is being underwritten by capitalist subsidies in the form of massive US aid (for although Professor Rao is non-committal on this score (see p. 88), there can be no doubt that foreign aid has been indispensable to the pursuit of a dirigist policy in India). It is even more paradoxical that, here and elsewhere, aid has served to obstruct progress, and not least by encouraging the diversion of scarce administrative talent from the performance of the essential functions of government.

The concept of 'self-sustaining and self-accelerating economic development' (see p. 73) is much in vogue. It is nevertheless meaningless. Growth can never be self-sustaining in the sense that it depends simply upon the attainment of a particular level of capital investment, or that it can continue regardless of other internal and external factors. Professor Rao may forecast that provided certain conditions are fulfilled, the Indian economy 'is sure to reach the take-off stage by the end of the current decade, *though it will still continue to be faced by balance of payments problems*' (see p. 92) (my italics). But since balance of payments problems can presumably only be resolved by external subventions, this situation hardly seems to merit the description 'self-sustaining'. Again, Malaya is one country which should be judged to have passed the 'take-off stage', if such a point existed: yet, as Mr Lim's analysis so clearly shows, postwar growth in Malaya has been markedly cyclical, and each cycle has been export-induced (see p. 100). Cyclical growth is scarcely self-accelerating, any more than export-induced growth can be said to be self-sustaining: and there are, of course, numerous past examples of societies which have reached a comparatively high level of material attainment only to fall into decline.

This point is by no means academic. The acceptance of the

idea that there exists some future point at which a less developed country will 'take off to self-sustaining growth' has the important practical effect of encouraging the provision of aid by holding out the prospect that there will come a time when the need for aid will cease. But since the concept itself is meaningless, aid commitments which are based upon it are in fact entirely open-ended. If public memories were longer, the idea of a 'take-off' point might by now have been discredited. For example, it is already five years since the late President (then Senator) Kennedy explicitly stated that India was on the point of take off into self-sustaining growth.[1] Now, according to Professor Rao, at least five more years are still required. So large a margin of error ought to make any standard of measurement suspect: nevertheless, the concept is still in fashionable use, and still widely adduced as an argument justifying foreign aid programmes, usually with the assurance that the 'take off' point is almost in sight.

These criticisms are not presented as an argument against aid in any form or on any scale. The intention is rather to stress the importance of abandoning misleading and meaningless catch-phrases, and returning to the consideration of first principles, when any reassessment of foreign aid is undertaken. Conventional advocates of aid may have come to use the same sort of double argument that is employed by the committed planners, and for similar reasons: if aid has been a success, they say, then more should be provided; if aid has not been successful, this is because it has not been sufficiently generous, and so, again, more should be provided. But to accept this argument is not merely to impose upon the more developed nations an economic burden that will increase progressively and indefinitely: it is also to ignore most, if not all, of what is known about the real causes of economic growth.

CONCLUSIONS

Economic development does not depend wholly, or even largely, upon governmental action. There are many factors, such as climatic influences, the availability of natural resources, the economic qualities of the population, and the prevalent

[1] In a speech to the United States Senate on February 19 1959.

customs and social institutions, which are only marginally susceptible to official action. It is not coincidental, for instance, that almost all the less developed countries lie in the tropical or semi-tropical regions of the world. There are definite limits to the pace and extent of material advance in such countries, and these cannot be overcome either by the assumption by government of comprehensive powers over the entire economy, or by accepting the income aspirations of developing countries (see p. 35) as a categorical imperative.

However, it is clear from the studies of Part 1 that governmental action has often served to obstruct progress in these countries. In assessing official economic policies, it must of course be remembered that economic arguments often gain political support for reasons widely different from their ostensible aims. The advocate of policies which inevitably create balance of payments problems, and which demand close control over the economy as a whole, is not necessarily naive or unsophisticated, or ignorant of economics. A balance of payments crisis may well be welcome to him as an excuse to call for foreign aid. Or again, the imposition of economic controls may be thought desirable as an instrument for the establishment of a centralized and closely regulated society.

But when economic arguments are invoked in support of far-reaching policies, it is quite legitimate that these arguments should be examined on the same level. This is perfectly compatible with recognition of the fact that the merits of particular economic policies cannot be assessed solely on the basis of technical economic discussion, and that they depend ultimately upon their probable effect on the total social situation, compared to the effect of alternative policies. Critical discussion can still fairly extend beyond the realm of technical economic argument.

The declared aims of all the governments in this region include the promotion of the material progress of their peoples. The evidence which has been examined in this analysis must, however, serve to show that many of these governments have pursued and are pursuing economic policies which are actually detrimental to their peoples' prospects of progress. An honourable exception can be made in the case of Malaya, and also of Thailand. But for the rest, the contributions in Part 1 clearly reveal the presence in varying degree of some or all of the following as major features of policy: the general neglect of the essential functions of government, the adoption of rigid and uncritical attitudes to economic planning, the concentration of effort and resources on uneconomic development projects, the imposition of controls and restrictions on private commerce and industry, the erection of barriers against foreign private enterprise, the consequent exclusion of fresh capital and new techniques, the neglect of the basic needs of agriculture, and the statutory reinforcement and extension of social factors hostile to advance.

There are other features of official policy which would qualify for more than a passing mention if space permitted. These include the inadequate development of communications, inefficient and inequitable taxation systems, and severe restrictions on the immigration of foreigners and their terms of work, all of which occur in more than one country in this area, and which also significantly affect development prospects. But whilst this evidence provides many specific examples of inappropriate government action as a contributory cause of continued poverty, it must be stressed yet again that development is not essentially a matter of government action.

At the same time, the fact that official policies have almost certainly obstructed material progress is a serious matter for both rich and poor countries alike. The results must be very serious for the peoples of the less developed countries, who have been denied the rise in living standards that should otherwise have accrued to them. They must also be of the closest concern to the peoples of the more developed world, because of the political and economic interdependence of rich and poor nations. It must be recognized that the responsibility for this state of affairs lies partly with those governments in less developed countries which have adopted policies that are not conductive to economic progress, in the sense of a general rise in living standards. But there can be no doubt that a major share of the blame must be borne by the more developed nations, because it is their governments that have condoned or encouraged the pursuit of such policies, and which have provided the financial support without which these policies could not have been sustained.

This suggests that the policies of rich countries will continue substantially to affect the economic prospects of poor ones. But so long as it is accepted by both sides that a general rise in living standards is desirable – and this seems unlikely to be questioned – it follows that all responsible governments should pursue policies that are likely to promote such progress, and that they should encourage others to do likewise. This clearly involves some radical changes of policy. And since the initiative for any change must in the circumstances come from the more developed nations, this analysis would not be complete if it did not examine the extent to which official policies and attitudes in the West require to be revised.

It may seem, at first sight, that there is little practical scope for such a revision. There are powerful political, administrative, financial and intellectual vested interests involved in the continuation of existing policies, on a national and an international level. Many of the more developed nations have made considerable sacrifices through their aid programmes, and much courage would be needed to recognize that these had been misdirected or wasted. Few governments in the less developed countries would lightly abandon their established policies or admit that these had been misconceived. All the Asian governments in this region are politically sovereign and independent and thus in theory free to adopt whatever policies they choose.

But these arguments do not weaken the case for a radical revision. In India and elsewhere, the current orthodoxy of economic development may rest upon the assumptions that progress is only attainable through comprehensive official intervention in economic activity, and that it must be backed by massive infusions of external capital through the medium of foreign aid programmes. But however popular they may be, both these assumptions are still unwarranted. It is clear that policies that are designed to promote trade, to widen external contacts, to provide incentives to progress, and to encourage structural changes are more likely to promote economic advance.

The time has therefore come for the governments of rich countries to adopt, both at home and abroad, policies which are genuinely likely to promote general material progress, and to withdraw or withhold their financial support from governments elsewhere which refuse to follow suit. This means, in practice, that Western governments should consciously direct their policies towards the greatest possible expansion of trade: that they should promote structural change in their own economies, and not obstruct it; and that they should make any future provision of aid, in the form of capital transfers to the less developed world, subject to certain definite conditions.

These conditions should not be political, in the sense that they demand any special alignment in international affairs. Nor should they be confined to specific stipulations about individual development projects. They should be concerned strictly with the overall economic policy of any would-be recipients of aid, and applied impartially to all of them. They should require in short that before it can qualify to receive financial aid, the rulers of any less developed country must be able to show that their economic policies are genuinely expansionist, and that they are carrying out the essential functions of government to the best of their ability. Those governments which are honestly trying to maintain law and order, to operate an efficient and fair system of taxation, to preserve the stability of the currency, to allow the maximum scope for individual enterprise and consumer preference, to encourage external economic contacts, to develop the country's basic public facilities, and to promote a suitable and liberal institutional framework for the activities of their people, can fairly claim to qualify for external aid. Those that cannot satisfy such conditions are neither entitled to expect external aid, nor capable of putting it to economic use.

It would probably not prove possible to obtain general agreement amongst all donor countries on the acceptance of these conditions. Communist donor countries certainly have an active interest in encouraging the emergence of dirigist government and a dominant public sector in any less developed country. However, much of their effectiveness in this is at present due to the tacit co-operation of the West: and whilst it is often argued that the West cannot afford to reduce existing aid programmes for fear of leaving the Communists a clear field, it remains a fact that prevailing Western attitudes often tend to serve Communist purposes. It is also true that, even within the West, there exists a considerable degree of competition for political and economic influence through the medium of foreign aid programmes. So long as this is so, it is perhaps reasonable for any one donor country to be reluctant to create, by the reduction of its own aid programme, an opening which will simply be filled by another Western competitor, if not by the Communist bloc. But the fact that this is so merely underlines the need for collective and responsible action on the part of Western donors and of the United States, as the West's major donor, in particular.

It might also prove difficult in practice to reach agreement on the extent to which such conditions were actually being fulfilled. Nevertheless, individual governments are constantly setting standards of their own, whenever they frame their internal policies, and there seems to be nothing to prevent them from working out analogous standards for external purposes. Indeed, this would have the important advantage of restoring some control over governmental spending on foreign aid to the electorate of the donor country, by enabling these standards to be put to the test of the vote. This would greatly assist donor governments to meet what amounts to a double obligation in respect of their aid programmes: first, to ensure that the resources which they levy from their taxpayers are not wasted, and second, to allocate aid, for which the demand far exceeds the supply, where it will do most good, rather than to ration it on any other basis.

It is safe to forecast that any move to introduce such criteria would also meet with several immediate objections. It would be argued, for instance, that the imposition of these or any other conditions would amount to an unwarrantable intrusion into the internal affairs of independent states: that any attempt to enforce them could only result in the complete alienation of the less developed nations from the West, and a corresponding increase in the influence of the Communist bloc; and that the poorest countries, whose need is greatest, would in any case be unable to qualify. These arguments are spurious. The independence of these countries is already qualified by their reliance on foreign aid. Foreign aid, as has already been noted, necessarily affects the domestic political situation in the recipient country, and thus involves the donor country in the internal affairs of the recipient. Acceptance of the proposals outlined above seems more likely to reduce the extent of such involvement than to increase it.

229

Again, governments would remain free to choose whether to accept or reject aid under such conditions. A free society which is likely to be sympathetic to the West can only develop where these conditions are met, and the West ought not to underwrite the creation of any other type of society. The resources of the Communist bloc are certainly neither inexhaustible nor unconditionally available. Lastly, national poverty should surely encourage a government to concentrate its resources on the essential tasks of government, rather than inhibit it from doing so.

It is still undeniable, and the contributions in Part 1 provide ample evidence of this, that the poverty and lack of progress of many less developed countries is being enhanced by official errors of omission and commission, in the neglect of essential governmental tasks, and in the pursuit of policies which obstruct economic advance. Any continuation of this state of affairs can be of no benefit either to the more developed or to the less developed countries.

One final aspect of the problem still remains to be considered. The aim of any aid policy should clearly be to ensure that all available resources are put to the best possible use, so that aid itself ultimately becomes unnecessary. It must therefore be undesirable in principle that the countries of the less developed world should bear economic burdens which may be necessary in themselves, but which can be discharged more effectively by others. For this reason, it is economically important that action should be taken to relieve the less developed nations of the burden of providing for their own external defence. This could be achieved by the introduction of a system of guaranteed frontiers. Such a system would have the immediate and important effect of removing the need for further defence expenditure on the part of the less developed nations, and thus would free considerable resources for peaceful use. By putting an end to the proliferation of armaments, which is politically dangerous as well as economically wasteful, it would represent a major contribution towards the lowering of international tensions. It would also reduce or remove some of the main drawbacks to the provision of foreign aid: it would reduce the involvement of individual donor countries in the internal politics of recipient states: it would separate defence aid from general economic aid and, by ending the former, enable the latter to be put to genuinely productive uses: it would diminish the force of invidious comparisons between the amounts of aid granted to different countries: and by eliminating the need for expensive arms purchases from overseas, it would greatly ease the strain on the balance of payments of many less developed countries.

To take a specific example, the guaranteeing of India's frontiers would relieve the Indian economy of the present strain and future burdens that must be caused by a single-handed attempt to build up defensive forces sufficient to resist a possible repetition of Chinese aggression. It must be plain that a situation wherein the Indian government is acquiring arms from the USA, from Britain and from Russia, as well as diverting further resources to the creation of a war-economy, can only make good sense to India's enemies. And though it is entirely understandable that Professor Rao (p. 91) should seek to rationalize the existing position, there can be no real doubt that the impact of the Indian government's decision to bear almost the whole burden of external defence needs, or rather to place this burden on the Indian nation, must make the country's prospects of achieving significant economic progress still more remote.

India's present case may be an extreme one. But even before the emergence of the Chinese menace, both India and Pakistan were devoting a considerable part of their available resources to the maintenance and development of their armed forces: and the fact that India's capability was primarily designed for defence against Pakistan, and vice versa, coupled with the fact that the resources concerned were partly of common Western origin, serves to highlight the situation. In such circumstances, it is surely logical that the more developed nations who already possess and can afford to maintain an effective military capability should between them evolve a system which would enable the resources concerned to be put to uses of general benefit. Indeed, there are already instances, as in Thailand and Malaya, where the greater part of the burden of national defence has been taken up by more developed countries under treaty arrangements.

It may be objected that even in a politically advanced region such as Asia, there is still a long way to go before a general system of guaranteed frontiers becomes a practical possibility.

It would need to be understood, for instance, that a guarantee of existing frontiers against aggression does not necessarily imply an unconditional endorsement of the *status quo*. Where boundary disputes exist, as in Kashmir, or may emerge, those concerned could not rely solely upon the right of occupation. It would still be incumbent upon the parties to such disputes to submit them to international judicial arbitration: and it might prove necessary for a frontier guarantee to be withdrawn if one state subsequently refused to cede territory to another in spite of a judgment that it should do so.

There are also other obstacles to be overcome. Considerations of national pride alone might appear to make such a system unattainable. Military aid has become a powerful instrument of foreign policy. In many less developed countries, political power has fallen into the hands of military oligarchies, and such regimes are unlikely to welcome a reduction in the status of the armed forces. The problem of internal security requirements would not be easy to resolve. Most important of all, a system of guaranteed frontiers which did not include the Soviet Union amongst the guarantors would seriously increase the dangers of military confrontation between the major power blocs.

But these objections are not necessarily insuperable. Even where a state's frontiers and those of its neighbours were guaranteed, this would still leave its government free to create a military capability if it chose to do so, though it would neither need it for defensive purposes nor be free to use it in aggressive ventures. However difficult Russian participation might be to obtain, its refusal would nevertheless amount to an admission that Communist policy regards the less developed world as a desirable battleground. Nor would a system of guaranteed frontiers conflict with the spirit of the United Nations, whose members already bind themselves not to commit aggression. Finally, the introduction of such a system need not necessarily depend upon the consent of the states whose frontiers were to be guaranteed. Indeed, frontier guarantees could justifiably be imposed, since the principles involved are not susceptible to negotiation or to compromise.

These proposals may require a radical departure from the policies which have been generally followed over the past fifteen years. This is no argument against such a change. The overwhelming weight of evidence shows that past policies in this field have in most cases provided little lasting benefit either to the more developed or to the less developed countries. Mutual interests in change are therefore very strong indeed: but if change is to come, it must fall to the more developed partner to make the first move. The missed opportunities and the waste that are characteristic of so much of development experience in this region, and the harmful economic and political effects that can be so clearly seen in India and elsewhere, have occurred primarily because the more developed nations have lacked the courage or the foresight to use their power to prevent them. A grave responsibility lies upon the West: and it is the duty of Western governments, and of the United States government in particular, to see that the resources of their peoples should no longer be used in ways more likely to retard than to promote the material progress of the peoples of Asia, or of any other part of the less developed world.

INDEX

Administration, 183; Burma, investment in, 13; Ceylon, 33; India, 71, 89; Pakistan, 139, 148–149

AFPFL (Burmese Political Party), 6, 14

Agriculture
Burma, 3, 6, 8, 11, 13, 202; State Agricultural Marketing Board, 17, 25, 209; shortage of plough cattle, 19, 214; priority to, 26
Ceylon, 30, 31, 65, 202
India, 72, 73, 75, 77, 79, 81, 88, 90; key economic activity, 68; need for increased output, 88–9
Malaya, 112–16
Pakistan, 125, 127; dependent on weather, 131; basic problem of development, 132; plans for, 133
Thailand, 168; foundation of economy, 151; growth in, 161–163
disincentives to export of products of, 202, 210
importance of, 204–5
effect of 'landlordism' and indebtedness on, 206–7
new land and better communications for, 208
effect of controls and taxation on, 209–10
see also under individual agricultural products

Agricultural Development Corporation (Pakistan), 132–3

Aid, see Foreign Aid

America, United States of, 229; aid to Burma, 7, 22; economists and engineers visit Burma, 7, 8; technical aid to Burma, 16; trade mission visits Burma, 22–3; synthetic rubber production in, 38; aid to India, 85–6; imports from Malaya, 96; importance of to Malaya, 109; aid to Pakistan, 140–1; advice to Thailand, 154; Economic and Technical Co-operation Agreement, with Thailand, 156, 158; change of attitude towards external aid, 222; see also Public Law 480

Balance of Payments, 180, 225; Burma, 9; Ceylon, 60; India, 73, 74, 75, 88; Malaya, 100, 106; Pakistan, 123; Thailand, 166–7 (incl. table)

Bank of Thailand, 152

Benham, F. C., 97

Birth control, 43–4, 144–5, 215

Brahmanand, P. R., 27

Britain (British), investment in Burma, 20; export prices, compared with Burma (table), 24; tea market in, 39; imports from Malaya, 96; Colonial Office, 107; aid to India, 85; aid to Pakistan, 140–1

Budget, Ceylon, 59; Malaya, 101, 111–12; Thailand, 152

Budget Procedures Act (Thailand), 155

Burma (Burmese Government), 182, 186, 187, 196, 201, 210, 214;

235

INDEX

International Finance Corporation, 83

International Labour Office, 34

Investment:
Burma, rate of for Eight-Year Plan, 8; low level of, 10; misdirection of, 10; influenced by socialism, 15; foreign in, 20–3; Burma Investment Act, 22–3; domestic (table), 21

Ceylon, 53–9

India, 72, 73, 75, 81, 90; low rate of, 68–9

Pakistan, 130–1; in Six-Year Development Programme, (table), 121; increases in (incl. table), 123; in First Five-Year Plan (incl. table), 124–5; in industry (table), 134

Thailand, foreign private needed, 172

definition of, 185

discussion of importance of, 185–188

foreign private, value of, 199–200

Irrigation, Burma, 11, 13; Ceylon, 31, 65; India, 72, 73, 81, 90; Malaya, 104, 115; Pakistan, 120, 126, 133; Thailand, 155

Israel, aid to Burma, 16

Japan (Japanese), 3, 9, 20, 22, 85, 95–6, 140; export prices of compared with Burma's (table), 24

Jute, 119, 147, 165, 201–2

Kashmir, 67–8, 219

Kelantan (Malayan State), 115

Kenaf, 151, 162, 165

Kennedy, President J. F., 224

Korean War boom, 7, 98, 99, 122, 136, 153, 201

KTA plan, see Burma, Eight-Year Plan

Labour, Burma, 26; Ceylon, 33–4; India, 83; Pakistan, 145

Land: Burma, under cultivation, 19–20; Ceylon, 30–1; India, 73, 89; Malaya, development schemes, 103, 104; fragmentation of, 114; availability of, 116–17; Pakistan, 132; Thailand, 172; new, importance of for agriculture, 208

'Landlordism', 114, 206

Land Nationalization Act (Burma), 6

Language, 49, 215

Law and Order, 6, 102, 183

Lim, Chong-Yah, Mr (author of Malaya section), facing page 95, 180, 182, 184, 185, 198, 204, 205, 206, 207, 208, 211, 212, 223

Mahalanobis, Professor P. C., 189, 198

Maize, 151, 162, 165, 168

Malaya, 178, 180, 190, 201, 202, 204, 211; general description of, 95; rubber and tin key products of, 96, 108; under Japanese occupation, 95–6; loss of export markets under occupation, 96; post war rehabilitation, 96–7; sources of and calculation of growth statistics, 97–8; growth statistics, cyclical economy, 98–9, 223; rubber and tin prices, 100–101; effects of emergency, 101; government faith in free enterprise, 102, 103–4, 194; rubber replanting programmes, 102–3; land development programme, 103–4; First Five-Year Plan, 109, 112; Second Five-Year Plan, 103, 109, 110, 112; government aid to industry, 104; government investment in infrastructure and social services, 104–5, 212; currency stability, 106; Draft Development Plan, 107, 108; World Bank Mission, 107–9; economic plans dependent on tin and rubber prices, 108–10; export dominated economy not controllable by government, 109,

239

INDEX